Beyond the Vanguard

Beyond the Vanguard

*Everyday Revolutionaries in
Allende's Chile*

———

Marian E. Schlotterbeck

UNIVERSITY OF CALIFORNIA PRESS

University of California Press, one of the most distinguished university presses in the United States, enriches lives around the world by advancing scholarship in the humanities, social sciences, and natural sciences. Its activities are supported by the UC Press Foundation and by philanthropic contributions from individuals and institutions. For more information, visit www.ucpress.edu.

University of California Press
Oakland, California

Parts of the introduction and epilogue of the present work appeared in a slightly different version in "Chile: Reflecting on the Revolutionary Left," *Berkeley Review of Latin American Studies* (Fall 2015): 28–31. Reprinted courtesy of the editors.

Library of Congress Cataloging-in-Publication Data

Names: Schlotterbeck, Marian, author.
Title: Beyond the vanguard : everyday revolutionaries in Allende's Chile / Marian E. Schlotterbeck.
Description: Oakland, California : University of California Press, [2018] | Includes bibliographical references and index. |
Identifiers: LCCN 2017053913 (print) | LCCN 2017057577 (ebook) | ISBN 9780520970175 (E-book) | ISBN 9780520298057 (cloth : alk. paper) | ISBN 9780520298064 (pbk. : alk. paper)
Subjects: LCSH: Working class—Political activity—Chile—History—20th century. | Chile—Politics and government—1970–1973.
Classification: LCC HD8298 (ebook) | LCC HD8298 .S35 2018 (print) | DDC 983.06/46—dc23
LC record available at https://lccn.loc.gov/2017053913

Manufactured in the United States of America

26 25 24 23 22 21 20 19
10 9 8 7 6 5 4 3 2

For my parents, John and Barbara

CONTENTS

MAPS

ACKNOWLEDGMENTS

Over the past decade, I have had exceptional interlocutors and mentors who transformed the inherently solitary activities of intellectual inquiry and historical research into collaborative endeavors.

The seeds for this project began at Oberlin College, on September 10, 2001, my first day of class. The aftermath of 9/11 and the anti–Iraq war movement informed my generation of Oberlin students' engagement with the meaning of U.S. power in the world. In this search, I was fortunate to find a lifelong mentor in Steve Volk. As a graduate student in the early 1970s, he lived in Chile during Allende's presidency and the September 11, 1973, military coup. His willingness to bring personal experiences into the classroom brought that history to life. In 2003, he organized a weeklong seminar around the thirtieth anniversary of the Chilean coup. Instead of the anticipated dozen Latin American studies majors, nearly two hundred students attended. My experience in that seminar encapsulates so much of what made Oberlin a stimulating and generous intellectual community. I can only hope to one day be as dedicated a mentor and as innovative a teacher as Steve. At the 2003 seminar, I also met Peter Kornbluh from the National Security Archive in Washington, DC. Working as Peter's assistant on the Chile and Cuba Documentation Projects challenged me to engage U.S. accountability, to make headlines out of history, and to write for wider audiences. My relatives Chris and Nick Scanniello graciously opened their home, allowing me to take an internship at the National Security Archive.

At Yale University, Gil Joseph models compassionate mentorship of graduate students. I am grateful for his unwavering support throughout this project. During an early phase of research in Chile, as I mulled over possible case studies, Gil had simple advice: write a history that people will want to read. His keen sensibility for finding the stories that are worth telling has always been a good standard to follow. Each of my dissertation committee members contributed to this project's development. Peter Winn from Tufts University graciously agreed to serve as an outside reader, and I benefited immensely from his vast knowledge of Chilean history and his attention to detail. At critical junctures during my sixteen months of research in 2010 and 2011, Peter and I fortuitously overlapped in Santiago. Each conversation sharpened my analysis and gave new direction to remaining research. His longstanding ties to Chile are an inspiration that I can only hope to emulate. As a scholar, teacher, and mentor, Lillian Guerra embodies bold critical thinking and inspires the questioning of conventional interpretations. Michael Denning's insights drawn from leftist political cultures and social movements enhanced this project's analytical frame. During graduate school, I also benefited from conversations and courses with Stuart Schwartz, Seth Fein, Moira Fradinger, and Patricia Pessar.

My Yale peers, all generous and energetic thinkers, include Lisa Ubelaker Andrade, Jenny Lambe, Ingrid Castañeda, Erika Helgen, Mike Bustamante, Christine Mathias, Drew Konove, Carmen Kordick, Kirsten Weld, Louise Walker, Lisa Covert, and Andra Chastain. From the moment I saw him on a cold spring day in a Berkeley hoodie outside the Yale Hall of Graduate Studies, I knew Fredy González and I would become fast friends. Through many ups and downs, multiple time zones, and bad internet connections, Fredy has always been there to offer encouragement. During my first summer of graduate school, Alison Bruey showed me the ropes of archival research in Santiago and since then has been an exceptional interlocutor. Her generosity in helping a new generation of Chileanists navigate the field knows no bounds. In New Haven and New York, I am indebted to the friendship of Matthew Vernon, Suzy Newbury, Allison Gorsuch, Aaron Wenzloff, Ariel Duncan, and Carmen Solíz.

Sponsored by Rotarians in Greencastle, Indiana, I first lived in Chile in 2006 as a Rotary Ambassadorial Scholar at the Universidad de Concepción, where Alejandra Brito Peña introduced me to Chilean social history and Jaime Fierro Carrasco pushed me to think critically about citizenship and democracy. The friendships formed that year have endured several long absences and many joyful reunions: to Pamela Santa Cruz, Margarita Martínez, Carolina Landaida, Bernardita Roa, Karina Sepúlveda, and Paulina Arancibia—*las chicas de siempre más* Antoine Caullet—*mil gracias por las amistades y convivencias*. Starting with an impromptu conversation about Subaltern Studies, it has been gratifying to embark on an academic career in the company of Raúl Rodríguez Freire. Over the years several Chilean families have welcomed me into their homes; a special thank-you to the Paillacar Mútizabal family in Osorno, the Espinoza Goecke family in Santiago, and the Monsalves Urrea family in San Pedro and Coronel. Betweem 2010 and 2011, Julia Brown-Bernstein, Josefina de la Maza, Fernando Garrido, Susana Costamagna, Claudio Barrientos, Sebastián Acuña, Andrés Estefane, and Valentina Orellana in Santiago and Gina Inostroza, Aníbal Navarette, Darwin Rodríguez, and Alejandra Ruíz in Concepción provided friendship and good cheer. The years I lived in Chile, 2006 and 2010–11, coincided with resurgent student protest. The exhilaration of watching these movements unfold, joining marches, sitting in on assemblies, and debating their meaning with everyday Chileans has informed my thinking about movement politics and Chilean history.

The courage and optimism of the many Chileans I interviewed continues to inspire me. I hope in this book they will recognize their many contributions. Miguel Soto in Concepción, Darwin Rodríguez and Juan Reyes in Tomé, and Hugo Monsalves in San Pedro went to great lengths to facilitate many of these interviews. In addition, Jody Pavilack, Sebastián Leiva, and Eugenia Palieraki generously shared their interviews and research materials with me. Chilean research assistants Antonia Garcés, Paulina Bravo, and Alejandra Torres, all talented young historians, accompanied me for many hours in the Hemeroteca of the Biblioteca Nacional in Santiago, and Mariel Ruiz Muñoz, Gina Inostroza, and Marco Contreras carried out additional interviews in Concepción and Talcahuano. The efficiency of transcribers Katherine Cáceres, Colomba Orrego, Fabián Rodríguez, and Julio and Ursula Jáuregui enabled me to provide interviewees with copies of our conversations and to begin writing from hundreds of pages of interviews. I am deeply grateful for the professionalism of the archivists and librarians in Santiago and Concepción who facilitated access to materials at the Biblioteca Nacional, the Archivo Oral de Villa Grimaldi, the Archivos Judiciales de Concepción, the Archivos Generales, Biblioteca Central Luis David Cruz Ocampo, and Centro de Estudios Regionales at the Universidad de Concepción, and the now-defunct NGO Servicios de Estudios Regionales. Aníbal Navarrete allowed me to consult the Bellavista-Tomé textile union minutes. I am indebted to Armindo Cardoso for documenting this history and allowing me to use his photograph on the cover.

The best scholars are also the most generous ones. There is no better way to describe Mario Garcés Durán. When we first talked about writing a social history of revolution in Concepción, Mario never doubted that this history mattered. He experienced those years of militancy firsthand in Concepción. His personal insights, critical distance, and deep intellect enriched my own thinking immensely and kept this project grounded in everyday lives. Over the years conversations with Steve Stern, Florencia Mallon, Julio Pinto Vallejos, Heidi Tinsman, Camilo Trumper, Patrick Barr-Melej, J. T. Way, Tori Langland, Aldo Marchesi, Fernando Purcell, and Jeffrey Gould have sharpened this project. I am grateful for the careful and critical manuscript feedback provided by Nancy Postero, Katie Hite, Raymond Craib, Angela Vergara, Greg Downs, Lisa Materson, Andrés Reséndez, and Chuck Walker. UC Davis student research assistants Kenia Mungia and Jessica Araya helped track down citations, and, at a critical midpoint in revisions, Sara Phelps edited every page of the manuscript with aplomb. Molly Roy's capacious cartography skills produced beautiful maps. Matthew Vernon's support was constant during long stretches apart for research and while writing and revising the dissertation for publication. I will always be grateful. Arnold Bauer, Ari Kelman, Michael Lazzara, Jennifer Adair, Alison Bruey, Claire Goldstene, Audrey Russek, Lisa Ubelaker, Fredy González, Mario Garcés, Rachel Jean-Baptiste, Michael Lemon, Ariel Duncan, Erika Helgen, John Schlotterbeck, and Barbara Steinson offered incisive feedback and editing expertise.

·I had the good fortune to complete this book as a member of the University of California, Davis, history department. I am constantly humbled to be in the company of so many talented historians. Teaching UC Davis graduate and undergraduate students has enriched my thinking about social revolutions and radical politics. Their commitment to social justice and engaged scholarship is a daily affirmation that the kids are all right. The friendship of Hannah Chale, Alissa Kendall, Kenny Sims, Ben Pearl, Lily Balloffet, Alyssa Ney, Ian Campbell, Lindsey Malta, and Quinn and Sophie Javers has made California feel like home.

During multiple stages of research and writing, I was fortunate to receive financial support from the Hellman Family Foundation, the University of California Humanities Research Institute, the Mrs. Giles Whiting Foundation, the Social Science Research Council, the Fulbright-Hays Doctoral Dissertation Fellowship, the Andrew W. Mellon Foundation, the Smith-Richardson Foundation, the Tinker Foundation, the MacMillan Center for International and Area Studies at Yale, the Rotary Foundation, and, at UC Davis, the Humanities Institute, Social Sciences Institute, Academic Affairs, and Academic Senate Committee on Research. During the final stages of writing the dissertation, my colleague Chuck Walker graciously facilitated office space at the Hemispheric Institute of the Americas. At UC Press, the attentive support of Kate Marshall and Bradley Depew is everything an author could hope for in editors. Ràymond Craib, Alison Bruey, and Margaret Chowning read the manuscript for UC Press. Their comments made it a much better book. All errors are, of course, my own.

My brother, Jesse, and his wife, Alina, offered valuable professional advice and sibling love. My niece, Ava, born in 2006 when I was living in Chile, has grown up alongside this project. Ellie, the scruffy terrier, arrived in my life just as I started a sabbatical in 2016. Her insistence on long walks provides much-needed writing breaks and a constant reminder to be in the present. This book is dedicated to my parents, John Schlotterbeck and Barbara Steinson, who have offered unwavering support and love in all my endeavors. I hold them responsible for my decision to become a historian.

Introduction

"All this time no one ever asked about the people," retired textile worker Juan Reyes said softly. The words hung in the air on a warm spring day in the southern Chilean town of Tomé in October 2011. I had met Reyes through my research on Chile's iconic, controversial, and often misunderstood Movimiento de Izquierda Revolucionaria (MIR; Revolutionary Left Movement). Over the past months, he had arranged and often accompanied me on interviews with former members of the MIR and its student and labor fronts.

Looking back on this process of recovering historical memory, Reyes enumerated the dramatic political shifts in twentieth-century Chile—the attempt at a democratic path to socialism under Marxist president Salvador Allende (1970–73), the seventeen-year military dictatorship headed by General Augusto Pinochet (1973–90), and the long transition to democracy (1990–2010)—before reflecting on Chile's collective amnesia, a deep inhibition born of fear and self-preservation that had for decades prevented the country from asking what happened in people's lives and how they felt about it. He paused before admitting that even as former revolutionaries, "we never talked about it either."[1] The silencing of Chile's recent history, particularly what came before the 1973 military coup, was so complete that Reyes initially had been surprised that I wanted to know about his involvement with the MIR. When the local textile mill closed in 1997, Juan Reyes was the oldest employee—a distinction that earned him a handful of local history interviews. No one had ever asked about his politics.

In September 1970, Chile captured the world's attention when it elected as president physician turned Socialist senator Salvador Allende Gossens. Allende and his Popular Unity coalition promised a peaceful, democratic transition to socialism—

1

a revolution by ballot box that would redistribute wealth. In the midst of the Cold War, Chile appeared to offer the world an alternative development model to both U.S. capitalist liberal democracy and Soviet-style Communism. The opening of a democratic revolutionary process in Chile expanded the constellation of radical political projects across the continent. At a time when enthusiasm for the 1959 Cuban Revolution had tempered as Fidel Castro moved into the Soviet orbit, Allende's improbable victory in 1970 fueled a progressive, leftist imaginary around the world. Alongside the proliferation of revolutionary Lefts that validated armed struggle as legitimate for carrying out a revolution, the Popular Unity project offered a top-down model that would not destroy the state but occupy and transform it.

As novel as a peaceful revolution appeared in 1970, Allende's victory was deeply rooted in the Chilean political system. It represented the fulfillment of the Chilean Left's decades-long strategy of channeling social struggle through electoral participation. Within Chile's tradition of multiparty coalition governments, Allende's Popular Unity coalition was the first time representatives of the working class—the Socialist and Communist Parties—led the government. With the goal of creating a state-run economy, Allende expanded many reforms begun during his predecessor Christian Democrat Eduardo Frei's "Revolution in Liberty" (1964–70). Allende campaigned on a platform to end foreign and monopoly control of the economy, grow the public sector, and deepen democracy through the creation of worker control in state-run factories. Within a year of taking office, Allende's government had nationalized the American-owned copper mines with unanimous congressional approval and acquired other key industries, including coal mines, textile mills, and steel mills. In just eighteen months, his government implemented one of the most extensive land redistributions in world history without widespread violence.[2] The Popular Unity government hoped that economic strength would translate into political support as it sought to persuade the majority of Chileans to vote for socialism by the end of Allende's term in 1976. Allende faced stiff opposition from Richard Nixon's administration in Washington, Chilean business elites, and the military, as well as sharp criticism from leftists inside and outside his governing coalition. To the very end, Allende steadfastly eschewed the idea that violence was necessary for revolution and relied on his skills at political negotiation to carry him through crisis points.

He did not complete his six-year term as president. On September 11, 1973, the Chilean military overthrew Allende's government in a coup that brought General Augusto Pinochet to power. Chile's 1973 coup marked a turning point in the consolidation of right-wing military dictatorships across South America. During seventeen years of military rule, Chile became both an international pariah, synonymous with human rights violations, and a poster child for neoliberal economic restructuring. State terror decimated the armed and the unarmed Left. Guided by neoliberal economists, many trained at the University of Chicago, the Pinochet regime implemented shock doctrine economic policies. Justified as necessary to find Chile's competitive niche in global markets, these reforms undercut the foundations of Chile's pluralistic democratic society. In 1973, the Chilean junta cast itself as a reluctant actor that stepped in to save the country from Marxist subversion and economic chaos. Over time, as Pinochet consolidated his hold on power, the narrative shifted to argue that the benefits of economic growth outweighed the human cost of political repression.

This narrative about the necessity of authoritarianism held sway for decades. Even after Pinochet's stunning arrest in London in 1998, when Chileans experienced renewed "irruptions of memory," these "memory battles" were largely concerned with accounting for the human rights violations committed during the dictatorship.[3] Despite the triumph of a human rights movement that eventually made the public defense of the dictatorship untenable, what had come before, as Juan Reyes suggested, remained taboo.

This is a book about radical politics in Chile in the decade before the Pinochet dictatorship. Alongside Allende's institutional project for a democratic transition to socialism, a multiplicity of understandings of revolutionary change emerged. *Beyond the Vanguard* is about those other meanings. It charts the untold history of how ordinary people challenged the existing social order. It examines the lost opportunities to create a democratic revolution in Chile as well as the lasting, everyday transformations in society that endure in spite of defeat. It concludes by suggesting how the legacies of 1960s revolutionary movements continue to resonate in Chile and beyond.

Spanning the thousand days of Salvador Allende's presidency (1970–73), the Popular Unity period is one of the most exceptional moments in Chile's history, yet it has inspired few social histories.[4] Instead, most accounts are overdetermined by the finality of the coup and present Chile's experiment with socialism as an inevitable march toward destruction. The Popular Unity project in this retrospective light takes on the air of a noble but naive dream destined to fail. With time, the responsibility for its failure increasingly moved away from the military and civilian leaders who plotted and carried out the coup to rest instead on a divided, ideological Left and a "hypermobilized" politicized citizenry.[5] The political context section of the 1991 Truth Commission report, written by the conservative Chilean historian Gonzalo Vial Correa, exemplifies this democratization of responsibility.[6]

In the literature on the Allende years, the Chilean MIR is typically presented as the troublesome Far Left that remained outside of the governing Popular Unity coalition and that pushed Salvador Allende so far that the coup was inevitable. The MIR's support for illegal land takeovers in the city and countryside challenged the controlled pace of a revolution planned from above. Voices across the political spectrum at the time, and particularly in retrospective accounts, accuse the MIR of pushing the radicalization of Chile's socialist experiment to a breaking point. During the dictatorship, the military targeted the MIR as an internal enemy of the state and systematically disappeared its militants—more than four hundred men and women in the first two years of the dictatorship alone.[7] The governing junta pointed to the MIR's defense of armed struggle in the 1960s to justify relentless repression. Even after the return to civilian rule in 1990, the social taboo around 1960s armed struggle foreclosed a critical examination of the origins of the continent's revolutionary leftist movements, the MIR among them.[8] At best, many observers saw these young revolutionaries as misguided idealists turned victims of state terrorism; at worst, as the main provocateurs of violent repression turned on themselves and society at large.[9] It should hardly be surprising that no one had bothered or dared to ask Juan Reyes about his politics. The stigma of association with leftist politics had real consequences for decades.

RETHINKING CHILE'S RADICAL PAST

The year 2011 turned out to be a watershed for Chileans to rethink their radical past. In the largest social movement since the dictatorship, high school and college students occupied the streets and their schools en masse. Like the nearly simultaneous Arab Spring and Occupy Wall Street movements, the "Chilean Winter" struck a deep chord of discontent over growing social inequality. What started as protests against Chile's privatized education model quickly moved on to challenge the dictatorship's market-driven neoliberal policies—and by extension, the legitimacy of a political and economic system that still maintained them twenty years after General Pinochet had left office. Born after the return to democracy in 1990, the students belong to the so-called generation without fear. These young people captivated the nation and the world with creative repertoires of protest that heralded a return not only to the streets but also to politics. Observers proclaimed 2011 as the "awakening of Chilean society," as powerful social movements once again succeeded in transforming the national political agenda and the nation's conscience.[10]

That year also marked an awakening of historical memory. Amid intense debates about Chile's future in living rooms and on street corners across the country, many individuals who had been silenced by fear, like Juan Reyes, openly acknowledged past activism. The Popular Unity years persist in popular memory as an experience that continues to form a central part of the identity of millions of Chileans.[11] For Reyes and his *compañeros* from the textile factory, watching the student protests on TV—and sometimes even accompanying their grandchildren to marches in nearby Concepción—gave a sense of urgency to telling their own stories. The palpable sense of expanding horizons in 2011 invited the question, What did revolutionary change look like in 1970s Chile?

In scale, effervescence, and intensity, the 2011 student movement evoked another moment in Chilean history when young people like Juan Reyes had mobilized for radical change. Forty years earlier, Chileans had similarly searched for alternative forms of politics, built cross-class alliances, engaged in collective actions, and shared the exhilaration of being part of a larger movement. Decades of authoritarian military rule had suppressed but not ultimately resolved these perennial questions about democratic participation. In the early twenty-first century, in Chile and around the world, protests once again led predominantly by young people put these questions at the center of political debate.

Oral history happens in the present and is, by its nature, retrospective. The oral histories that form the core of this book are, necessarily, the stories of survivors—those who lived to tell and those who chose to speak.[12] Memories of the Popular Unity years were filtered through seventeen years of military dictatorship with widespread repression, detention, torture, and exile for some and broad disenchantment with the unrealized promises of the 1990 democratic transition. This process of remembering was not easy, not only because—as Juan Reyes had suggested—their experiences during the Popular Unity had been suppressed for so long, but also because many leftist militants faced what the cultural critic John Beverley has described as the "paradigm of disillusion"—a refusal among 1960s activists to find anything positive in an experience that ended so badly.[13] Many college-educated former revolutionaries have written ex post facto apologies for their youthful flirtations with revolution and armed struggle.[14] As Beverley reminds us, these narratives by "repentant guerillas" often tell us more about the neoliberal present than they do about revolutionary politics in the 1960s. By contrast, most of the more than sixty grassroots activists I interviewed had not been prominent public figures. They were not accustomed to telling their stories and did not have neatly packaged narratives of heroic deeds. Rather, it was the sense of possibility and hope in the present that generated an opening for previously unspoken memories. For the first time in many years, it appeared that all those sacrifices in the past might have been for something.

For one thousand days in the early 1970s, Chileans experienced revolution not as a dream but as daily life. I use the term "everyday revolutions" to differentiate the local, contingent, everyday pursuit of change from the simultaneous national, globally mitigated, top-down battle for a peaceful revolution in Chile. The election of a compañero president, who promised state force would no longer be used to repress, afforded an opening for grassroots movements on an unprecedented scale. The perception of expanding horizons enabled many Chileans to imagine revolutions beyond the promises of the Popular Unity platform. By widening our conceptual framework for revolution to mean something more than just the seizure of state power, other processes become visible. When given the opportunity to act, what did people do? What was the content of their radical dreams? How does the ordinary become revolutionary?

I argue that revolutionary change took the form of quotidian transformations in people's everyday lives. These smaller-scale transformations might seem less threatening than the specter of armed insurrection, but they were no less of a challenge to the status quo: not in the ideological sense, but in the very real, material remaking of lives. The experiences at the heart of this book might appear wonderfully mundane: to acquire a political education not as indoctrination but as critical thinking, to speak before one's peers in an assembly, to occupy empty land and build one's home, to take over a bakery and ensure that bread reached those who needed it most, and to feel capable of shaping one's own destiny. It was through these collective efforts to reorganize daily life and democratize relations in classrooms, workplaces, and even the spaces of the home that Chileans started to enact a transformation of the social order. These efforts to redefine the terms of inclusion and overturn social hierarchies were driven not by violent destructive forces but by empowering creative energies.

By foregrounding how local experiences of radical, participatory democracy formed the backbone of revolutionary Chile, I reveal the extent to which a Cold War framework based on polarization and ideological conflict confounds more than it explains political conflict in Latin America. Through a local study, it is possible to see the complex working through of different notions of politics, democracy, and revolution. During the sixties and early seventies, as Chilean students, workers, *pobladores* (urban poor), and peasants became increasingly visible political actors, their participation drove the democratization of Chilean society. The Nixon-facilitated 1973 military coup sought not just to overturn a Socialist president and a democratic transition to a Socialist economy but also to turn back the decades-long struggle of working people for full inclusion as citizens. Rather than consign grassroots projects to defeat, I recover and reassess projects for popular sovereignty that affirm both the transformative potential of democracy and the ability of people to be agents of change. In this sense, the impact of radical politics cannot always be measured by immediate political victories but rather in the capacity for long-term social transformation. Understanding this history enables us to comprehend the present-day challenges that students and other activists face as they seek to envision new social contracts.

DECENTERING THE REVOLUTION

Decentering this history, moving it away from Santiago and national political actors, opens up new understandings of both Chile's revolution and Chile's misunderstood revolutionary Left—the MIR. In Chile, as in many other Latin American countries, the capital metropolis often stands in for national history. *Beyond the*

Vanguard foregrounds the local experience of Chile's revolution. By looking beyond the center of state power, a different story emerges about the convergence of workers, students, professionals, and urban poor in Chile's "red zone." The locus of this study is the provincial, port city of Concepción and its surrounding industrial enclaves located 500 kilometers to the south of Santiago.[15] Pedro de Valdivia, Spanish conquistador and "founder" of Chile, established the city of Concepción at the mouth of the Bío Bío River in 1550, marking the southernmost boundary between the Spanish Empire and the autonomous indigenous-controlled territories. The Mapuche people resisted Spanish rule, and Concepción remained a frontier until the late nineteenth century when the Chilean state waged a genocidal military campaign to incorporate the lands to the south. Concepción figures prominently in the national history of Chile, as Bernardo O'Higgins, liberator of Chile, declared independence from the city's central plaza in 1818. Throughout the nineteenth century, creole elites challenged Santiago's hold on central power. In the twentieth century, residents drew on Concepción's dual meaning as frontier and as alternative to Santiago to develop a strong regional identity based on cultural and economic autonomy and novel political formations. (See map 1.)

Concepción long prided itself on being a middle-class city. It boasted the country's first private university, founded in 1918 by local professionals associated with the Masonic temple. Dedicated to the "free development of the spirit," the Universidad de Concepción (UdeC) remained autonomous from the control of both the state and the Catholic Church—unlike the Universidad de Chile and the Pontificia Universidad Católica de Chile in Santiago. Even as it attracted students from across southern Chile and became an important cultural mecca, Concepción retained the feel of a provincial city. Nothing was more than a short walk from the self-contained campus and *barrio universitario* (university neighborhood). Students routinely marched from campus to the central plaza, which bordered sprawling working-class neighborhoods. For university students in Concepción, the sites of local power as well as urban poverty were never far away. When coal miners and textile workers arrived by train and by foot to occupy the city center, students often joined them. (See maps 2 and 3.)

As an important site of labor and student activism, Concepción occupies an outsized place in the history of the Chilean Left. Beginning in the late nineteenth century, capitalist expansion in the export sectors transformed peasants into industrial workers in the nitrate fields of northern Chile and to the south in Concepción province's Lota and Coronel coal mines and Tomé textile mills. Between 1880 and 1930, Chilean workers organized, joining with other working-class sectors and with the Chilean Communist and Socialist Parties. Chile's radical, Marxist-oriented labor movement extracted key concessions from the state in the 1920s and moved the entire political debate to the left. Chile, like many other industrializing countries in South America, went through a period of populist

MAP 1. Central Chile. Map by Molly Roy.

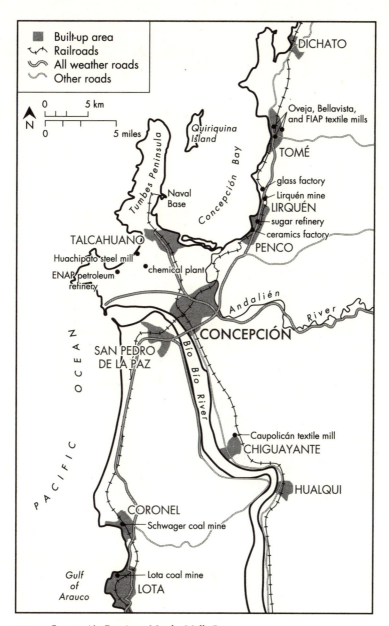

MAP 2. Concepción Province. Map by Molly Roy.

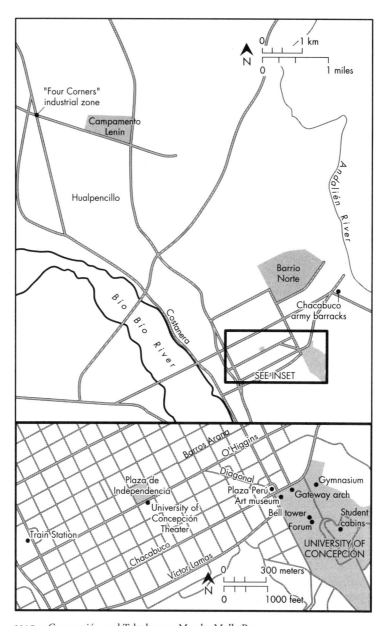

MAP 3. Concepción and Talcahuano. Map by Molly Roy.

governments, particularly in the 1930s and 1940s, when multiparty Popular Front governments, which included Socialists and Communists, came to power. The historian Jody Pavilack has demonstrated how in Concepción province the Popular Front, as a national and international political project of multiclass alliances, acquired its own local expression when Lota and Coronel coal miners, closely allied with the Communist Party, succeeded in gaining control of local government and radicalizing the scope and reach of welfare and labor policies in the region.[16]

These expressions of working-class agency did not go unchecked. In October 1947, coal miners launched a legal strike. In response, the Chilean military occupied the coal zone. The military rounded up hundreds of labor organizers and Communist Party members and sent them to northern detention camps, foreshadowing by a quarter century the ferocity of repression unleashed nationally in 1973.[17] President Gabriel González Videla pushed through a national security law that banned the Communist Party, stripping nearly forty thousand Chileans of their rights as citizens to participate in politics and union organizing. The antidemocratic legislation backed by state terror targeted not just Marxist ideology but also the region's militant working-class culture.

In Concepción province these experiences of working-class agency and state repression endured in local memory. Just as the national political alliance of the Popular Unity coalition drew on the legacy and experiences of the 1930s and 1940s Popular Front coalitions, Concepción residents carried forward the sense of agency that social relations could be modified. In the 1960s, demands of "Power to the People!" echoed around the world. Chile was no exception when *poder popular* (popular power) became the rallying cry of radicalized leftist sectors. While terms such as this were not used during the Popular Front era, the experiences of empowerment associated with them were not unique to the sixties and early seventies. During the Popular Unity, people in Concepción drew inspiration from both the promise contained within the national government's program and a highly militant working-class culture. These traditions of worker radicalism and territorial autonomy explain the strength of grassroots movements in Concepción in the 1960s that preceded Allende's election and that multiplied in the wake of his 1970 victory.

In the 1950s and 1960s, state development strategies centered on import substitution industrialization transformed Concepción province into one of the country's leading industrial hubs. In addition to the coal mines located twenty miles down the coast in Lota and Coronel, the country's first modern steel mill opened in 1950 across the bay in Talcahuano, along with a petroleum refinery and navy shipyard. To the north of the provincial capital, lighter manufacturing operations, like ceramics and glass factories, joined the well-established nineteenth-century textile mills in Tomé and Chiguayante. Migrants from the countryside and southern Chile arrived in the region in search of steady employment. Between 1940 and 1970, the population of Concepción province more than doubled, from 310,663 to

642,163.[18] By 1970, one-third of all residents—among them many recently arrived workers—lacked access to adequate housing. The basic need for a home would fuel urban land takeovers by the homeless poor and unhoused workers. By the 1960s, Concepción had a surplus of both students and workers.

RECOVERING THE REVOLUTIONARY
LEFT FROM BELOW

Chile's homegrown revolutionary Left, the Movimiento de Izquierda Revolucionaria, came into being and enjoyed its widest popular support in Concepción province. Despite being founded in 1965 in Santiago by ideologically pluralistic groups, including many dissident Socialists and Communists with roots in labor organizing, the MIR rose to prominence within the University of Concepción in tandem with the university reform movement. At the time, the MIR's endorsement of armed struggle and its admiration for the Cuban Revolution were not unique in Chile or Latin America. What differentiated the MIR from other Latin American revolutionary groups was its ability to work within the Chilean political tradition and engage in grassroots organizing. Contrary to stereotypes of the MIR as a middle-class student movement, during the Popular Unity years the MIR in Concepción became a cross-class movement of workers, pobladores, and students.

For decades, the dominant narrative about the MIR has been one of resistance, repression, and defeat. This story of the MIR's failure is a national story told from Santiago. Shifting perspective to view this history from the grassroots upends existing narratives, ranging from those that emphasize the state repression that decimated these groups to those by militant apologists that celebrate masculine revolutionary martyrdom. Similarly, previous histories of the MIR largely drawn from official party documents and biographies of top leaders re-create an image of what the MIR wanted to be—a revolutionary vanguard—rather than what it was in practice—a grassroots movement for revolution.[19] Under Marxist-Leninist theory, the national MIR leadership rationalized its support for grassroots struggle as intensifying class struggle to produce an inevitable future confrontation. Yet on the ground, the MIR's methods and goals were more about promoting popular participation than overturning the state.

Moving beyond an image of sixties and seventies Latin American revolutionaries as bearded guerrillas hiding out in the mountains or young people building bombs in cities, *Beyond the Vanguard* foregrounds their contributions to grassroots social change.[20] Like the Black Panther Party in the United States, the Chilean MIR was more than a militant organization. In his study on the origins of Black Power and the Black Panther Party in Lowndes County, Alabama, the historian Hassan Jeffries argues that "the radicalization of local people stemmed from specific movement experiences rather than a general interaction with supposed movement messiahs."[21] This framework underscores how movements unfold in a context of open contingencies. Latin American history is replete with examples of how those in power blame external agents as agitators behind popular mobilization. Ideology becomes a convenient scapegoat to deny legitimate, basic demands for human decency.[22] Rather than individual leaders being the sole drivers behind a movement, it was local people and organizing practices that redefined the goals, orientation, and actions of the MIR in Concepción, transforming it from a nascent guerrilla movement into a successful and highly radical social movement.

What follows is the untold story of how the MIR was far more than the masculine, Leninist, armed "ultra-Left," as it has often been portrayed. Disproportionate to its size, the MIR became an important ally in experiments of popular democracy and grassroots empowerment during the thousand days of Salvador Allende's presidency. The ability to build a united leftist front with the Popular Unity parties in Concepción province belied the national MIR's own rhetoric of rupture with Allende and the Old Left. Indeed, the MIR's appeal to broad sectors derived from its ability to fuse new calls for revolutionary change with the Old Left's time-tested strategies of direct action, grassroots activism, and participatory democracy. In response to local conditions and labor traditions, Concepción MIR militants temporarily and strategically defied the rigid Marxist ideological orientation of national MIR leaders and sought to make revolutionary change more pragmatic and less dogmatic by challenging power relations in factories, communities, and even families. The conflict between national and regional MIR leaders over how to understand the array of experiences happening in Concepción speaks to the tension between the abstract goal of revolution and the complex realities of everyday politics. This dilemma is not unique to Chile. Rather, the tension between hierarchical internal party structures and horizontal political practices remains a perennial problem for grassroots movements and their relationship to political parties.

Studying this history through oral history interviews with grassroots activists not only adds new voices to the historical record but also makes it possible to historicize how people discovered a sense of themselves as political actors. Chilean historiography remains weak on the question of subjects and their experiences. Most scholarship on this contentious period in Chile's history hinges on explaining "the breakdown of democracy" from different partisan political perspectives and privileges national actors and political institutions.[23] Yet one of the defining features of the Popular Unity years was the profound sense of historicity—the sense of agency that many ordinary Chileans experienced at having made history.[24] My extensive oral histories with grassroots activists shed light on who joined, why they joined, and how they actually spent most of their time. These kinds of questions move us toward the realm of subjectivity in which we consider historical actors and their motivations, hopes, and values. By setting aside the viability of a particular political project, this approach enables us to ask what gave a revolutionary movement meaning—then and now.

Decades later, the privileged place that the Popular Unity years occupy within individual memories speaks to the power that people continue to derive from having been participants in a process of collective transformation. Under the grandiose rhetoric of revolutionary utopias in the sixties and early seventies, spaces for participation emerged that brought people into politics in new ways. The literary scholar Kirstin Ross observed how in Paris in 1968 "the synchronizing of two very different temporalities"—students and workers—made manifest new political subjectivities and gave rise to a vision of equality that was "verified subjectively, declared and experienced in the here and now as what is and not what should be."[25] As the everyday became radical, politics became part of daily life and were no longer solely the domain of state institutions and electoral politics. In understanding how people came to make revolutionary politics their own, this study offers new insights into the repertoire of action that underwrites successful social movements: developing personal relationships, engaging people's dual identities, organizing around basic needs, creating a platform for people to be heard, providing educational opportunities, and building on the affective experience of joy that accompanies social effervescence. The experience of personal transformation through political participation represents an important legacy of radical politics for both the sixties generation and present-day activists.

This book moves chronologically and thematically. The first three chapters trace the emergence of the MIR among students, workers, and pobladores in Concepción. These different sectors converged in the 1972 Concepción People's Assembly, a unique experiment in popular democracy chronicled in chapter 4. By late 1972, the Allende government faced its greatest challenge in the "Bosses' Lockout." Chapter 5 uncovers how grassroots activists mobilized to save the government by ensuring access to basic foodstuffs. The final chapter examines how militants experienced the internal contradictions within the MIR and Chile's unraveling revolution by charting their frustrations at being unable to reverse the counterrevolutionary onslaught and their belief that continued organizing and sacrifice might well make a difference. At the center of this narrative are—as the textile worker Juan Reyes suggested—the people themselves, the men and women who carried out everyday revolutions.

"We Lived Those Years with a Lot of Passion"

University Reform and the Rise of the Movimiento de Izquierda Revolucionaria

At seventeen, Margarita González left home to enroll in the University of Concepción. Like many other college students, she felt a mix of excitement and uncertainty as she left behind the comfort and safety of her family. As a student, she gained newfound independence: "I stopped being a girl sheltered by a large family and became a young university woman in charge of my own life." Without house chores and curfews, Margarita had freedom to decide how she spent her time and with whom. She had time for classes and studying but also for debate and reflection with her peers. Growing up with nine siblings, she was used to sharing close quarters, but the residence hall's sheer diversity of students—"from wealthy families to working-class families to very poor families, from northern Chile to central and southern Chile, from cities and rural areas"—was thrilling. Politics, she soon discovered, was the currency of intellectual exchange. Margarita had arrived in this southern industrial city and its campus at a very particular moment: March 1968.[1]

Student protest and calls for university reform came to the fore around the world in the mid-1960s and peaked in 1968. Chile was no exception.[2] Campus activism often began by questioning power structures within the university, then challenged the status quo as a whole. In the process, students transformed both society and themselves. In Chile, university reform movements swept through the Catholic and state universities in Valparaíso, Santiago, and Concepción.[3] Students called for a co-government arrangement that would grant faculty, staff, and students shared administrative power.[4] In tandem with this desire to democratize the university, students fought to expand access to higher education. Nothing in these Chilean student demands in 1968 was new; rather, they drew inspiration from the

1917 "Grito de Córdoba," which had launched university reform in Argentina.[5] The difference was their success.

By 1969, student movements had transformed every major Chilean university—from the more abstract allocation of resources and power to the more palpable questions of what students could study, who taught them, and who gained admission. The 1960s saw a fivefold increase in university enrollments across Chile, from approximately 25,000 to 145,000.[6] In Concepción, enrollments doubled between 1961 and 1968, from 2,685 students to 5,770, and tripled during Margarita González's years on campus. As a direct result of the university reforms, Concepción enrolled nearly 20,000 students in 1973.[7]

Margarita's experience as a university student in the late 1960s was indelibly shaped by the sense that she was living in an exceptional moment in her country's history. Decades later she recalled, "We lived those years with a lot of passion. It was a turbulent time: the birth of the MIR [Revolutionary Left Movement], calls for university reform, real possibilities for a Socialist president and a socialist project in Chile. These were experiences that shaped my life forever. As students, we made decisions. We took political stances. My second year studying medicine [coincided with] a moment of important political effervescence and I became a militant [of the MIR]."[8] How did Margarita come to see political militancy in a revolutionary organization as the most promising avenue to confront the injustices ingrained in Chilean society? Her personal and political transformation allows us to ask, Why did university students reemerge as political actors in the mid-1960s? And why specifically in the Chilean context did Concepción become the epicenter of a revolutionary movement?

At the University of Concepción, I argue, the university reform process was mutually constitutive with the turn to revolutionary politics. Despite being founded in Santiago in August 1965, Chile's iconic and controversial revolutionary Left—the MIR—has long been closely associated with Concepción and its combative student movement. The struggle for university reform (1964–69) heralded the MIR's arrival on the national political scene and provided a training ground for the generation of student leaders who took over the MIR's national leadership in 1967.[9] Against the backdrop of student protests, Concepción and then national MIR leaders Miguel Enríquez, Bautista Van Schouwen, and Luciano Cruz deepened their commitment to building a Marxist-Leninist vanguard party. The former Concepción medical students restructured the party toward that end in 1969, tightening membership requirements, taking the party underground, and sending Concepción students out to build the party in other regions. By 1973, most of the top national and regional leaders were former Concepción students. This is the known story of the university reform movement and the MIR: the audacity of its student leaders in radicalizing the Concepción movement gave the MIR greater visibility and catapulted the medical students turned MIR leaders into the national spotlight.[10]

Yet the struggle for university reform generated much broader ripples in Chilean society, transforming not just the MIR as a political organization and regional politics in Concepción but also individual students' lives. The push to democratize the university became linked to the democratization of daily life. These other legacies of the 1960s student movement shaped the regional experience of Chile's revolution in the years ahead. Armed with little more than radical aspirations and Marxist ideals, young militants in Concepción successfully forged networks of militancy across class lines. This cross-class political project started on campus with students like Margarita González.

This chapter examines the particularities of Concepción student politics to explain how the university reform movement accelerated a revolutionary project on and beyond the campus. In the face of authorities' intransigence and police brutality, student demands radicalized. Even as the national MIR's public declarations defended the legitimacy of violence to usher in socialist revolution, the Concepción university reform was a democratic process shaped by transforming an institution from within. The university reform movement laid the foundation for the MIR's subsequent modus operandi—not as armed insurrection, but as grassroots organizing driven by mass participation, direct action, and radical democracy.

FOUNDING THE MOVIMIENTO DE IZQUIERDA REVOLUCIONARIA, AUGUST 1965

In September 1964, Chileans went to the polls to elect a new president. After the heated campaign cycle, Christian Democrat (DC) Eduardo Frei Montalva won an unprecedented absolute majority (56%). The leftist Frente de Acción Popular (FRAP; Popular Action Front) coalition candidate Salvador Allende finished a distant second (39%) in a two-way race. It was the third electoral defeat for the Socialist physician, whose support had increased from 1958, when he narrowly missed being elected president with 29% of the vote in a four-way race. Debates arose within the ideologically diverse Chilean Left over whether the decades-long strategy of Popular Front coalition politics was spent. These conversations were not confined to party leaders but also took place across Chile, in factories, schools, and universities. For radical sectors outside the Socialist and Communist Parties, Allende's defeat confirmed their conviction that change would not come from the ballot box. The radical Christian labor leader Clotario Blest had spent years trying to unify Chile's dispersed revolutionary Left factions. This project became a reality when sixty delegates converged on an anarchist shoemakers' union in Santiago on August 15, 1965, to found the Movimiento de Izquierda Revolucionaria.[11]

The MIR presented itself as the Marxist-Leninist vanguard that would lead a socialist revolution in Chile. Its founders purposefully used the term "revolutionary Left" to differentiate the MIR from the "reformist" Chilean Communist Party and "movement" to signal their distrust of political parties' tendency to divide the working class. The MIR's founding charter criticized the "bureaucratic leaderships of the traditional left," who "defraud workers' hopes" by offering "reforms to the capitalist regime" and who "deceive workers with a permanent electoral dance, forgetting direct action and the revolutionary tradition of the Chilean proletariat."[12] With the explicit goal of "overthrow[ing] the capitalist system and [replacing it] with a government of workers and peasants," the MIR embraced class struggle and endorsed armed popular insurrection as the only means to bring socialism to Chile. At the first congress, Miguel Enríquez presented the Concepción delegation's "Political-Military Thesis" outlining the MIR's proposal for popular insurrection. Although many in the MIR admired the 1959 Cuban Revolution, by 1965 the disastrous attempts to export revolutionary guerrilla *focos* to other Latin American countries were sufficiently graphic to dissuade the Chilean organization from pursuing the same strategy.[13] Instead, to ensure that armed groups would have wide support, the older generation of leaders tempered the Concepción students' proposal by specifying that sufficient radicalization of popular movements was a precondition to launching an armed insurrection.[14]

Despite the MIR's self-fashioned rupture, according to the historian Eugenia Palieraki, its origins lay in the history of the Chilean Left and Chilean political culture. From the moment of its founding, the MIR was a heterogeneous mix of generations, ideological influences, and political organizations. Its creation in 1965 provided important continuity between the 1920s and 1930s generation of Trotskyists, Socialists, and radical syndicalists and the 1960s generation of young self-styled revolutionaries.[15] The majority of its older militants had been expelled from the Central Única de Trabajadores de Chile (CUT; Chilean National Labor Federation), the Socialist Party, and the Communist Party in the 1950s, many of the younger ones from the Socialist and Communist Youth Parties in the 1960s.[16] Founding members brought their political formation in the Old Left to bear on the internal organization of the MIR, adopting the Socialist Party's internal party structure based on cells and the Communist Party's same Leninist principle of centralized decision making as binding for all members.[17] More than just an inherited, hierarchical party structure, the newly formed MIR also drew on the Old Left's successful methods of direct action, grassroots activism, and participatory democracy and reinvigorated them with renewed calls for revolutionary change. The MIR's grassroots expansion during the Allende years resulted from its ability to work within the Chilean political tradition, not outside it.

EL MOVIMIENTO UNIVERSITARIO DE IZQUIERDA:
CONCEPCIÓN'S PROLOGUE TO THE MIR

Leftist students at the University of Concepción launched a grassroots movement, the Movimiento Universitario de Izquierda (MUI; Leftist University Student Movement), in October 1964, preceding the creation of the MIR by nearly a year.[18] "The basic organizational principle guiding the MUI," noted a student journalist, "is revolutionary democracy, which means decisions are not made by the leaders who turn their backs on the masses but rather by the masses themselves in direct form."[19] The will of the majority resolved any dispute in university-wide assemblies.[20] The MUI combined assembly-based participatory political culture with highly visible direct actions, including marches and skirmishes with police in the city center and strikes and the occupation of buildings on campus. This combination of assembly politics and direct action created a repertoire of activism that underwrote the MIR's rapid expansion in Concepción province from a minority of Marxist students to a broad movement in favor of transforming not only the university but also society at large.

Enzo La Mura, a history student, was among the dissident Communist and Socialist students in the education and medical schools who came together to form the MUI. He had arrived in Concepción to finish high school in 1959. In contrast to a life "spent chasing after a bus" in Santiago, La Mura found that the provincial "Concepción offered time for other things." With more time to dedicate to reading, La Mura discovered his passion for history and for politics. Inspired by the Cuban Revolution, La Mura joined the Communist Youth (JJCC) in 1960. He immediately noticed a difference between the seriousness of the older generation of Communists, who had lived through the repression and clandestine phase (1948–58), and those who had joined out of "affinity with el Che [Guevara]." He balked at the internal rigidity of the Party and the Stalinist tendencies of some of its members. "They made the mistake of trying to discipline me," he explained. "My circle of friends was a bohemian, party group, who liked to go out singing and to smoke hookahs. We were irreverent." The final straw for some Communist Youth like La Mura came when the Chilean Communist Party sided with the Soviet Union instead of the Cuban Revolution following the Sino-Soviet split in 1962.[21] Despite being expelled from the organized youth wings of the Socialist and Communist Parties, many students like La Mura actively campaigned for Salvador Allende in 1964. It was afterward that the real disillusion set in, recalled La Mura, "and it radicalized things. Many of us stopped voting. I annulled my vote in 1965."[22]

Yet the campaign experience inspired the desire for a new kind of politics. Allende himself admitted the failure to mobilize independent voters outside of party structures through autonomous committees that might be sustained after the election. The Communist and Socialist Parties tended to compete against each other to recruit people directly into their parties. Instead, La Mura recalled, "what was needed was a grassroots movement, and we identified with this idea because we had done something similar in the engineering school."[23] The goal to build a campuswide grassroots organization that would unify all leftist students regardless of their party affiliation required not only expanding their supporters to include left-leaning independents but also overcoming suspicion and accusations of "divisionism" between the Socialist and Communist Youth Parties and the students who had left or, in some cases, had been expelled from them. In addition to open membership requirements, the MUI's internal organization differentiated it from other political entities. As La Mura explained, "Political parties functioned in bases or cells, predicated on obedience to party hierarchy. By contrast, the MUI functioned horizontally in assemblies, independent of any oversight" from regional or national party structures.[24] Within the space of a few years, the MUI succeeded in bringing together diverse ideological tendencies around common goals: advance student struggles inside the university and advance toward socialist revolution in society.

The horizontal political practices of the MUI mirrored the University of Concepción's unique political culture where politics were practiced as a sport. Unlike other Chilean universities, Concepción student politics functioned as "a kind of direct democracy . . . [in which] everything was resolved in the assembly arena before hundreds of students."[25] Decisions to go on strike were not made by the executive council of the Federación de Estudiantes de Concepción (FEC; Concepción Student Federation) but rather were put to a vote before an open FEC general assembly. These assemblies took place in the largest gymnasium on campus and routinely drew audiences of several thousand. The students sat by political bloc: Christian Democrats and supporters of the relatively moderate Radical Party congregated on the north side bleachers alongside the Right's small presence; and at the south end, New Left students (MUI) filled the stands next to Communists and Socialists.[26] Assemblies frequently "opened with songs, chants, and taunts from one side to the other" before student leaders addressed the audience from the gym floor.[27] The quality of their performance would be assessed by boos and applause. As an autonomous New Left coalition that operated outside party hierarchies, the MUI enjoyed greater freedom to radicalize student demands.

The raucous, direct democracy of the student federation general assemblies was just one element that differentiated student life in Concepción from elsewhere in Chile. The University of Concepción stood out with its self-contained campus, student residential halls and cabins, and common first-year core curriculum. Enshrined in its motto—"For the free development of the spirit"—the University of Concepción educated not just the children of local elites but also the sons and daughters of the aspiring middle class and, increasingly, the working class. Students from humble origins obtained scholarships and university-subsidized housing in Concepción that

was not available elsewhere. The backgrounds of early MUI leaders reflect the changing social composition of the study body. Raised in Concepción, Miguel Enríquez
was the son of a physician; Luciano Cruz, the son of a military officer; and Bautista
Van Schouwen, the son of a low-level engineer.[28] Juan Saavedra, a law student, was
the son of a provincial accountant in southern Temuco. Enzo La Mura's mother
worked as a seamstress in Santiago, but he lived with his grandparents in Concepción. Nelson Gutiérrez, born in the remote central town of Cauquenes to a rural
primary school teacher, enrolled in Concepción in 1965—the inaugural year for the
Propedéutico, the common first-year core curriculum.

The residence halls and cabins were spaces of encounter between students
from different regional and class backgrounds. This fluidity contributed to the
politicization of the student body and facilitated building a cross-class student
movement. Early on, the MUI consolidated its leadership of the Federación de
Hogares, representing students from outside Concepción who lived on campus.
Expanded enrollments in the 1960s had produced a corresponding demand for
subsidized housing and dining. In addition to students from other regions, the
cabins and dormitories housed many students from the immediate surrounding
areas, including Tomé and Coronel, who lived on campus during the week and
returned home on the weekends. These students served as points of entry for political organizing in their hometowns. The MUI worked within these spaces—
through conversations with classmates and roommates—to bring students with
little previous political experience into active engagement with campus politics.
The regional and social class diversity of UdeC students facilitated the movement's
expansion into surrounding industrial enclaves and Chile's far-flung provinces.

In the mid-1960s, the MUI engaged in the "ant work" of building support by
competing in student center elections across campus—in other words, in classic
grassroots politics.[29] MUI leadership within student centers proved critical for
launching the university reform movement in Concepción in 1965. The rapid
growth of the student body coupled with inadequate facilities and understaffed
classes produced an opening for student protest. The UdeC institutes and schools
with MUI-dominated student governments disproportionately became involved
in nascent protests against insufficient staff, incompetent professors, and poorly
designed curricula. By publicizing university authorities' consistent refusal to
negotiate with students, the MUI successfully elevated these school-specific
demands into campuswide issues. On the basis of local grievances, MUI students
gained the FEC's endorsement, often in the form of general assembly votes for 24-
or 48-hour campuswide solidarity strikes.

At a time when the Christian Democrats' hegemony was unrivaled nationally—
indeed, this was in the midst of President Eduardo Frei's Revolution in Liberty,
whose moderate social and economic reforms were funded by the U.S. government's Alliance for Progress—the MUI in Concepción gained ground in student

elections as a dynamic alternative within the Left that surpassed the national coalition, the Popular Action Front (FRAP), led by the Communist and Socialist Parties. Yet the MUI was more than just an electoral coalition. Built from the bottom up by leftist students, it was a burgeoning movement that sought to challenge the system from within. As they competed against Christian Democrats in campus elections, the MUI soon challenged the Frei government in the streets.

TAKING PROTEST TO THE STREETS, 1965

In April 1965, the MUI succeeded in paralyzing Concepción over the 50% fare increases for public transportation announced by the Frei administration.[30] High school students in Concepción and Coronel first went on strike in protest on April 19, 1965.[31] The following day, the MUI seized the opportunity to oppose the newly elected Christian Democratic administration by calling for a march. Mounting popular discontent over fare hikes in April 1965 echoed the April 1957 *revuelto popular* (popular revolt), when students and workers poured into the streets and brought Santiago to a standstill for two days.[32] At thirteen, Miguel Enríquez and his childhood friend Bautista Van Schouwen experienced their first political action; they joined workers, pobladores, and students occupying Concepción's main streets on April 2, 1957.[33] Eight years later, the event remained an important touchstone for the MUI students as they made a foray into mass politics.[34] What began as a protest over fare hikes by fifty university students quickly transformed into two thousand students mobilized in defense of university autonomy.

The MUI's first public demonstration on April 20, 1965, had many elements that would be repeated in the days and years to come. The march traced a familiar circular route between the university campus and the adjacent city center. Although the specific targets—the American cultural propaganda office (USIS), the Christian Democratic Party office, the local governor's office in the Intendency (local seat of government), *El Sur* newspaper offices—varied, the movement through the city remained a constant. Marches always began in the Plaza Perú in front of the main campus entrance and proceeded down the diagonal avenue to the Courts of Justice on the edge of downtown. As they marched, MUI students derided President Frei with chants like "Old big-nose just hiked fares on us!" and "Revolution in Liberty, that's a real good joke, ha ha ha!" When they turned left down Concepción's main thoroughfare, O'Higgins Avenue, their message changed from criticism of the Christian Democratic government to condemnation of U.S. imperialism: "Yankees, get out of Vietnam!" After a brief stop in front of the USIS offices, where a rock hurled from the crowd shattered the front window, the students marched to the Plaza de Independencia, where Chilean independence was declared in 1818 and where the Intendency still stood. As they moved through the city center, newspapers reported that "the people waiting at bus stops applauded the students, while the bus owners proceeded to divert their vehicles."[35] Joined by high school students in the plaza, the demonstrators sat down at the intersection of Barros Arana Avenue and Aníbal Pinto Street, where they blocked all remaining transit. Afterward they doubled back toward the university on Barros Arana, stopping in front of the Christian Democratic Party headquarters to ridicule Frei's Revolution in Liberty one last time before turning down Colo Colo Street, to criticize the conservative daily *El Sur* for false reporting. The march ended without larger incidents. While the USIS officials later expressed bewilderment over their broken office window since the object of the protests had been fare hikes, for the students, contesting the "anti-popular" policies of the Christian Democratic administration slid easily into protesting U.S. imperialism.[36]

In the following days as Concepción students again took to the streets, they came face-to-face with the repressive side of the state. Their rocks and occasional Molotov cocktails were met by water cannons, tear gas, and bullets. Even the local press, which was not particularly sympathetic to the students or their demands, registered shock at the violent repression.[37] Following police confrontations and the arrests of dozens of students, the MUI presented daily resolutions to continue campuswide strikes to protest both fare hikes and police repression. The MUI campaigned for the release of detained students regardless of their political affiliation. In general assembly debates with Christian Democratic students, MUI students' resolutions won majority support, and the strikes and marches continued unabated.[38]

As almost daily street clashes between university students and the Grupo Móvil riot police extended over several days, the wider Concepción community came to the students' defense. Unionized teachers and railroad workers denounced the fare hikes and police brutality and celebrated "the virile attitude of the protesting students."[39] When the local branch of the CUT, Chile's largest labor federation, called a rally on April 24, their invited guest speaker was the medical student and MUI leader Luciano Cruz, who embodied the contentious, combative style of the Concepción student movement. Amidst "wild applause," Cruz proclaimed the demonstrations were no longer about fare hikes but "a demonstration by Chile's poor against the rich."[40] His ability to cross over from student leader to social protest leader blurred the boundaries between university and city in a community already deeply invested in its local university. The CUT rally followed accusations that the police had come onto the campus, which violated the long-standing tradition of university autonomy. Cruz offered vivid testimony of how students had valiantly stood their ground after the police had launched a surprise attack, noting that "in the defense of the Barrio Universitario all students participated regardless of political ideas."[41] What mattered, Cruz emphasized, was their willingness to put their bodies on the line.

The police incursion onto the campus fueled growing support for the students and their cause. On April 24, university authorities confirmed the discovery of tear gas canisters on the campus grounds. In response, they requested an explanation directly from President Frei for the "violation of university autonomy" and demanded a special congressional inquiry into the incident.[42] Seven days after the initial protests, two thousand university students—roughly two-thirds of the student body—attended an assembly on campus. Afterwards, MUI students led a march that culminated in a peaceful sit-in in the Plaza de Independencia.[43] By contrast, despite controlling the student federation (FEC), Christian Democratic students were reticent to challenge the local governor, Alfonso Urrejola, a UdeC professor and a Christian Democrat. In April 1965, an issue ostensibly external to the university—fare hikes—galvanized the university community. The events marked the MUI's debut outside campus.

The sense that the university was a space to be defended came under a different challenge in November 1965 with the arrival of U.S. senator Robert Kennedy. By this time, several of the MUI students, including Miguel Enríquez, Bautista Van Schouwen, Luciano Cruz, Edgardo Condeza, Ricardo Ruz, Jorge Grez, and Sergio Pérez Molina, had participated in the founding of the MIR and sat on its Central Committee.[44] Kennedy's goodwill tour through Latin America and his scheduled speech at the University of Concepción gymnasium posed a dilemma for leftist student leaders. As self-proclaimed revolutionaries, admitted then law student Juan Saavedra, "we could not tolerate allowing such a distinguished representative of imperialism to speak at our university without at the very least attempting to stop him."[45] In an afternoon meeting with student leaders at Senator Kennedy's hotel, Miguel Enríquez engaged in a quick-witted exchange with Kennedy and warned him to stay away from campus. The MUI publicly reiterated its position that individuals "whose hands are dirty with sister blood should not be allowed to enter the campus."[46] Kennedy, however, was not dissuaded and arrived that evening to address some two thousand students in the university gymnasium. The MUI students became increasingly desperate to show their opposition to the American senator and the recent U.S.-led invasion of the Dominican Republic. As the microphone drowned out their jeers, Sergio Pérez cut the PA system and other MUI students hurled eggs and fruit at the stage.[47] Robert Kennedy eventually left without speaking.

The confrontation with Kennedy was largely symbolic, a gesture of hostility that gained the MUI press coverage and notoriety. While the MUI students had succeeded in preventing Kennedy from speaking, they had not forcibly expelled him from campus as the leftist press claimed.[48] And as Saavedra admitted, the "reaction in the university was complex." Upon exiting the building, Christian Democratic students pounced on the protesting students and roughed them up.[49] Unlike the fare hike protests, the Kennedy incident did not garner widespread support for the MUI from the study body or the wider Concepción community. It did however, showcase another side of the revolutionary Left's budding political culture: audacity. In their eyes, the students had stood up to U.S. imperialism and won. Although the students most directly involved were all members of the recently formed MIR, at the time they appeared in the local press as the MUI. The incident served to boost the MUI's anti-imperialist and revolutionary credentials and reinforced the leadership of Miguel Enríquez, gaining him attention within wider revolutionary circles.[50]

The highly visible events led by the MUI in 1965 were largely about forces outside of the university: massive street protests in opposition to the Christian Democratic government's fare hikes and a vociferous minority audaciously confronting U.S. imperialism in the form of Senator Kennedy. Both incidents enabled the MUI to take up the mantle of defenders of the university, understood as autonomous territory. In 1966, the UdeC itself would be at the center of a reinvigorated student movement. Simultaneously with challenges to the power structures of the university and its role in society, protests of external factors did not disappear. Rather, through their leadership of the Concepción university reform movement, the MUI codified its opposition to U.S. imperialism and to the Christian Democratic government.

UNIVERSITY REVOLUTION, 1965–1967

While nationally the MIR experienced slow growth between 1965 and 1967, Concepción was the exception. Early on, MIR student leaders called for a "university revolution" in Concepción, not just reform.[51] In his unsuccessful MUI-backed bid for FEC president in October 1965, Miguel Enríquez declared, "We are fighting for a university revolution that will transform the university into the principal motor for development, democracy, and openness to all ideologies."[52] He continued, "The [student] federation should work alongside the poblador and the campesino to organize them and together we will build progress for our patria. We believe the current university defends class interests . . . [and] remains dominated by foreign influences and pressures alien to our social reality."[53] Enríquez's October 1965 call for students to organize the urban and rural poor—sectors traditionally outside of Chilean politics—anticipated what would become the MIR's principal rallying cry and organizing strategy. In the short term, the MUI concentrated efforts on removal of foreign influences from the University of Concepción, which received more U.S. Peace Corps volunteers than any other university in Chile, as well as significant funding from the United Nations Educational, Scientific and Cultural Organization (UNESCO) and the Ford Foundation to implement administrative and curricular changes.[54]

Through their engagement with student politics in the 1960s, revolutionary Left students in the University of Concepción challenged and, ultimately, redefined the role of the university within society. Since 1958, when UNESCO designated the University of Concepción a pilot program for Latin American universities, development through modernization held sway as the model to emulate. This vision centered on creating a science-driven university, capable of bringing efficiency, modernity, and prosperity to a capitalist society. The Ford Foundation and the University of Minnesota provided economic and intellectual support in developing the "1958 Modernization Plan" for the University of Concepción, signed by Rector David Stitchkin in 1959. The plan called for administrative and curricular restructuring and the expansion of the campus urban plan. International experts from UNESCO, the Ford Foundation, and the University of Minnesota regularly visited campus to evaluate progress on its implementation.[55] Neither intrinsically anti-American nor stubbornly intent on politicizing educational issues, the MIR students understood the university as a key space of contestation—not just for its long-standing tradition as a microcosm of national politics, but also as an institution that reproduced social and class structures.

The MUI's grassroots strategy to compete in student center elections laid the foundation for the university reform movement. In November 1965, a MUI-Radical ticket won control of the pharmacy school's student center, breaking the seven-year hold by the Christian Democrats. The same year, the MUI candidate was elected first-year student body president. These victories were significant, because in 1966 both the first-year students and the pharmacy students went on strike over curricular issues. In September 1966, pharmacy students initiated a series of protests that lasted for nearly three months. The university authorities responded by annulling the enrollments of striking students.[56] In response, students occupied the university's main buildings.

As the Concepción student movement gained traction in 1965 and into 1966, the university administration refused to negotiate and even retaliated by cancelling students' dining scholarships. Faced with administrative intransigence, students soon moved from school-specific issues to demand more transcendent reforms centered first on co-government and then, with New Left (MUI-MIR) influence, on anti-imperialism. Unlike reform movements in state and Catholic universities in Santiago and Valparaíso, anti-imperialism became a central plank in the Concepción reform movement because as a private university UdeC relied heavily on international funding, principally from UNESCO and the Ford Foundation. By 1966, by unanimous general assembly vote, Concepción students demanded nothing short of the complete democratization of their university:

> The problem in the Pharmacy School, which continues without solution, is a reflection of a wider crisis in the University of Concepción, which itself is the product of a general crisis in society. And since social change is underway, the university should transform to draw closer to its higher ideals and its truly revolutionary mission. This crisis in the university is manifested principally by the lack of democratization, the creation of professionals without social conscience, research without focus on national development, and haphazard expansion in higher education.[57]

As an indication of how far student politics had moved to the left, Christian Democratic students presented this proposal as an attempt to respond to growing MUI-MIR demands. The call for university reform—first proposed by New Left students in October 1964—would be consolidated during a special student federation congress in October 1966, where Miguel Enríquez presented his "University Revolution" proposal.[58] The accords from this congress formed the basis for Concepción students' struggle for "the democratization of the university, the defense of its autonomy, greater access to the university for workers and peasants, and the struggle against U.S. penetration [on campus]."[59] For the first time, Concepción students demanded 20% representation in university administration (*consejo universitario*) and the immediate expulsion of "the U.S. Peace Corps agents from campus."[60]

In building a movement for university reform, the MUI confronted the entrenched power of the Masonic Order. Within the University of Concepción, the order exercised de facto power.[61] Its members made up the majority of full-time teaching faculty and the Assembly of Associates—a group composed of Concepción's most distinguished gentlemen—who had unilateral power to appoint the university rector and board of directors (Directorio). While Concepción students demanded that their university respond to changing social currents, the university authorities remained impassive under the ineffectual leadership of Rector Ignacio González Ginouvés.[62] In October 1966, Rector González lamented privately to the board of directors, "There is moral cowardice in the majority [of students] and much audacity in the minority." Referring to the MUI, the rector acknowledged that "the extremist groups are not the majority, but they are extraordinarily well-trained in propaganda and action."[63] Rejecting claims that outside agitators had infiltrated student protests, he placed the blame for the prolonged strike on the Christian Democratic student leaders "who initiated it, [but] did not know how to handle it. . . . I told them they would pay the consequences for unleashing this movement, and that's what happened. Soon after it started, they were no longer in control."[64] The Christian Democratic students' ineffective leadership in Concepción may have stemmed in part from their preoccupation with internal party conflicts playing out nationally. Yet the rector failed to appreciate the extent to which many University Christian Democrats (DCU) in Concepción had moved to the left.[65] In the November 1966 FEC elections, the DCU again narrowly defeated the MUI. Yet this time, the more radical sectors of the DCU, including Eduardo Aquevedo, took over the FEC, mirroring the rise of the left-wing Christian Democratic youth nationally.[66]

University authorities offered a preliminary step toward resolving the prolonged student conflict in November 1966 with the creation of a tripartite commission. Composed of equal numbers of students, faculty, and administrators, it was tasked with identifying solutions to specific curricular problems.[67] As a punishment for UdeC authorities who had given in to the students' demands, the Frei administration levied a 15% tax against the lottery, which was the private university's main source of income. An indignant local citizenry mobilized in "defense of their university" and went on a provincewide strike.[68] The Chilean Senate under pressure from Concepción authorities rejected the lottery tax. The action, however, served to galvanize the wider community to defend UdeC's autonomy and that of the nascent reform process.[69] With the proposed tripartite commission, students gained a seat at the negotiating table, which they would use to their advantage in the years ahead.

UNIVERSITY REFORM IN CONCEPCIÓN, 1967–1968

The Concepción student movement radicalized the following year. The MUI benefited from this process as its members took protests for university reform into the streets and pressured the university authorities through repeated strikes and occupations of campus buildings. In the second half of 1967 alone, New Left students made headlines nationally for daring protest tactics, including kidnapping a police officer in exchange for detained students (September), MIR leader Luciano Cruz escaping from police custody (September), commemorating Che Guevara's death by lowering the Chilean flag on campus and raising a Cuban one (October), and imprisoned student leaders launching hunger strikes (November). As an affirmation of this new brand of audacious student activism, MIR leader Miguel Enríquez celebrated "the example of the Concepción students," who understand better than the Old Left that "the only way to stop a reactionary and repressive offensive—to stop a legal dictatorship or a military coup—is not to give in, dress in lamb's skin, and swear on your knees to pacifism and legalism; [but instead] to confront the repressor, to fight him without giving ground, to denounce each and every of his sinister steps, and to press forward, making him retreat, not to his starting position, but further back."[70] In November 1967, Concepción students elected mirista Luciano Cruz president of the FEC on a combined MUI-Socialist ticket.

When Margarita González arrived on campus in March 1968, the university was consumed by heated elections for a new rector in which FEC president Luciano Cruz directly challenged the power of university authorities and the Masons. For the first time, the FEC nominated its own candidate for rector: Senator Carlos Altamirano, leader of the left wing of the Socialist Party. The MUI students had no pretensions that Altamirano would win; indeed, former rector David Stitchkin (1956–62, 1968), backed by the Masons, won by an overwhelming majority. Instead, New Left students used Altamirano's candidacy to generate awareness of the undemocratic nature of rector elections.[71] Campaigning alongside Senator Carlos Altamirano in Concepción, Luciano Cruz asserted that not only students but also all part-time faculty deserved the right to vote—a position widely supported by faculty and students.[72]

In his March 1968 inauguration speech, Rector Stitchkin affirmed his commitment to university reforms, including changing the university bylaws. Moreover, he promised an "open dialogue" with students, "whose opinions will be considered without prejudice."[73] In June 1968, Stitchkin created a 128-member reform commission with 60% faculty and 40% student representation. The MUI, which already held the majority of the seats on the student federation's executive council, actively campaigned to get its members elected to the various commissions that negotiated the terms of the reform. In November 1968, the University of Concepción became the first university in Chile to ratify new bylaws redefining the mission of the university in society.[74]

In the span of a few years, Concepción students had succeeded in transforming the power structure governing their university. Students won 25% representation on the Consejo Superior—the university's new top administrative board—and 40% representation in the Claustro Pleno to elect university authorities. This expanded role for student participation was further decentralized to the more day-to-day operations. Students gained the right to vote in matters relevant to their department, school, or institute with a 25% student to 75% faculty representation.[75] This new system of co-government gave students a say in their own education and in university administration. With this power, they vociferously advocated for the university to make a stronger commitment to social and economic rights. For example, students demanded that university authorities formally endorse the right of urban poor to occupy land and build shantytowns—even when the illegal takeovers were on university-owned lands. Stitchkin fulfilled his promise to step down once the reform was implemented. In December 1968, for the first time students, professors, and staff participated in the selection of the university's top authority.[76] Nearly ten thousand votes were cast. When the results came in, the new rector was the left-leaning Socialist Dr. Edgardo Enríquez Frödden, director of the UdeC medical school and father of MIR founders Miguel, Edgardo, and Marco Antonio Enríquez and father-in-law of Bautista Van Schouwen.

The passage of the university reform in 1968 democratized the University of Concepción in ways that had a direct impact on the regional expansion of the MIR. Under Rector Enríquez's leadership, campus enrollments expanded fivefold, to nearly 20,000, and the number of students receiving economic assistance went from one in ten in 1969 to one in three by 1972.[77] Prior to the reforms, students had vehemently complained about the lack of adequate faculty. For example, the Modernization Plan (1958) mandated the creation of a sociology institute, yet the faculty hired for its inaugural year in 1965 lacked sufficient training—a fact that students, led by Nelson Gutiérrez (MIR), wasted no time in protesting between 1965 and 1968.[78] The reformed university promised to raise "the quality of research and academic standards."[79] To that end, unqualified professors were soon replaced by leading Marxist intellectuals, including many fleeing military persecution in Brazil and

Argentina. Among them were Néstor D'Alessio, Ruy Mauro Marini, and Eder Sader, who joined Chileans Fernando Mires and Luis Vitale.[80] Some of these intellectuals joined the MIR as active militants during the Popular Unity years. Between 1968 and 1973, the UdeC sociology institute became an internationally renowned center for Marxist thought and dependency theory. Students engaged in applied research and fieldwork dedicated to studying Chile's social conditions. These Marxist and Trotskyist professors, many of them closely allied with the MIR, had a profound impact on the intellectual trajectory of Chile's nascent revolutionary party.

By the time Luciano Cruz was elected FEC president in November 1967, he had leveraged his local celebrity as a student leader into successful political organizing outside the university. At the peak of student mobilizations, Cruz contended that MIR students were "not going to limit ourselves to university protests[;] . . . we have other more important political work."[81] He spent the last five months of his FEC presidency in Cuba, representing both the MIR and the Concepción student federation. Cruz returned to Chile in December 1968 more convinced than ever that organizing the party and its work with pobladores and workers should take priority over the student movement. By then, he was the MIR's principal leader of the student movement and also among important sectors of workers. At a MIR Central Committee meeting, Clotario Blest even proposed that he and Cruz launch a nationwide speaking tour of factories and *poblaciones* (urban poor and working-class neighborhoods).[82]

The MIR (which still competed in student elections as the MUI) retained its control of the FEC from 1968 to 1971, which gave it access to important resources, networks, and regional prestige to support social activism and establish contacts with grassroots activists. Through the student federation, students projected revolutionary politics outside the university. Summer volunteer teams and more regular local activities enabled MIR students to build ties with expanding popular movements. With varying degrees of success, the MIR adapted the MUI's model of assemblies and direct actions regionally and nationally as it sought to organize other mass fronts during the Popular Unity years (1970–73).

Despite being a relatively small and new political organization, the MIR quickly succeeded in amassing a large following among Concepción students. Margarita González's experience is illustrative of how this expansion worked. When she arrived in Concepción in early 1968, student politics remained at the center of campus life, particularly as university reform campaigns reached their climax: "I went to many assemblies and listened to all the different political options. I was drawn by the appeal of something new, something younger, something with so much energy, something with strong a desire for change, regardless of the costs— that's why it was called the Revolutionary Left Movement—it declared itself in favor of armed struggle. [In 1969], at the end of [my second] year, I joined the MIR out of ideological conviction."[83] González's trajectory as a medical student reinforced her commitment to revolutionary politics. The same social conscience that led her to study medicine drew her to the radical positions espoused by the MIR student leaders, who were also her classmates. By 1969, the MUI increasingly operated as the MIR's public student front from which promising recruits could be identified.[84] As left-wing Christian Democrats became increasingly disillusioned with their party's failure to fulfill the expectations raised by the Revolution in Liberty, many joined the MUI in Concepción, where they were later recruited into the MIR.[85] It was not just audacious national leaders who emerged from the Concepción university reform movement, but a second generation of MIR militants recruited from high school and university students. It was this second generation that remained in Concepción and that, along with the Marxist intellectuals at the university, took over the regional MIR leadership during the Popular Unity years.

TOWARD A VANGUARD PARTY: THE MIR'S CHANGING BALANCE OF POWER, 1967–1969

The success of the Concepción university reform movement catapulted its student leaders to national leadership positions within the MIR. From their new positions, they initiated an internal reorganization to bring the MIR closer to the concept of a revolutionary vanguard. Shortly after Luciano Cruz's election as FEC president, Miguel Enríquez, then a twenty-three-year-old medical student, was elected MIR general secretary.[86] Enríquez's election at the MIR's second congress in December 1967 marked a shift in the balance of power, as a younger generation of student activists gradually displaced the older Trotskyists and labor organizers.[87] Under Enríquez, the MIR's five-person national leadership (Secretariado Nacional) was composed exclusively of students, among them, Luciano Cruz, Bautista Van Schouwen, Sergio Pérez, and Sergio Zorilla.[88] The new national leadership introduced a debate over the party's future, distributing a document titled, "Only a Revolution within Ourselves Can Lead to a Revolution in Chile" (May 1969).[89] Inspired by Che Guevara's writings, the students sought to settle internal differences over what kind of party to build and what organizational work to prioritize.

Throughout the late 1960s, the MIR discounted the Chilean Left's electoral possibilities and continued to pursue preparations to become a guerrilla movement. In early 1969, MIR general secretary Miguel Enríquez declared, "No to elections, armed struggle is the only path," and called on the MIR to boycott the upcoming presidential elections in September 1970. His position sparked an internal polemical debate. From Santiago, Enríquez advocated for the MIR to become a revolutionary party of professional cadres. His more openly militaristic vision strained relations with the Trotskyists, among them Concepción history professor Luis Vitale. In May 1969, Vitale met with Bautista Van Schouwen and Luciano Cruz to discuss the MIR's plans for a fourth congress to be held in August 1969. Inspired by the party's growing support in Concepción province, Van Schouwen proposed that it was "the moment for the MIR to become a party with influence among the masses."[90] To do so, Cruz contended, the MIR would first need an internal realignment that firmly "prioritized open organizing work among exploited sectors in the city and countryside over clandestine activities that could lead to a more vertical organization."[91] Vitale was given the task of drafting a proposal orienting the MIR to greater insertion in Chile's popular movements. He left the meeting optimistic about their proposal's prospects.

The unresolved question of whether the MIR would prioritize clandestine preparations for future armed confrontation or aboveground political organizing came to head in June 1969, when a Concepción-based MIR operative group briefly kidnapped the conservative journalist Hernán Osses Santa María.[92] As the editor of the afternoon tabloid, *Las Noticias de la Tarde,* Osses regularly pilloried Concepción student leaders, advocates for university reform, and the MIR. At Van Schouwen's personal request, local schoolteacher Lily Rivas allowed "a compañera from Santiago" to stay at her apartment in Concepción. This visiting mirista "was used as bait" to lure Osses out on a date, whereupon he was kidnapped. For her role in the incident, Rivas spent five days in jail and earned local notoriety as "the woman from the MIR." His captors held Osses for several hours, taking compromising photographs of him before leaving him naked outside the university gymnasium, just as a crowded freshman variety show was letting out. If Luciano Cruz and his companions saw the operation as "a test of the MIR's structure and its capacity for action," they were unprepared for the serious consequences the "Osses incident" unleashed on both the MIR and the University of Concepción.[93]

The Christian Democratic administration denounced the kidnapping as an attack on the free press and launched a wide-ranging campaign of repression against the MIR and the newly reformed University of Concepción. Disregarding the long tradition of university autonomy, President Frei authorized an early morning police raid on the campus, including the largest men's dormitory and the offices of the student federation. Police carried out an additional two hundred raids on homes in Concepción and in Santiago shantytowns with suspected MIR connections.[94] The Frei government declared the MIR an illegal organization and, under the Law for Internal State Security, issued arrest warrants for thirteen MIR leaders. "Wanted! Fugitives from Justice!" notices bearing the images of miristas soon circulated throughout the country.[95] The Frei administration's proscription of the MIR pushed its top national leaders underground.

Unlike Chilean Communists, who had experience with periods of repression and underground organizing in the 1940s and 1950s, MIR militants scrambled to adapt. Some saw it as an opportunity for much-needed internal housekeeping and restructuring.[96] Although Miguel Enríquez claimed no prior knowledge of the operation and roundly condemned the Osses kidnapping, the new reality of life on the run prompted the MIR's top leaders to abandon their studies and "profession-alize" as revolutionaries.[97] Soon afterwards, the national leadership announced the suspension of the MIR's August 1969 congress.[98] Many of the older Trotskyist labor activists believed the Osses attack had been planned to hasten the MIR toward an armed guerrilla phase.[99] At a Central Committee meeting on July 27, 1969, citing insurmountable differences over elections and plans for military action, Miguel Enríquez announced the MIR's division.[100] All told, the MIR lost nearly a fifth of its members and nearly all of the party's older generation, including the distinguished labor activist Clotario Blest and the Concepción history professor Luis Vitale.[101]

In response to their departure, Enríquez pushed forward to reorganize the party. To fill the vacancies created in the top leadership, the Secretariado Nacional started to appoint new members to the Central Committee unilaterally rather than electing them at party congresses.[102] Enríquez also redeployed Concepción MIR students to create new MIR structures in other regions.[103] In a document provocatively titled, "We Will Advance Faster without Dead Weight" (July 1969), Enríquez criticized the MIR for being too open and too indiscriminate in the selection of its members.[104] Outlining planned changes for MIR bases, Enríquez asserted, "The type of militant who joins the MIR will be different from before. The *aficionados* should leave the organization. Meeting times will no longer be casually observed. . . . Dedication [to the MIR] should be total. The organization will decide if a militant should work or not, should study or not, and where they will live."[105] These measures went against the participatory, democratic culture of student politics, but top leadership justified them as "the only way to create a solid, disciplined, efficient organization, capable of discussing less and operating clandestinely."[106] From this point on, to join the MIR, it was necessary to first prove oneself by passing through different intermediate stages: one month as an unorganized sympathizer (*simpatizante*), two months as an organized aspiring militant (*aspirante*), and finally five to six months of political formation as a militant in training before becoming a full-fledged MIR militant.[107]

The conquest of power, for Miguel Enríquez, required the construction of a more homogeneous, hierarchical organization characterized by strong central leadership and the absence of internal opposition.[108] The hallmark of this top-down restructuring was the creation of the Grupos Políticos-Militares (GPM, Political-Military Groups) as the primary unit of party organization in place of the assembly-based brigade model.[109] Organized territorially, each GPM contained political bases, as well as operative, technical, and infrastructural ones led by a single leader: the *jefe del GPM*.[110] The aim was to promote integrated development of the party with better-prepared militants ready to "combine armed actions with political work in mass fronts."[111]

In the years ahead, the relative weight given within the national MIR to political or military tasks remained an ongoing question. In the short term, the military side won. After failing to secure Fidel Castro's financial backing, national MIR leaders launched a series of bank robberies to fund the party and prepare it for the next stage of conflict. Between June 1969 and June 1970 as a clandestine organization, the MIR dedicated its attention nationally to armed operations, carrying out a series of bank "expropriations" to finance the professionalization of its militants. Significantly, no robberies took place in Concepción province, allowing a relative degree of freedom to expand party work with popular movements in places like Tomé and Coronel.[112] The Santiago bank robberies—rare in Chile's history—generated intense media coverage that augmented the MIR's image as *"los Robin Hood chilenos,"* while other outlets dismissed them as common criminals.[113]

The advent of the 1970 presidential elections and Salvador Allende's candidacy led the MIR to suspend its armed actions and to turn instead to organizing mass fronts. Yet the tensions already revealed in 1969 between the democratic practices of assembly-driven mass fronts—a legacy of the student movement in Concepción, even as the MIR sought to shed its student origins—and the centralized hierarchy of a vanguard party of professional militants had not been resolved. The exponential growth of the MIR during the Popular Unity years remained in constant tension with its leaders' vision for a revolutionary party. It would resurface as a conflict between the national and regional leadership in 1973.

Through the reform movement, the MIR consolidated itself both as a successful social movement in favor of university reform and as a vanguard of the *juventud rebelde* (rebel youth). The MIR's early trajectory reveals the coexistence of divergent visions for the revolutionary organization as a vanguard party and as a democratic grassroots movement. As a party in the process of building itself, student militants lived this tension; a single action could be driven by multiple overlapping motivations that were not always mutually exclusive. For example, an anthropology field trip to the countryside to encourage the creation of peasant cooperatives left one student militant debating the extent to which his superiors in the MIR were genuinely interested in people or just in the theoretical applications of the Cuban Revolution's foco theory.[114] In this instance and others, in the process of scouting for guerrilla locations, MIR students "discovered" a social struggle. The ascendency of popular mobilization during the Popular Unity years reoriented the national MIR to prioritize social struggle over armed struggle—temporarily differentiating it from other armed revolutionary Lefts in the Southern Cone.

In seeking to understand how revolutionary movements emerge through efforts to democratize everyday life, the ability to transform the university's power structure had a direct impact on students' lives and course of study. As a student during the university reform era, Margarita González benefited from the restructured university curriculum. Through their newfound positions of power within the university, students proposed curricular changes to facilitate direct contact with workers and promote social justice. For example, medical students lobbied the university to create new clinics in shantytowns and working-class neighborhoods, where the students could complete their medical training. González soon became involved in a student-led movement to "socialize" medicine and relocate student residences to shantytowns.[115] By 1970, as a third-year medical student, she completed her rotations in a public clinic in the working-class Barrio Norte neighborhood. The extension of essential services like health care to Chile's marginalized population fulfilled the student demands in the university reform movement to reorient the university to the service of all Chileans. For students like Margarita, witnessing this profound reordering of power relations inside the university affirmed their belief that a similar capture of power could be possible in other areas and could be achieved through political activism. Students' desire to transform the university from within worked in tandem with their growing commitment to engage radical change outside of the university.

As a MIR militant, Margarita González was assigned to the more clandestine party work of gathering intelligence—never openly acknowledging her militancy or taking on a public role in student protests. Yet rather than see her integration into the MIR's party structure as being at odds with either the Popular Unity government or her medical studies, she experienced them as overlapping and mutually reinforcing political and ethical projects. "Working in a clinic meant always talking to people," she explained. "It wasn't exactly 'evangelizing' but rather putting out there the ideas that we, as MIR militants, promoted." When speaking to women, she urged them to defend their rights: "'Señora, you have a right to an education and a right to health care, but you must demand them.'" González concluded, "It's not that people didn't know this—they knew they had rights as citizens and as humans—but you as a [revolutionary] had to incentivize them to be more demanding with their rights."[116] Providing medical attention to marginalized populations represented a praxis experience for revolutionary medical students like González. She emphasized that her conversations with female patients broached topics such as birth control and family planning: "You generate [empathy] with people as you learn about their problems and needs. And they, in turn, realize that we were fighting for the same things." As her reflections indicate, rights talk was central to the creation of revolutionary politics in Chile.

Decades later, former militants like Margarita González recalled these kinds of experiences with much greater frequency than particular ideological stances or political positions vis-à-vis national politics. While some scholars have observed the tendency among former student activists to distance themselves from their youthful flirtations with revolution, by contrast, González's political commitments remain an enduring affirmation of her agency: "In this time of changes, I went down the path that I chose, and about which I have no regrets today." These cross-class encounters centered on the promotion of rights forged the meaning—and memory—of revolutionary militancy from below.[117]

For MIR student militants who remained in Concepción after the departure of the national leaders to Santiago, the university reform movement offered key lessons for subsequent grassroots organizing. Student politics in Concepción were driven by direct democracy. Students who came of age during the reform and who joined the MIR brought these experiences of general assemblies and open participation with them as they sought to organize other social groups, including pobladores in Campamento Lenin and union democracy in coal mines. At the same time, the university reform movement demonstrated the efficacy of pressure tactics—strikes from classes, occupation of the university, street protests and skirmishes—to force authorities to negotiate with students' demands. From the university reform movement, the juventud rebelde came to embrace a vision that political action was not based in the state, congress, or institutional channels but in the streets. This ability to translate micro politics into mass politics would be replicated in the years ahead.

2

"To Create a More Just Society"

*Coal Miners and Textile Workers
in the Revolutionary Workers Front*

"Ever since we were kids—all our lives—we have been against capital," explained textile worker Eulogio Sanhueza. Growing up in Tomé, an industrial port 35 kilometers north of Concepción and the heart of Chile's textile industry, Sanhueza learned the meaning of class struggle from a young age. He did not need to be convinced that a socialist revolution would spell the end of capitalism—the workers' greatest enemy. Yet by the late 1960s, he was skeptical that the existing political system could bring about the liberation of workers. The alliance forged between labor unions and the Communist and Socialist Parties in the early twentieth century had won significant concessions for workers but at the cost of subordinating the labor movement to party bureaucracies and political negotiations. In 1967, Sanhueza along with two other textile workers and a trade school student brought the MIR's revolutionary message to their hometown.[1] Climbing the steep hilly neighborhoods, they talked to fishermen, handymen, and textile workers about the need for a different kind of political organization. They first learned of the MIR's existence when "some pamphlets arrived in Tomé." It wasn't very hard, Sanhueza added, "with the University of Concepción so close by to make contacts there. . . . We had talked to everyone about it, then some *compadres* from Concepción arrived and gave a talk about politics, about the party itself and all this." For Sanhueza, the appeal of the MIR derived from its rejection of elections and politics as usual. He sought a complete transformation of the system, and the MIR appeared to be the vehicle through which to achieve it.[2]

The autonomous formation of the MIR in Tomé by a group of workers in 1967 was not an anomaly. On several occasions, students sent to make contacts for the MIR in remote areas arrived only to be greeted by individuals already identifying themselves as the MIR. These local MIRs had organized in the late 1960s. Their existence points not to the organizational capacities of the MIR, which were fairly limited before 1970, but rather to the desire among wide swaths of the Chilean populace for a transformation of the social order and their conviction that revolution was the means to achieve it.[3]

As revolutionary subjects par excellence, workers represented the MIR's ideal constituents. The party's founding platform in August 1965 called for the "liquidation of the bourgeois state's repressive apparatus and its replacement with a direct democracy of the proletariat and armed militias of workers and peasants."[4] MIR leaders never wavered in their belief in a "proletariat revolution," and they anxiously sought to build up the party's legitimacy with working people. The MIR accused the Communist and Socialist Parties of abandoning their commitment to revolution and promised to pick up the historic mantle of the Chilean working-class's struggle, particularly of figures like Luis Emilio Recabarren, founder of the Chilean Socialist Workers Party (POS, 1912). The MIR fashioned itself as a Marxist-Leninist vanguard that would channel the energies of the "most advanced" working-class sectors and, in doing so, spread revolutionary consciousness to the masses.[5]

Yet, not surprisingly, as a new political organization the MIR struggled to find legitimacy among unionized workers, who by the 1960s had built a powerful Marxist-oriented labor movement and who were already well represented in the political system by the Communist and Socialist Parties. Nationally, the MIR had limited success attracting unionized labor between 1965 and 1973; textile workers and coal miners in Concepción province proved the rare exception. Tracing the routes through which some workers joined and how they came to understand their mission sheds light on how the MIR in Concepción pivoted from a small, student-dominated organization that dabbled with armed struggle in the late 1960s to a broader movement that embraced social struggles on the road to socialist revolution. Why did Eulogio Sanhueza and his fellow workers seek out the MIR? And how did their embrace of radical politics transform the MIR from within?

For workers like Eulogio Sanhueza, the MIR drew on strains of radicalism that had existed within the Chilean labor movement since the late nineteenth century. These anarchist currents—particularly direct action tactics—were rearticulated in the wake of the revolutionary process opened by Allende's victory in 1970. To win support among these highly politicized, class-conscious communities, the MIR had to engage the political system in ways that would ensure its transformation. To this end, the MIR unveiled the Frente de Trabajadores Revolucionarios (FTR; Revolutionary Workers Front) in mid-1971 and actively fielded candidates in elections for local unions and the national labor federation (Central Única de Trabajadores de Chile [CUT]). The MIR's labor front won union victories in the coal zone, and the FTR's national spokesperson, Alejandro Alarcón, was a young Tomé textile worker.

MIR-affiliated workers sought to defend the autonomy of the labor movement vis-à-vis the state; they refused to be completely subordinated, even to a compañero president. During the early 1970s, the MIR and its FTR labor front advocated for democratic practices within a union culture that had been consumed by bureaucracy. Local union victories, so widely celebrated by national MIR leaders, came from engaging the system, promoting grassroots democracy, and deepening worker participation. As the Concepción MIR was forced to adapt and respond to people's needs, pragmatism often won out over dogmatism.

This chapter examines the appeal of the MIR's call for revolutionary change and the ways that ordinary people came to make it their own. It argues that networks of committed activists and preexisting traditions of labor radicalism underwrote the expansion of the MIR in two working-class industrial enclaves, Tomé and Coronel. The Concepción MIR forged a cross-class alliance by building on personal relationships, providing political education, defending union autonomy, and adapting to local conditions. This repertoire of actions explains how working-class support for the MIR derived not from a narrow focus on workers or by embracing a narrow radical ideology but by organizing across different sectors.

THE CRADLE OF THE REVOLUTIONARY WORKERS FRONT: TEXTILE WORKERS IN TOMÉ

Christian Democrat Eduardo Frei Montalva's landslide election in 1964 marked a turning point for the Chilean Left. The electoral defeat laid the groundwork for the formation of the multiparty Popular Unity coalition that would select Salvador Allende as its candidate in 1970. It also inspired diverse sectors to renew their commitment to revolution and unity across the Left—leading to the MIR's creation in 1965. As the previous chapter revealed, the dismal electoral showing led some to search for strategies centered on grassroots organizing. On the university campus in Concepción, students organized a united front—the Leftist University Student Movement (MUI)—to contest not just the hegemony of Christian Democrats in student elections but also the university administration, the Frei government, and the incursion of "Yankee imperialism" on campus.

Up the coast in Tomé, workers similarly weighed their options. Bellavista-Tomé worker Juan Reyes explained that "a dilemma began to present itself for many people: Should we wait six more years? And what if we don't win again, can we wait another six?"[6] As Juan Reyes and his fellow textile workers began questioning the ability of the current political system to resolve their demands, he noted that "without realizing it, those of us who thought the same" began to congregate, often in the factory lunchroom. By 1968, it appeared that the Christian Democrats "after three years [in office had] made a mess of things." Some of Reyes's coworkers had become impatient and appealed to insurrectionary language: "We're tired of waiting! Why not bring it down now?" But others countered, "No, we must wait for [the elections in] 1970." At that moment, Reyes reflected, someone must have overheard them and thought, "Let's see now, these guys think more or less like the MIR." Then one day in early 1968, a compañero at the mill, Eulogio Sanhueza, invited Reyes to a meeting, warning him that he "had to keep a secret."[7]

Juan Reyes set off apprehensively at dusk for the Punta de Parra overlook outside of town. At the time, his largely favorable impression of the MIR had been shaped by the news media. Like many textile workers in Tomé, he followed the news daily, reading anything he could get his hands on. As stories about the MIR started to appear, Reyes liked what he read, including incidents such as the 1965 confrontation with Robert Kennedy in the University of Concepción and subsequent bank robberies in Santiago. Yet he had never heard of the MIR being active in Tomé. When he arrived, he discovered that his lunchroom friends had been secretly invited, one by one, to join the MIR. Reyes suspected they attracted more attention by going all the way up the hill than if they had met out in the open in the town plaza. But the MIR "had its methodology, and you couldn't oppose it," so he said nothing.[8]

The MIR's revolutionary masculine bravado, embodied in combative Concepción student leaders such as Luciano Cruz, had crossover appeal among workers.[9] An air of excitement enveloped the MIR as the "new it thing," with its militant posture and hard-line stance. At the meeting, the discipline the MIR demanded—with an attitude of "what's said here, compadre, doesn't leave here"—made an impression on Reyes: "I liked that attitude because it made us feel like men." Reyes left the meeting feeling confident that the MIR university students "had taken me seriously."[10] In 1959, Cuba put socialist revolution on the horizon of possibility. In seeking to identify people who shared their beliefs, MIR students would approach people by asking, "Do you like Che?"[11] The parallels between these students and the Cuban revolutionary were not lost on Tomé residents: "They were doctors, like Ché, from the university."[12] The MIR succeeded in combining the Old Left's tradition of grassroots activism and working-class militancy with the New Left's revolutionary discourse and commitment to direct action.

Unlike the peasants and pobladores whom the MIR sought to organize, textile workers in Tomé did not need to be convinced of the need for revolution. Many of the people who joined the MIR had prior political formation and organizing experience. For example, Eulogio Sanhueza and the other men who helped start the MIR in Tomé had initially gotten to know each other at Socialist Youth meetings, much like many of the Concepción students who later joined the MIR.[13] In contrast to the coal zone, where the Communist Party's hegemony was undisputed, Tomé had always been more ideologically diverse, and the Socialist Party and independent leftists frequently won union representation. The relationship between the nascent MIR and the Socialist Party in Tomé would be one of competition but also collaboration.

In both Coronel and Tomé, workers and their families had a strongly developed class consciousness born of decades of labor struggles that mobilized their communities. "In Tomé we have our own way of thinking," retired Bellavista worker and MIR labor front member Nicanor Ibáñez explained. "You start by looking back on how our fathers sacrificed to raise us. My old man earned 10,000 pesos [in the Bellavista-Tomé mill] and they paid him only 4,000. The *patrón* kept the other 6,000. Looking back on these things, you say, *this,* this is what we're fighting for. I'm a leftist because of the sacrifices my father made."[14] Reflecting on the hardships he faced as a child, Ibáñez recounted going to school in his father's hand-me-down shoes as the only alternative to going barefoot. When he was first approached about joining the MIR, he reasoned, "The ideas of the kids [*cabros*] [in the MIR] were good, and so [I decided] I'm going to fight for this so that my children don't have to go through what I did."[15] His coworker Juan Reyes similarly credited his upbringing with contributing to his decision to embrace the MIR: "Ever since I was a kid, I had a sense of ideals from my father. Even though he wasn't very educated, he read a lot and knew backward and forward the history of compadres like Elías Lafferte and Emilio Recabbaren." When Reyes visited his mother's family in the countryside, he saw how exploitation there was different from that in Tomé: "We were poor, but it wasn't so bad because my parents had work at the Bellavista mill. But then I started to ask myself, why are we poor if both my father and my mother work?"[16] This generationally transmitted sense of injustice and class struggle formed the backbone of a working-class community defined by life in the mills. As the sons of textile workers, they grew up knowing that they too would enter the mills: their parents insisted they "learn to read and write, and then it was off to work at Paños Bellavista."[17] The whistles of shift changes set the rhythm of life in the company town, punctuated by the labor strikes that mobilized entire families. The Bellavista factory complex cast a long shadow over the neighborhood where Juan Reyes, Rolando Espejo, and Nicanor Ibáñez raised their families. "We were not educated" in a traditional sense, explained Reyes, "but we had an intellectual capability, we understood easily. When [union organizers and the MIR] explained to us, we assimilated it at once."[18] The textile workers were largely literate and more educated than their counterparts in the coal zone.

The anticapitalist worldview of textile mill workers in Tomé was rooted in the history of Chile and the Chilean Left. Reyes and his companions had grown up hearing stories of the 1948 repression against Communists and union leaders in Tomé. They saw themselves as part of a longer history of labor struggle in Chile. "What rebounded in us," reflected Reyes, "came from long ago, from the ideas of Recabarren and the idea of unionism."[19] From its origins in 1953, the CUT defined as its goal the creation of a classless society. Among its founders was the renowned Christian anarchist labor leader Clotario Blest, who retained a deep distrust of political parties as responsible for dividing the working class.[20] Blest played an instrumental role in founding the MIR and introduced these strains of radical unionism centered on the goal of uniting revolutionaries beyond political parties.[21] The formation of the MIR in 1965 bridged two generations—the 1920s and 1930s Trotskyists, socialists, and radical syndicalists and the 1960s youth predominantly from Concepción.

The MIR's Marxist-Leninist ideology reflected familiar anticapitalist narratives for Tomé workers that were affirmed in their daily experiences, steeped as they were in the working-class culture of Tomé and the values they had learned as children. As textile worker Rolando Espejo noted, "Ever since I was little, I believed that there shouldn't be rich people or poor people, not the extreme difference between them that you saw." At the time, he saw revolution as a means "to make the world a better place, to create a more just society."[22] The MIR's commitment to equal rights motivated Eulogio Sanhueza to join Chile's revolutionary movement: "This was the socialism that we practiced: that the poor didn't keep getting poorer, that there would be education for all the people."[23] These ideas about equality found material expression in Tomé. The desire for revolutionary change often centered on very basic needs. As Reyes reflected, "In the streets the people said they wanted socialism. But what's that? It's an abstract idea. What they wanted was bread, work, and freedom. Nothing more."[24] By the late 1960s, the ideals that had shaped the worldview of Reyes and his neighbors increasingly appeared possible to attain, even in their lifetimes. If the MIR's anarchist radical syndicalism appeared familiar to Tomé workers, it was the messenger in the form of university students that drew more skepticism.

BUILDING A CROSS-CLASS MOVEMENT

The challenge for the MIR in attracting support among Tomé workers stemmed not from workers' lack of class consciousness but rather from their suspicion of cross-class alliances. Tomé textile workers, who joined the MIR in the late 1960s and formed its labor front in the early 1970s, had a clear sense of who they were and what animated their class struggles. It was less apparent to them why college-educated kids would support the destruction of the social order. As Reyes put it succinctly, "Why is a rich person worried about the poor?" He explained, "As a worker and a union member, I always questioned this part—I thought the rich can't defend the poor because in a given moment they will side with the other rich people."[25] His coworker Nicanor Ibáñez similarly doubted whether the students could relate to his and his neighbors' struggles, especially since "we had such different lives. When we met the kids running the MIR, they were sons of doctors. Just imagine, the Enríquez brothers were sons of the rector of the University of Concepción."[26] Middle-class university students in Concepción took pains to prove their working-class credentials and sought to "proletarianize" the party and themselves. Although these efforts appeared artificial to some, the accessibility of young MIR leaders soon convinced some workers that their commitment to revolutionary struggle was genuine. The proximity of Concepción to Tomé facilitated sustained contact with MIR student leaders, even as social differences mediated how these encounters were understood.

Through personal relationships with students and the circuits of exchange that solidified them, these textile workers began to change their minds about the MIR. In May 1971, just six months after Allende's election, "revolutionary workers and revolutionary students at the University of Concepción" developed and implemented a study plan for workers at the sociology institute.[27] Juan Reyes and Nicanor Ibáñez, along with a dozen other workers from Tomé, took part in this program. They attended daily classes for six months on consciousness-raising and political formation taught by some of the most preeminent Marxist intellectuals in Chile, including Néstor D'Alessio, Fernando Mires, and Luis Vitale.[28] "I thought to myself," recalled Reyes, "this is why these kids turn out so smart because they study here. I believed they could do nothing short of run the world." When the textile workers met with Concepción MIR leaders, like lawyer Pedro Enríquez Barra, Reyes was surprised that he did not condescend but spoke to them "as if we were university students." Reyes worried that "maybe no one had told him that we were just workers."[29] Textile workers experienced these interactions as "leveling the difference" of the opportunities separating them from the MIR students.[30]

In 1964–69, MIR students had pushed to democratize the University of Concepción through the reform movement. The formal instruction of textile workers in the early 1970s and their presence on campus—a symbolic space of social capital in the region—appeared to fulfill the reformed university's promise to open its doors to all social classes. Lectures on the political economy of capitalism versus socialism echoed the same consciousness-raising classes (*clases de concientización*) that the MIR had successfully formalized as part of the university's common first-year curriculum. More than just fulfill the MIR's strategy to have well-informed union leaders, the study plan for workers on campus contributed to the transformation of subjectivities, a hallmark of any revolutionary project.

In trips to Concepción, textile workers began to appreciate the sacrifices made by MIR students, and their own commitment to the movement grew. When Juan Reyes was invited to the homes of MIR leaders in Concepción for *once*, the traditional Chilean afternoon tea, he made personal discoveries about the students that continued to resonate over the following decades:

I saw they were good kids and they lived in nice homes. Their mothers loved them. I saw how much she worried for her son, maybe because she knew that he didn't have any reason to get involved. He already had everything he could want. [Then I realized,] this [the MIR] has to be something really great for people like them to join. That we were drawn in wasn't so novel because we had always been poor. We had always struggled for the rights of workers and to improve our wages, work, and living conditions. But they hadn't, they already had everything. That's why I've always said, there was never a better generation than that one, with loyalty and strong ideals.[31]

What mattered to the textile workers was not the students' material conditions but their radical aspirations and commitment to action. Textile worker Rolando Espejo marveled that as "attractive, young professionals [the MIR students] could have lived any way they wanted." But instead, "they came here [to Tomé] to give these teachings to me—I accepted them as if it were the Gospel." The social difference separating middle-class students from workers did not inhibit the expansion of the party; rather, it worked in the MIR's favor. Reyes and his fellow textile workers characterized the experience as meeting in the middle of a ladder: "[The students] stepped down from the privileges they had and they brought us higher with the knowledge they gave us. They lowered themselves and we raised ourselves up, arriving just a few rungs below them."[32] The MIR's investment in forming militants was also an investment in transforming people—instilling a sense that each voice mattered and everyone had something to contribute to the revolutionary struggle in Chile. By building personal relationships and gaining political education, Juan Reyes, Nicanor Ibáñez, and Rolando Espejo came to identify with the MIR and take it as their own.

ORGANIZING ACROSS THE COMMUNITY

While workers might initially have been suspicious of the Concepción MIR students, local high school students had fewer qualms. In a place like Tomé, to organize MIR supporters among high school students meant organizing textile workers' sons and daughters. By the time the MIR began targeting Tomé high school students, the exploits of MIR student leaders in Concepción were legendary, from street fights with police to the kidnapping of journalist Hernán Osses in 1969, which conferred outlaw status. In addition to the small age differences separating college and high school students, the MIR's carefully cultivated revolutionary mystique increased its appeal among young people.

Just as MIR leaders had called the Bellavista workers to meet in secret on the Punta de Parra hill outside of town, they invited high school students in 1969 to a clandestine nighttime gathering on the beach. Decades later, Jorge González, son of a Bellavista textile worker, recalled the sense of adventure he felt as he set off with his classmates. Instructed to put out their cigarettes as a precautionary measure, they scrambled across the rocky beach with only the light of the moon to guide them. Suddenly they came upon a seated group. Among those waiting for them were the MIR's top leaders: Miguel Enríquez, Bautista Van Schouwen, Luciano

Cruz, all still fugitives from the law. As the high school students took their seats in the circle, they listened with rapt attention to the MIR leaders' speeches. When mid-meeting a lookout's whistle warned, "The police!," the meeting was over as suddenly as it had begun. "In a matter of minutes the compañeros had vanished, climbing the hill in the direction of the cemetery," Jorge González recounted. "From there they made their escape in Citroëns. We were left behind, alone on the beach. When the police arrived minutes later, they asked what we'd been up to. 'Midnight fishing,' we replied."[33] Although the tactics of intrigue and revolutionary mystique played to the MIR's advantage as it recruited grassroots supporters, it was the party's investment in them as people that most effectively drew workers, their children, and their neighbors into Chile's Revolutionary Left Movement.

Throughout the late 1960s and early 1970s, as the MIR established contacts with workers, students, and pobladores in Tomé and Coronel, it functioned largely as an underground organization. During 1969, the MIR's national strategy was still oriented to preparing for an armed guerrilla struggle in the countryside.[34] Although these plans remained in an embryonic state, the MIR's revolutionary rhetoric and commitment to action served to increase the party's appeal among some sectors.[35] During this early phase of clandestine recruiting, the MIR invested time, energy, and resources in the political formation of its aspiring militants. Through reflection and consciousness-raising with young MIR leaders from Concepción, working people came not only to support the MIR's revolutionary project but also to feel an integral part of it.

After initial contacts, like the beach meeting, the next step was the creation of political "bases," the smallest unit of party organization, each composed of four or five militants. Juan Reyes belonged to a base of textile workers and Jorge González to one of high school students. Eulogio Sanhueza noted approvingly, "Everyone got the same political formation, that's why I liked being there." González detailed the format: "First you started with a political discussion, an analysis of the national political situation, and each person had to say what he or she thought about the current political reality." Through this systematic process, MIR members honed critical analysis skills that could be applied to any situation. As an example of praxis, the meeting then pivoted to defining concrete tasks for each person to carry out in the week ahead.[36]

These weekly meetings functioned as spaces of critical reflection that facilitated personal growth. In a period marked by intense ideological debates, the political preparation of militants could have resembled indoctrination classes. Yet even as militants recall hours spent studying various Marxist texts, they underscored that the meetings covered more than "just politics." Their transformative potential rested on how, through participation and discussion, MIR militants began to think of themselves and others differently. Textile worker Rolando Espejo observed that the MIR taught "me to believe in people, to believe in the individual. This makes you see beyond yourself . . . [because] to believe in politics makes you more universal and not so sectarian."[37] This holistic approach to political education embraced the notion of self-transformation espoused by top MIR leaders: "Only a revolution within ourselves can lead to a revolution in Chile."[38] Finally, while direct action was a hallmark of MIR-oriented politics, grassroots militants were not treated as interchangeable pawns sent out to "do some tasks."[39] The MIR's investment in the education and preparation of its members credentialed them as revolutionaries, capable of analyzing a situation and implementing a plan of action.[40] To this day, many Tomé workers and students emphasize how their participation in the MIR expanded personal and collective horizons. This sense of empowerment remains at the center of the meaning people continue to derive from these experiences.

FROM GUERRILLA RECONNAISSANCE TO UNION VICTORIES: THE MIR IN THE COAL ZONE

While in Tomé highly politicized textile workers formed a local MIR, the Communist Party's hegemony in the coal mining town of Coronel posed a serious obstacle to the MIR's expansion. In 1966, Concepción students and MIR founders Miguel Enríquez, Luciano Cruz, Bautista "Bauchi" Van Schouwen, and Manuel Vergara first met with four people in the coal zone. At that time, their primary interest was still oriented to the possibility of creating rural guerrillas. These local contacts acted as guides, taking the students out on rudimentary military training exercises—resembling extended camping trips—in the nearby Nahuelbuta Mountains.[41] Yet these exploratory efforts at a rural insurgency were jettisoned following Allende's 1970 election, when the MIR pivoted nationally to organizing an aboveground movement. How did support for the MIR in Coronel expand from just four recruits in 1966 to winning victories in coal miner union elections in 1972?

As in Tomé, local people who joined the MIR in the 1960s facilitated the grassroots organizing that made possible the MIR's expansion in the coal zone. The original 1966–67 local leadership reflected a mix of class and occupational backgrounds: a coal miner, a white-collar employee at the mines, a construction worker, a fisherman, two high school students, and a schoolteacher.[42] Between 1967 and 1968, the Concepción MIR assigned Manuel Vergara, then a sociology student in Concepción, to organize in Coronel. In these formative years, the MIR in Coronel structured itself around the horizontal concept of brigades. Modeled on student politics in Concepción, the brigades were governed by general assemblies and open debate.[43] This horizontal participatory political culture outlasted the MIR's national strategy to become a rural guerrilla insurgency and underwrote subsequent union victories and collective community actions.

The existence of other smaller revolutionary groups that occupied an oppositional status to the Communist Party played a critical role in the MIR's expansion into the coal zone. When these groups merged with the MIR in the late 1960s, they brought their local members with them. When the MIR formed in 1965, it united several dispersed revolutionary groups, among them the Vanguardia Revolucionaria Marxista (VRM; Revolutionary Marxist Vanguard).⁴⁴ As a boy in the early 1960s, Lautaro López listened as his father, Daniel López, held meetings for the Concepción chapter, which was composed mostly of dissident socialists and Trotskyists. On Saturday afternoons the house was filled with his father's political friends—lawyers and economists from "the most educated sectors of society"— who would spend hours debating ideological questions and political matters. When the family moved to nearby Coronel in 1968, Lautaro, then a young teenager, encountered a different reality, in which "salt of the earth people [*gente común y corriente*] spoke their own language—one that wasn't inflected by ideology. They weren't going to analyze a situation with historical materialism; there was another kind of history there." In contrast, "when the Vanguardia would meet, I heard their revolutionary discourse, but I didn't see it. They spoke of class, but I didn't see it. In Coronel, all there was—my classmates at school, the people in town—was all part of this *pueblo* that I had heard about in the Vanguardia meetings." When he attended the only high school in town, he fully grasped "the message of that revolutionary discourse." He explained, "I began to connect what I had heard since I was little at home with what I saw every day in the reality of life in a poor community with a working-class tradition." These cross-class encounters inspired López to seek out a "popular militancy"—one that combined revolutionary discourse with "responses that came from the people themselves."⁴⁵ In 1968, the same year medical student Margarita González joined the MIR in Concepción, Lautaro López joined the MIR's high school student wing, the Frente de Estudiantes Revolucionarios (FER; Revolutionary Student Front).⁴⁶

As in Tomé, organizing high school students in the late 1960s became a way into workers' homes. In Coronel's only high school, the children of miners, like Hugo Monsalves and Grecia Quiero, mixed with Coronel's small middle class, among them Lautaro López and Aníbal Cáceres. By the time the MIR started actively organizing mass fronts after Allende's victory, Cáceres explained, "the students were already prepared. They began to speak up and challenge ideas at home. The father was no longer the only voice that mattered." Cáceres observed how "when a miner's son managed to study in high school, he gained authority as the professional in the household, as the thinking son, because his coal miner father had never finished primary school."⁴⁷ Despite the likely preference of fathers for the Communist Party, their children introduced revolutionary politics into Coronel households.

Similar to experiences in Tomé, when Coronel students continued their studies at the University of Concepción and became politicized on campus, they brought their new politics home with them. Their early recruits were often younger siblings and childhood friends. For Aníbal Cáceres, it was his older sister, then a student at the University of Concepción, who in 1966 introduced her fifteen-year-old brother to revolutionary politics. At the time he was dating a woman in the Communist Youth and went to a Communist May Day rally. When suddenly "someone yelled, 'There are provocateurs here! Let's beat them up!,'" he saw his sister among the accused: "Then and there, I switched sides. I was going to be a Communist, and thanks to that day I became part of GRAMA, the Grupo de Avanzada Marxista [Advanced Marxist Group]," which would soon merge with the MIR. The people in GRAMA "defended my poor sister, the only woman in the group, and when they left, I went with them." In the moment, familial bonds proved stronger than political inclination or romantic attachment. On the spot, Aníbal Cáceres found himself deputized into the MIR by Concepción leader Arturo Villavela, who declared, "You're a militant now. You're our militant." Founded by University of Concepción engineering students, the GRAMA joined the MUI when it formed in 1964. As support for the MIR expanded on campus, it absorbed other smaller radical groups, including the GRAMA and the VRM. By an assembly vote in 1967, GRAMA officially dissolved and its members became MIR militants, among them Aníbal Cáceres and his older sister. Many of this first and second generation of MIR militants had prior political formation in other leftist groups.[48]

When the MIR turned to organizing mass fronts among workers, pobladores, peasants, and students in the early 1970s, it was not students coming in from the outside but rather the local activists who had joined the MIR in the 1960s who carried out this work. The fluidity of small-town dynamics in Coronel meant that middle-class students drawn into revolutionary Left politics had ample points of contact with the working-class culture of their coal mining hometown. According to schoolteacher Enzo La Mura, tasked in 1971 with expanding the Revolutionary Workers Front (FTR), there was fraternization between workers and students through "football, which was incredibly important, as were jokes and neighborhood humor." He also observed, "People knew one another, they were on speaking terms ... and this enabled the MIR's ideas to circulate." According to Grecia Quiero, a lifelong member of the Villa Mora neighborhood sports club, "The MIR became involved in everything related to the social organizations, especially the sports clubs." For Quiero, the youngest of ten children, just as for Cáceres, the MIR was a family affair. "The political discussions in the house were tremendous," she noted, and watching all of that, "I followed my sisters and brothers into the MIR," joining in 1968 as a high school student. She joked that the family's house "was practically the [Coronel] headquarters." Their backyard shed became the center of MIR propaganda production, and their mother's sewing machine was requisitioned to make the MIR's red and black flags.[49]

Similar to Tomé and other small towns, organizing on multiple fronts in Coronel drew on personal relationships and people's dual identities to expand the party. As a seventeen-year old, in 1968, Aníbal Cáceres had his first experience recruiting someone into the MIR. After the May Day incident with his sister, he stopped regularly hanging out with neighborhood kids. One day, they called him over to ask if it was really true that he was "going around with the people in the MIR." No sooner had Cáceres answered affirmatively, then one of his close friends swore on the spot that he wanted to join. Cáceres informed him, "The first thing you have to do to join is dedicate yourself to your studies. And so we started studying together. I got him to join and then two or three more friends joined and I had myself my own base." Aníbal Cáceres, who had joined the GRAMA at fifteen, by seventeen was in charge of his own base of aspiring MIR militants in Coronel. They sold copies of *El Rebelde* and carried out "agitation and propaganda" operations—usually under the cover of night—painting a prominent wall in town with the latest MIR slogan. In his capacity as base leader, Cáceres also coordinated their political formation, which—as in the case of Tomé and elsewhere—took the form of study groups centered on discussion and reflection. He noted that their weekly meetings "covered everything—up to and including who we dated," explaining, "Supposedly this was to be a clandestine party, so you couldn't go out with a conservative girl. Our girlfriends had to be trustworthy because we had important information."[50] Throughout the late 1960s, the MIR remained a semiclandestine organization, combining rudimentary military training with social and political activism.

The material resources of the Concepción Student Federation, whose presidency the MIR held from 1967 to 1970, proved crucial to building networks across the surrounding region. Starting in 1966, the student federation summer volunteer teams (*trabajos de verano*) and summer schools exposed Concepción students to both precarious social conditions and regional traditions of struggle.[51] These trips, funded and organized under the auspices of the reformed university, served multiple and sometimes competing goals within the nascent revolutionary group. On the one hand, a more instrumental approach understood these activities as allowing MIR students to explore the terrain for future rural insurgencies and to establish contacts for military and political instruction. On the other hand, for those who saw the MIR as a new type of political organization, the trips offered an opportunity to learn firsthand from the people the MIR hoped to recruit. By defining itself as a movement—and not a political party—the MIR signaled that it operated beyond the terrain of electoral politics. The summer school trips provided MIR students with the opportunity to engage local communities outside the framework of electoral campaign cycles. In the late 1960s, tensions existed within the MIR and within individuals themselves, particularly the earliest university student members, about just what kind of organization they were in the process of building.[52] Some saw it as an instrument for future armed struggle; others saw it as a vehicle to develop their social conscience and assist in struggles for social justice. With time, the MIR would use these summer volunteer teams as a way to build connections across different sectors of Chilean society. For example, a Tomé textile worker versed in praxis-based pedagogy would accompany university students in their efforts to recruit indigenous Mapuche activists in southern Chile.[53] Pobladores from the emblematic Campamento Lenin enthusiastically traveled on university-sponsored trips to meet with pobladores in other parts of the country.[54]

The summer volunteer work often paved the way for more systematic organizing. Starting in 1968, at the behest of FEC president Luciano Cruz, the MIR developed "schools for military instruction and political education" in the coal zone. Cruz had recently returned from a six-month visit to Cuba "ready to carry out direct actions."[55] Medical students and MIR leaders Luciano Cruz and Bautista Van Schouwen coordinated these training schools with the support of well-known University of Concepción professors, including the historian Luis Vitale and the sociologist Fernando Mires. Recent graduates from the University of Concepción took on the more quotidian work of sustaining these training schools. For example, Enzo La Mura, who first met with Coronel coal miners in 1967, acted as Cruz's assistant, developing the cultural and political components for these schools. "As a history and geography teacher," La Mura explained, "I was in charge of making maps by hand and teaching others how to read them, as well as a few aspects of theory and politics. Luciano served as the military instructor."[56] These points of contact between workers in the coal zone and university students continued regularly until the Concepción MIR's leadership was pushed underground by the kidnapping of Hernán Osses in June 1969.

With the MIR officially banned, its top leadership went into hiding to evade arrest. For months, the front page of local newspapers speculated as to the Concepción students' whereabouts, thus contributing to their status as celebrity outlaws. As the son of a lieutenant, Luciano Cruz famously spent this period hiding in the military barracks in nearby Talcahuano. During this early clandestine phase, the Concepción MIR leaders relied on MIR members in Coronel to provide a support network. Five of the thirteen MIR leaders with outstanding arrest warrants, including Bautista Van Schouwen and Arturo Villavela, took refuge in Villa Mora, a working-class neighborhood in Coronel. Van Schouwen designated seventeen-year-old Aníbal Cáceres to carry out "Operation Rinse." Dressed in commando gear, Cáceres visited the homes of MIR members in Concepción and Coronel for the purpose of burning party documents and removing any dynamite stockpiles. Meanwhile, high school student Grecia Quiero was responsible for bringing provisions to the MIR safe house in Villa Mora.[57] The MIR leaders' "clandestine" existence—an open secret in the region—served to enhance their status as rebels with a cause.

The 1969 Osses kidnapping and subsequent government repression precipitously forced the party underground and prompted an internal confrontation over the relative importance of military versus political organizing. National MIR leaders—including Miguel Enríquez, who favored a military approach—seized the opportunity to reorganize the party toward those ends in July 1969, creating the Political-Military

Groups as the primary unit of party organization and establishing stricter requirements for membership. Many prominent MIR students, including those hiding in Coronel, soon left the provinces for Santiago and national leadership positions. Other Concepción MIR students chose to focus on their studies. Many of them continued to identify with grassroots organizing, even if it was not their first priority. For MIR members of lesser rank who escaped government persecution, like Enzo La Mura, the internal reorganization brought unwelcome choices: "I stopped doing political work and switched to infrastructure in a [bomb-making] workshop."[58] This transition produced serious consequences for the MIR's relationship with its grassroots base, as the case of Coronel illustrates.[59]

In the coal zone, the national MIR's decision to create a revolutionary party of professional cadres produced a division between party militants, who joined clandestine operative units, and the majority of the grassroots militants and sympathizers, who were "cut loose." In accordance with general secretary Miguel Enríquez's call for "aficionados" to leave the MIR, Enzo La Mura explained, many in the grassroots were deemed "undisciplined" and could not be trusted with military actions, so "they were isolated from the party and cut loose."[60] Being "cut loose" did not mean abandoning activism or continued identification with the MIR. Members of these groups in Coronel went on to create the autonomous Brigada Sindical del MIR en Carbón (MIR Coal Zone Labor Brigade).[61]

Their strategy of union activism would ultimately outlast the national MIR's aborted strategy to form a guerrilla movement. In 1969–70, when the MIR's national leadership did not put "an emphasis on real political work," the "cut loose" coal zone labor brigade members continued identifying with the MIR and organizing themselves as miristas. Local traditions, particularly the spaces of cross-class sociability that existed in this small industrial town where "everyone knows everyone else," facilitated this autonomous expansion. On the initiative of MIR-identified people in Coronel, the elementary school principal, César Aguilera, began to write and circulate a newspaper called *El Rebelde Minero* (The Rebel Miner), a local version of the MIR's official party organ, *El Rebelde* (The Rebel). With the MIR banned by the Frei government in 1969, the official *El Rebelde* appeared sporadically. Yet *El Rebelde Minero* freely circulated every fifteen days in Coronel, and its content mixed local issues and "union news with news from Cuba or about el Che." As "El Mono" Escalona, an elementary school teacher and MIR member, explained, "Our editorial page always sought to elevate the revolution on the one hand and to identify the issues of the day that the revolution could attack," citing pragmatic needs like unfinished school buildings and the lack of indoor plumbing and electricity in many neighborhoods. Frequently "any little thing" could serve to enhance the cause; as he explained candidly, "These things worked to attract more supporters." In describing the paper's reception, he noted that "the person who picked up *El Rebelde Minero* read it and identified with it because it [spoke to] the reality

[and] the truth of the coal zone." The coal zone lacked a local newspaper, which accounts, in part, for the popularity enjoyed by El Rebelde Minero and its attention to everyday life in the coal mining community.[62]

More than simply reporting local news, the paper also drew community attention to the MIR and its combative politics. The front page of El Rebelde Minero, designed by Grecia Quiero's older brother, featured a symbol "of armed struggle in the image of a coal miner throwing a stick of dynamite." The cover image and the content depicted "propaganda for an armed struggle," which according to Enzo La Mura, served to differentiate the MIR from the Communist Party and to attract new supporters drawn from "people who were tired [of the status quo], young people, [and] a few former Communists." La Mura admitted that the newspaper played to people's emotions rather than their rationality, noting that "many people joined because they were fed up with the system." The cover image drew on the combative legacy of struggle by coal miners and fused it with the MIR's revolutionary message.

Even as the MIR in Coronel sought to present itself as an alternative to the Communist Party, the task of distributing the paper was not easy. As then high school student Aníbal Cáceres explained, "When we tried distributing El Rebelde aboveground, outside the mines, the miners often hit us and chased us away. Then when we distributed it inside the unions, the Communists attacked us directly." It was not until a local union leader, Guillermo Cánovas, one of the original 1966 coal zone contacts, starting bringing El Rebelde "down into the mines" that the MIR gained some acceptance among coal miners.[63] When it came to circulating El Rebelde Minero throughout the community, local sports clubs and other social organizations also played a key role. As sports club president, "El Mono" Escalona distributed El Rebelde Minero among older workers as well as the parents of his elementary school students. In this period of transition for the MIR, from the late 1960s into 1970, the local activists behind El Rebelde Minero functioned autonomously from the MIR's official party structure. Through the production and circulation of El Rebelde Minero these self-identified miristas laid the groundwork for the MIR's rapid expansion during the Popular Unity period. These preexisting networks made it possible to spread the MIR's vision for a different Chile.

"A VICTORY FOR THE WORKING CLASS": ALLENDE'S ELECTION, 1970

In the months before Allende's election, the MIR continued to serve as an inspiration for diverse sectors of Chilean society. However, what it meant for each person often differed widely. From the worker-created MIR in Tomé to the independent MIR union brigade in the coal zone, the MIR's early years offer ample examples of how local initiatives shaped MIR culture on the ground. The emphasis on being a movement situated the MIR outside politics as a contest for votes. As one Coronel schoolteacher explained, the MIR was "not a party, we started out by saying we were a movement and a revolutionary one, and so we threw ourselves into organizing workers and attracting mass support." For many local activists, this emphasis on grassroots organizing was the MIR's priority—not the more clandestine side of the party accessible only to the confidants of top leaders. During the Popular Unity years, competing visions continued to coexist within the MIR both over the emphasis given to political versus military tasks and to supporting Allende's government versus maintaining an independent position. The ambiguity of these positions enabled local activists to interpret their mission according to their own vision for revolutionary transformation. The national MIR political rhetoric and factionalism were often irrelevant to miristas at the grassroots level.

Overwhelming popular support for Salvador Allende's candidacy persuaded MIR leaders—including Miguel Enríquez—to reconsider their hard-line position on elections. In the midst of a heated campaign cycle, Allende and Enríquez met in private in June 1970. Allende promised he would give amnesty to imprisoned MIR leaders and lift the ban on the party. Enríquez never publicly endorsed Allende's candidacy. Instead, he called on MIR militants to not vote for the conservative candidate, Jorge Alessandri. He did, however, agree that the MIR would suspend all armed actions in June 1970, so as to not jeopardize Allende's chance for election. The MIR's bank robberies and plans for guerrilla struggle were set aside in favor of forming the Grupo de Amigos Personales (GAP), a personal security detail for Salvador Allende.

Despite the truce of sorts, the MIR's national leadership remained skeptical that Allende could win and argued that if he did, conservative forces would never allow him to take office and implement his program for a gradual transition to socialism. To that end, the MIR's clandestine intelligence wing infiltrated right-wing groups to collect intelligence on potential coup plots. These concerns were not unfounded given the U.S. Central Intelligence Agency's efforts to promote a coup in Chile between Allende's election in September and his confirmation by Congress in November 1970. The MIR's intelligence efforts uncovered evidence of the right-wing plot to assassinate General René Schneider in October 1970, which led many MIR militants to predict an imminent confrontation with the sectors opposed to Allende.[64]

Given the national leadership's own ambiguous and evolving stance on elections in general and Salvador Allende's candidacy in particular, it is perhaps not surprising that few grassroots members adhered to the MIR's proscription of elections. In the end, only the most disciplined MIR militants, most of them university students, cast blank ballots; meanwhile, the majority of the MIR's social base in Concepción province voted for the Popular Unity candidate and celebrated Allende's victory as their own. The MIR's refusal to support Allende created problems for workers because many were *allendistas* (Allende sympathizers). Despite the party's instruction to the contrary, Tomé worker Juan Reyes acknowledged that both he and his father voted for Allende: "The movement [MIR] should have been a part of the elections because it was a way to advance what we were fighting for." He emphasized, "It would have been absurd for us to cast blank votes. No, we all voted for Allende, and we marched in the streets when he won." "For us," added his coworker Nicanor Ibáñez, "more than a victory for a political party, Allende's election was a victory for the working class." All across Chile, in places like Tomé and Coronel, "the people took to the streets to celebrate" the election of their compañero president.[65]

Salvador Allende's historic victory in 1970 changed the MIR's trajectory. This change in orientation officially came from above, yet was driven by the possibilities that grassroots activists like those in Tomé and Coronel opened up. Whereas other Latin American revolutionary Left groups prepared to mount urban and rural guerrilla struggles against conservative, often authoritarian governments, the MIR faced a unique situation in Chile. As the culmination of a decades-long strategy by the Chilean Left to engage in the political system, the Old Left represented by Allende's Popular Unity coalition led by the Communist and Socialist Parties was now in power.

In this "prerevolutionary period" of open democratic reforms, the MIR had the opportunity to engage in aboveground organizing and to become a mass party. Behind closed doors, MIR leaders debated "the correct role for revolutionaries" and the future of the party. One side argued that the MIR should support the Popular Unity program since it had wide support among the popular sectors. This position concluded that the MIR should dedicate its energies to specialized military and intelligence activities to defend Allende's government against national and international enemies. On the other hand, the effervescence of Chilean popular movements in the late 1960s—coupled with the expanded possibilities for action that Allende's election inspired—meant that many miristas saw an opening for the MIR to promote more autonomous, independent popular movements, with an eye toward radicalizing the overall revolutionary process. In a characteristic hedge, general secretary Miguel Enríquez embraced the mass party option in principle but argued that in the short-term military preparations should take priority. As a consequence, until mid-1972 the MIR's national leadership remained oriented to anticipating a coup and lagged behind in building support among popular sectors.[66]

In the absence of official directives, the Concepción MIR enjoyed greater leeway and creativity to organize popular sectors and did so by promoting an assembly-based politics that validated grassroots participation. Local MIR activists working alongside student militants led the expansion in working-class enclaves like Tomé and Coronel. Prepared militants could reproduce the same political formation to recruit others. "To bring in more and more people," including women workers, Juan Reyes and his friends approached coworkers in the Bellavista factory, inviting their participation.[67] Local high school students and workers recruited one another. An older brother working in the mill might recruit his little sister in the high school, and the high school student president in turn might convince his parents and older siblings to support the MIR.[68]

Following the university reform, enrollments at the University of Concepción expanded exponentially. Like many college students from the surrounding area, students from Tomé lived at home; some students politicized by their experiences there kept a low profile on campus but began organizing for the MIR in their hometowns.[69] Bellavista worker Alejandro Alarcón first learned of the MIR in the late 1960s when his older brother brought home a new friend, "Pepe" Catalán, to board with their family in Tomé. Catalán's arrival was no coincidence. In 1969, as the MIR nationally started to develop a more systematic party structure centered on GPM, Miguel Ángel de Catalán Febrero was sent to Tomé to organize the party. A history major turned full-time revolutionary, "Pepe," or "Coliguacho," as he was affectionately known in the MIR, became a local fixture in Tomé as he organized MIR bases of high school students and workers.[70] No sooner had Alejandro Alarcón's coworkers in the weaving section elected him to be union delegate in Bellavista's Industrial Workers Union than someone in the MIR approached him about representing the revolutionary position in the factory.

In addition to drawing on personal relationships, existing labor conflicts generated openings for radical politics to spread. All across Chile, the 1970 presidential campaign—a hotly contested three-way race—produced an opportune aperture for popular mobilization. Concepción province was no exception, with escalating labor strikes and urban land takeovers.[71] In Tomé, the Bellavista textile factory faced financial crisis following a costly modernization of equipment and by 1970 verged on bankruptcy.[72] On April 1, 1970, Bellavista workers peacefully occupied the factory, initiating six months of conflict with the owners.[73] As negotiations dragged on, young workers in the metallurgical section announced a new 24-hour strike in late July.[74] From there the strike spread to other sections until workers occupied the entire factory.[75] Union leader Alejandro Alarcón explained the workers' decision to take the factory: "It was a simple calculation. If before the factory with slow production and old machines was capable of maintaining 1,500 families, afterwards we began to see that production with the new machinery was much faster. It tripled or quadrupled the productive output. If there was going to be greater production and the owner's profits would triple, how could it be that half of us were going to be laid off?" "It was absurd," he added, "so we took the factory. From that experience, we started joining the MIR because it was the MIR that supported us."[76] The MIR did not field candidates in the national elections in 1970; instead, it operated outside of electoral politics, giving it greater leeway to press for more radical solutions.

Similar to the radicalization of the university reform movement, the impetus for the labor conflict in Bellavista centered on a concrete material demand: better wages. As the movement unfolded, other, more radical demands followed. The prolonged factory takeover created an important space of sociability and exchange between workers of different political persuasions and workers and visiting MIR students. For Eulogio Sanhueza, the Bellavista worker who had first contacted the MIR three years earlier, the visit by Luciano Cruz marked a turning point. Cruz had emerged from the university reform movement as the MIR's most visible social leader with crossover appeal throughout the region. His three-hour speech in the occupied factory attracted hundreds of "people of all classes," and afterwards, noted Sanhueza, "everyone wanted to be miristas, and that's how we went about advancing our cause."[77] Decades later, workers still recall how "Luciano Cruz told us we had the right to strike" and how "those boys from the MIR came and planted the idea for nationalization."[78] The MIR students' presence boosted morale inside the factory and enabled MIR workers to organize more effectively. In short, it was the lived experience inside the occupied factory that expanded political horizons.

Striking Tomé textile workers, still at an impasse with owners, saw Allende's victory in September 1970 as their own: "We felt we would win after Allende won because he would have to solve" the conflict.[79] The demand for nationalization, which emerged from conversations inside the occupied factory, had within a few months garnered community-wide support. Just weeks after Allende's election, five hundred Bellavista textile workers and their families marched eight hours on foot to Concepción. Students and workers in Penco and Lirquén joined them en route to Concepción's central Plaza de Independencia, where President-elect Salvador Allende was slated to speak. The workers hoped to gain a personal interview with Allende to present their demand for back pay and make the case for expropriation.[80]

Within months of taking office, Allende fulfilled his campaign promise. On December 1, 1970, he decreed the nationalization of the Bellavista mill, making it the first industry nationalized by his administration. A few weeks later, on December 31, Allende returned to the region to nationalize the Lota and Coronel-Schwager coal mines.[81] "The region's textile mills, coal mines and steel now belong to the Chilean people," Allende proclaimed to exuberant crowds.[82] The Popular Unity government promised to transform industrial relations by institutionalizing worker participation within the nationalized sector.

Nationalization marked a key victory for workers. The real work came afterwards in the day-to-day question of how these nationalized factories would be run. On what terms would workers gain control over the means of production? Six months later, in June 1971, Bellavista Revolutionary Workers Front leader Alejandro Alarcón complained that "a period of stagnation" had set in and that "nothing was done to implement participation."[83] From its position outside the Popular

Unity coalition, the MIR called on Allende's government and the state-appointed administrators to ensure that sufficient mechanisms existed for worker participation. While critical of the government's slow pace, MIR workers in Tomé did not see themselves as challenging Allende's government. Rather, their call to fulfill the revolution's promise of worker control appeared to them the surest path to consolidate victories already attained.

Just as MIR students had mobilized to participate in the university reform commissions, Bellavista workers campaigned to get two MIR members, Juan Ávila and Hernán Mora, elected to the five-person Council of Administration, which would eventually oversee production in the mill.[84] Juan Reyes explained the MIR's approach to union politics: "The MIR was like an illegitimate child. How do you legitimate yourself before the people? You gain representation in the organizations that represent the interests of each group."[85] During Allende's presidency, MIR workers never displaced the Communist and Socialist Parties' leadership of the textile unions and the local and provincial branches of the national labor federation but gaining a seat at the table gave MIR-affiliated workers a voice and a vote in critical union matters through the FTR. Reyes explained, "After we had won a spot on the local CUT's governing board, for example, the Communists couldn't shut out the MIR. They had to listen to the FTR delegate because he had been elected by the workers' votes and his presence on the board legitimized the MIR."[86] Not all the workers who identified with the MIR and ran for union elections on MIR platforms would go on to become full-fledged militants. Many remained active in the newly created FTR, the MIR's mass front for workers.

The local organizing efforts begun in the late 1960s and expanded during the 1970s strike gave rise to the MIR's first Revolutionary Workers Front in the country. In June 1971, the national MIR debuted this new labor front with a flashy news spread featuring Alejandro Alarcón recounting the experience of the Bellavista strike and the nationalization. Yet as the experiences in Tomé and Coronel demonstrate, workers' support for the MIR preceded by several years the FTR's formal creation. It was no accident that the MIR chose to root its labor movement in the emblematic Bellavista factory and named Alejandro Alarcón as its national candidate for the 1972 CUT presidency. The MIR wanted to be associated with a younger labor movement, and Alarcón was the perfect figurehead. As a leather jacket–wearing, motorcycle-riding singer in a popular local rock band, he embodied the MIR's audacity, revolutionary masculinity, and counterculture appeal. That he was a little-known and relatively inexperienced union leader mattered less to the MIR's Central Committee than his association with the emblematic Bellavista textile industry, which lent working-class legitimacy to the MIR. If the symbolic origins of the FTR were located in the 1970 strike by Tomé textile workers, it was in the coal zone where the FTR achieved its most significant union victories.

REVOLUTIONARY UNION VICTORIES IN THE
COMMUNIST COAL ZONE, 1970–1972

After Allende's election in September 1970, the MIR could organize more freely as it sought to become an aboveground party centered on mass fronts of peasants, pobladores, workers, and students. As in Tomé, local MIR activists in Coronel were well positioned to lead this expansion. Despite initial success organizing students and pobladores, national MIR leaders, guided by Marxist thought, continued to consider workers the most important sector. In November 1970, Concepción MIR leader Bautista Van Schouwen called for "the democratization of unions so that rank-and-file coal miners can participate." He criticized the miners' exclusion from discussions about the impending December 1970 nationalization of the mines and instead asserted the need for an open assembly with grassroots participation. Even before the formal creation of the Revolutionary Workers Front, the MIR actively competed in union elections. Van Schouwen celebrated the MIR's nomination of Guillermo Cánovas, one of the original four local recruits, for the Schwager Industrial Worker Union's upcoming elections. He failed to mention the existence of the Brigada Sindical del MIR en Carbón, which ran its own candidate, Jorge García Dureu, also on a MIR platform.[87] While the MIR-designated Cánovas lost in the industrial union elections, the independent MIR brigade's candidate, García, won the most votes in the Sindicato Metalúrgico de Schwager (Schwager Metallurgical Union).[88] García's election came nearly a year before the MIR officially debuted the FTR in the Bellavista Tomé textile factory in mid-1971.

The 1970 coal zone union elections highlighted the existence of two parallel groups, each organizing locally in the name of the MIR. Motivated by a desire for unity, the two groups held a general assembly open to anyone who identified with the MIR to select the new leadership in the coal zone.[89] This represented a unique instance of participatory democracy within the MIR. By contrast, the national MIR leadership unilaterally appointed local and regional leaders with little input from the bases. In the coal zone, people associated with the official, and until recently clandestine, MIR selected "Huence," a fisherman and one of the original MIR recruits from Coronel to be second in command. They settled on a Concepción sociology student, Luís "Marmota" Pincheira, sent by the regional leadership the previous year, to lead public political organizing. The students and members of the independent union brigade who had been "cut loose" from the MIR in 1969 chose a local soccer talent, Eulogio "Duro Pablo" Fritz, a Coronel coal miner's son.[90] Yet as the former high school history teacher and now professional revolutionary Enzo La Mura explained, "They still didn't have anyone to lead because they had been divided, and so I gave guarantees to each side and this satisfied everyone and brought them together." La Mura's selection further reflected how personal relationships drove MIR activism in its early years. In 1962, La Mura spent a month substitute teaching in the Coronel high school, where he taught Sergio "Chico" Pérez, who became a national MIR leader, and Perucca Aguilera, editor of *El Rebelde Minero*. An original founder of the MUI during the university reform movement, La Mura also taught coal miners classes on Chilean labor history during the Concepción student federation–sponsored summer schools in the late 1960s. In 1971, he brought this grassroots organizing experience to his leadership role in Coronel. In less than a year, local MIR labor activists created one of the most successful FTRs in the country.

When President Allende symbolically gave the coal miners the keys to the mines in December 1970, people celebrated in the streets. Yet nationalization was not a utopic end in and of itself. A great distance separated socialized government ownership from workers' visions of shared management and shared profits. Former Communist union leader turned state-appointed general manager at the mines, Juan Bautista Bravo, embodied the tension of playing a "double role": "People believed that because the mines had been given to the workers, they could do whatever stupid things they wanted." Bravo had to ensure continued productivity: "It was necessary to stop this insolent attitude because we were the government, and as such, we had to defend the company, but the dilemma was that [we also had] to defend the worker."[91] From the perspective of some workers, Bravo's attitude approximated that of the old owners. As coal miner and FTR member Tito Carrillo contended, "When Allende took office, he considered the coal miners a solid constituency; thus, there was never much concern to improve salaries or working conditions for the workers."[92] This contradiction created a strategic opening for the MIR to advance demands for union democracy. "When it came to collective bargaining proposals," Lautaro López, a member of the Coronel MIR's student front, explained, "the MIR tried to democratize them, so that the people could say what they wanted." By contrast, "the Communist Party accepted the proposal from the government and said, 'We can't go any further.'" The "MIR tried to present the demands of the workers," but the "Communist Party, on behalf of the government, tried to diminish the possibility of a real wage adjustment."[93] To attract coal miners, the FTR strategically remained focused on the bread-and-butter issue of better wages.

It was in the coal zone where the MIR and its mass fronts directly confronted the hegemony of the Communist Party, which controlled practically all positions of local power. Tito Carrillo continued: "A Communist, Isidoro Carrillo, ran the national coal company. The governor, the mayor, the union leaders, they were all Communists. They were not in favor of making changes and were content with the way things were." With the idea that each worker equaled one vote and one voice, the MIR championed the need for union democracy. The institutional status of the Old Left, particularly the Communist Party, now a part of government and management, created an opening for the MIR to occupy an oppositional stance.[94] At union meetings, the FTR appeared as both a radicalizing and a democratizing force. In doing so, it tapped into a long tradition of union autonomy in the coal zone.

The Revolutionary Workers Front in the coal zone quickly became a model for FTRs nationally. Following the reunification in mid-1971, the Coronel MIR focused on organizing the FTR in accord with the MIR's national directive to prioritize mass fronts. On the basis of months of open discussion with local rank-and-file members, FTR union leaders wrote a platform for upcoming union elections without intervention from the local MIR leadership.[95] This document offers a glimpse into how the grassroots base of the MIR envisioned revolutionary change. Two points—"expropriate all the holdings of the *momios* [right-wing reactionaries] without paying indemnities" and create "real and effective worker participation in the management of the National Coal Company (ENACAR)"—coincided with the national FTR program.[96] As in Tomé, MIR-affiliated workers called attention to the absence of effective worker control in the state-owned enterprises and pushed for greater participation.

In 1971, the grassroots-generated FTR platform did not remain narrowly focused on labor conditions. Instead, drawing on traditions of worker and community activism, it offered concrete proposals for the redistribution of material resources and the overturning of social hierarchies: "Place the assets of the former private coal company at the service of the workers!" Mobilizing memories of struggle and exploitation, the union leaders called for a symbolic and material reordering of local power relations: "All the company's holdings are the product of centuries of exploitation," and as such they "should be utilized for the benefit of all." In this proposed redistribution, "the parks, houses, mansions, lands, etc., should no longer be the symbol of exploitation and class division. On the contrary, they should become in the immediate future a symbol for the revolutionary spirit." At once utopic in spirit but pragmatic in presenting concrete demands, the Coronel FTR proposed that "the houses should be given to the oldest workers and those with the largest families, the nonproductive lands should be given to [social] organizations, and the mansions and parks should be converted to rest homes, libraries, and day care centers."[97] In essence, MIR-affiliated coal miners proposed nothing less than the democratization of local space in Coronel—to take the sites associated with the employers' power and the exploitation of workers and make them available for the benefit of all Coronel residents. The FTR program's front cover depicted "a worker giving a member of the bourgeoisie a kick in the rear, and sending his briefcase flying"—an image suggestive of the desired transformations in social relations within Coronel.[98] In the imagined "immediate future" of a socialist Chile, the protagonists were not the owners but the coal miners and their families.

With its new platform, the Coronel FTR ran candidates in the coal mine union elections in early 1972.[99] Their candidates won the first majority in two elections: Jorge García in the Sindicato Professional Obrero Metalúrgico de Schwager (Metallurgical and Professional Workers Union of Schwager) and Guillermo Cánovas in the Sindicato Industrial Minero de Schwager (Industrial Workers Union of Schwager).[100] In the former, the FTR won three delegates to the Communist Party's two; thus, García assumed the presidency and the metallurgical union office became the local headquarters of the FTR. In April 1972, another of the original four recruits, Edmundo "Ademir" Galindo, won the first majority in the white-collar employees' union elections.[101]

More than any other group in Chile, coal miners embodied the Chilean proletariat. The national MIR's official *El Rebelde* affirmed that "the coal miners have always marched at the vanguard of their class brothers and their trajectory of struggle is part of the larger history of popular struggle in Chile." The MIR Central Committee celebrated the 1972 election victories in Coronel, asserting that they represented a "huge advance of revolutionary positions" among workers.[102] Nationally the FTR tended to attract support in small and medium-sized industries; by contrast, in the large industries like copper, coal, and steel, where the Communist and Socialist Parties had strong bases of support, the MIR struggled to gain a foothold.

Yet the story of the MIR's successful expansion in the coal zone and the FTR union victories derived not from ideological dogmatism but rather from the efforts of local people working with time-tested grassroots organizing strategies. First, the FTR candidates were well-known local leaders who enjoyed legitimacy within the labor movement and wider community. Unlike the Communist Party, which frequently invited "outsiders"—senators and other political figures—to participate in union meetings, "the FTR leaders were compañeros from around here."[103] During meetings, if the Communists tried to prevent FTR members from taking the floor, many miners came to their defense, arguing that each worker had the right to speak his mind.[104] The MIR's systematic political formation and investment in leaders also contributed to expanded support. As Aníbal Cáceres explained, "Our compañeros in the coal mines started to take a stand at union meetings, when before only Communists and a few Socialists would speak out. Now there was debate and discussion."[105] The union victories of the FTR, so widely celebrated in *El Rebelde*, were made possible by candidates who represented the coal miners' interests and who did not shy away from making concrete demands for better pay, better homes, and better social policies. They successfully inserted themselves into the opening to defend workers' rights vacated by the Communist Party, which was now officially part of the government and in control of company management.

Far from abstract notions of a socialist revolution, the MIR-affiliated workers defended participatory democracy in union politics. They also continued to champion workers' social and economic rights in the form of material gains, a practice that approximated the economic reformism of trade unionism that the national MIR shunned. While this approach marked a significant rupture with the traditional subordination of unions to political parties, it also highlighted a key disjuncture between the national MIR's official rhetoric of intransigence and the reality of their union gains in Tomé and Coronel.

The MIR's long-held aspirations of becoming a workers party were most realized in Tomé and Coronel during the Popular Unity years. Yet workers were only part of the story of the MIR's success. In less than eight years, the MIR had created functioning cross-class alliances in Tomé and Coronel. It pushed to democratize access to education, housing, and workplace participation. The importance placed on preparing militants through political education empowered individuals to see themselves as thinking subjects, capable of analyzing the challenges they confronted. In contrast to the ideological debates reverberating through the Chilean Left in the 1960s, MIR activists in Coronel and Tomé confronted a different set of traditions as they sought to organize working-class people. The autonomous initiatives of local activists often determined how the MIR expanded in these industrial enclaves. Support for the MIR grew when its political actions had a direct impact on the way people lived, which in turn empowered individuals to conceive of themselves, their neighbors, and their rights in society in new ways.

3

___

"By Our Own Means"

Building a Socialist Utopia in
Revolutionary Shantytowns

On the night of May 8, 1970, Iris Muñoz did not sleep. She waited surrounded by her nine children and husband, Santiago Sáez. Three days earlier, Santiago brought news home from the glass factory that tonight would be the night.[1] She took care to pack up the family's few belongings and what food there was. At two in the morning, a truck pulled up and university students helped the family climb in. When she descended from the truck into a grove of trees, Iris Muñoz did not know where she was. She had never seen this place before but would now call it home. Under the cover of a thick fog, she and her family made their way across a field. There, amidst other newly arrived families, they leaned a few pieces of wood together for shelter and raised a Chilean flag. Having staked a claim to the land, the Sáez Muñoz family huddled in the darkness and waited for dawn to come.

In the morning, the occupants took in their surroundings. A large field stretched out before them. On the far side ran Avenida Golondrinas, connecting the provincial capital Concepción to Talcahuano's booming four corners industrial sector.[2] The truck that carried them and others like it had driven through the night, making dozens of similar trips through Concepción's sprawling marginal neighborhoods.[3] The operation had been carefully planned, never stopping at random. A solidarity committee composed of thirteen local unions had selected the four hundred families transported that night.[4] In the early morning light, forty university students worked diligently, measuring off new streets and passageways. While the thick night fog had initially hampered police detection, by the morning their growing presence could not be ignored. As Iris Muñoz looked out over "Campamento Lenin," the police barricade stood as a stark reminder; she was not out of the woods yet.

By 1970, the *toma de terreno* (land takeover) had become part of a well-scripted repertoire of action by pobladores in Chile. As state development strategies turned Concepción province into an industrial center in the mid-twentieth century, the region experienced a rapid influx of rural migrants. Between 1940 and 1960, the population of Concepción rose by 72.5%, and the adjacent industrial suburb, Talcahuano, grew by 134%.[5] By 1970, one-third of Concepción province's half a million inhabitants had "urgent housing needs." Iris Muñoz was one of hundreds of thousands of Chileans who "took their plots" in the city, radically remaking Chile's urban landscape in the process. In subsequent negotiations with state officials, pobladores sought legal land titles and participation in state-backed housing programs. As one of Chile's most important twentieth-century social movements, pobladores redefined the terms of citizenship and inclusion in the nation.[6]

The MIR encouraged organizing grassroots social movements that did not look solely to the state for the resolution of their needs. The toma represented an effective form of mobilization by the dispossessed. For many pobladores, the idealistic MIR college students willing to lend their support represented a means to an end: a home. The students, in turn, saw the end goal of the housing struggle as socialism—the only solution capable of ending the exploitation of the Chilean working class.[7] In Campamento Lenin these two goals converged in the attempt to create revolutionary subjects in preparation for a future socialist society. Shantytowns organized around revolutionary principles went beyond meeting basic housing needs: they would bring about a wholesale transformation of social relations. The day-to-day process of working together opened up new spaces of participation for women like Iris Muñoz and generated local forms of community power. Shantytowns associated with MIR activism, like Campamento Lenin, became unique experiments in radical democracy.

"TO MOBILIZE PEOPLE, YOU FIRST
NEED TO KNOW THEM":
THE MIR AND HOUSING STRUGGLES, 1967–1970

By the time the MIR arrived on the housing activism scene in the late 1960s, urban land takeovers represented a well-tested strategy and an increasingly accepted political practice. Political parties, from Christian Democrats to Communists and Socialists, recognized the legitimacy of the pobladores' demands for housing and frequently assisted in the initial organization and distribution of land plots, and sympathetic politicians also facilitated access to negotiate with state bureaucracies to find a permanent solution. The Communists played an active role, most notably in supporting the emblematic 1957 La Victoria and 1967 Herminda de la Victoria land seizures in Santiago. Yet the Old Left's adherence to class-based analysis meant they tended to see housing struggles as a secondary issue to work-ers' rights.

With the rise of the Christian Democrats, pobladores found a new ally.[8] Influ-enced by the theory of marginality, Christian Democrats interpreted pobladores' and peasants' cultural and material poverty as responsible for isolating them from the benefits of modern society and making them incapable of overcoming poverty on their own. Instead, Christian Democrats believed that external agents in the form of the Chilean state and the Catholic Church should intercede to resolve prob-lems on behalf of the pobladores and thus facilitate their integration into society.[9]

Eager to court popular support, the administration of Eduardo Frei Montalva (1964–1970) institutionalized the participation of pobladores under the auspices of Promoción Popular (Popular Promotion). The Ley de Juntas de Vecinos (Neigh-borhood Councils Law), passed in August 1968, mandated that communities organize as a precursor to participation in government housing programs. Only legally recognized neighborhood councils could apply to create housing coopera-tives, whereby members would make monthly downpayments on the future gov-ernment-assisted construction of their homes. Yet these programs remained inac-cessible for the majority of improvished Chileans. The Frei administration introduced "Operación Sitio," a self-construction program that distributed subdi-vided land plots and building materials but did not provide even the most basic infrastructure like electricity, plumbing, and paved streets.[10] Pobladores remained responsible for building both their homes and their communities. By institutional-izing the participation of pobladores in official government programs, the Chris-tian Democrats hoped to deflect any larger challenges to the existing order.

The results proved mixed. The Popular Promotion programs incentivized com-munity organizing, but expectations quickly outstripped the capacity or willing-ness of the state to respond. By 1969, not only had the Christian Democrats' plans for housing construction fallen far short of the projected targets, but the Frei administration increasingly repressed illegal land takeovers. In March 1969, the Chilean national police killed ten pobladores, including an infant, in the southern city Puerto Montt. This widely publicized incident became a rallying call for the Chilean Left.[11] No longer encouraged by the Christian Democrats, the pobladores movement quickly exceeded institutional control.

In this context of escalating popular mobilization met with state repression, the newly formed MIR saw a political opportunity to organize the marginal urban and rural poor. In the 1960s, pobladores and peasants were still relatively new actors on the Chilean political scene.[12] As the previous chapter on Tomé and Coronel illus-trated, the MIR faced considerable competition in organizing Chilean industrial workers, who had long formed the backbone of electoral support for the Commu-nist and Socialist Parties. Shantytowns contained heterogeneous populations within a single territory. Thus, promoting urban land takeovers enabled the MIR to recognize the revolutionary potential of marginal subjects and to engage people's dual identities as both workers and pobladores in need of a home.

In the logic of an impending armed struggle, MIR intellectuals saw shantytowns as spaces that could potentially become liberated zones that would be defended by popular militias of pobladores.[13] Contradicting the theory of marginality, they held that peasants and pobladores were revolutionary subjects equal to workers and theorized land takeovers as a means to create territorial expressions of popular power.[14] As conceived by Marxist-Leninist theory, this popular power would form a counterweight to the bourgeois liberal state and would eventually be capable of destroying it. Unlike other parties, the MIR in 1969 was still a clandestine organization that existed outside electoral politics and state institutions. This outsider status gave rise to unique forms of organizing in MIR-connected shantytowns. Rather than channel pobladores' mobilization into the Christian Democrats' state housing programs or into electoral campaigns in support of a particular party, the MIR favored ongoing mobilization and direct action.[15] This combative approach appealed to pobladores, increasingly faced with police repression and frustrated with the slow pace of Christian Democrats' housing plans. Moreover, the 1970 presidential campaign offered a temporary reprieve, which pobladores seized as an opportunity for action. They found a willing ally in Chile's revolutionary Left and its many student militants.

As a new political organization, the MIR lacked the infrastructure and material resources of well-established political parties. Instead, the MIR in Concepción used the resources of the Concepción Student Federation to reach pobladores, just as they had initially done with workers in Tomé and Coronel. The MIR in Concepción, many of whose members were university students, approached organizing the popular sectors with the thoroughness of a senior thesis. "To mobilize people," recalled one former student, "you first need to know them." Under the guise of the FEC's social outreach committee, MIR leaders sent students to document people's housing needs. A student participant in these housing surveys explained, "We'd ask about income, family size, living conditions. . . . Then we'd systematize all this information and start looking for a solution. If you as a militant couldn't come up with a plan, then you'd ask your superiors in the party for guidance."[16] Working through the FEC lent the regional prestige of the University of Concepción to the urban poor's struggle for decent housing. Unlike Santiago, where land takeovers took place far from the downtown and universities, urban poverty existed in close proximity to the Concepción city center and campus. Students did not need to wait for summer vacation to engage in social and political activism. Their efforts to promote the inclusion of marginalized groups corresponded to their desire to democratize access to the reformed university and its many resources. Through their activism, the MIR affirmed that the right of citizens to a home superseded the liberal right to private property.

TO "DISTRIBUTE THE FAMILIES ON THE LAND":
THE TOMA OF CAMPAMENTO LENIN, MAY 1970

The May 1970 land takeover that created Campamento Lenin heralded the appearance of the MIR as an actor in the housing struggle in the southern Chilean province of Concepción. MIR university students eagerly played a supporting role, offering material resources, technical expertise, and solidarity. As in the coal zone and textile mills, local activists took the initiative. Javier Navarro, a thirty-five-year-old former Franciscan priest from Santiago, was a central figure in the introduction of revolutionary ideas to local housing struggles. By the time of the Campamento Lenin land takeover, Navarro was a familiar face to many pobladores, having been president of the adjacent población Puerto Montt, named in memory of those killed in 1969. In addition to participating in other land takeovers in Talcahuano, Javier Navarro had spent time in the polemical MIR-affiliated 26 de Enero población in Santiago.[17]

Navarro's personal and political trajectory mirrors the radicalization of housing struggle in Chile. In 1969, he identified as a Christian Democrat, but by the time he led Campamento Lenin, he was a sympathizer of the MIR.[18] Navarro described his own political awakening as a gradual evolution away from the Christian Democrats towards an embrace of Marxism: "I left the Franciscan convent in La Granja in Santiago because I saw that I could not fulfill myself that way. Reading Marxist books also influenced my decision. . . . Currently, I confess myself to be a Marxist."[19] Navarro's experience echoed a larger trend. By the late 1960s, the MIR increasingly drew support from individuals who had initially mobilized with Christian Democrats but had become disenchanted with the Revolution in Liberty. Just as students in Concepción had changed allegiances from the Christian Democrats to the more radical MIR during the university reform, a similar process happened among pobladores as the pace of radicalization outstripped the slow pace of reform.[20]

While the May 8, 1970, Campamento Lenin toma took local authorities by surprise, it was far from a spontaneous act. Thirteen labor unions had begun preparing the massive land takeover months earlier. The rapid expansion of the steel and petroleum industries had drawn many workers to the Concepción-Talcahuano area. For example, Víctor Rebolledo Plaza initially came to Concepción in 1964 on his honeymoon and decided to stay when he found good work as a welder for the Sigdo Kopper construction firm.[21] He organized the first Sigdo Kopper workers' union and soon began advocating for a permanent housing solution for some two hundred other workers with families.[22] Following the gendered approach that favored families over single men, several unions worked together to compile a list of four hundred families without homes. Even during the organizing stage, the union solidarity committee framed their housing activism as being about more than just acquiring homes. Composed of workers, students, and pobladores, the group advocated for joint actions that would "promote the destruction of the exist-ing social order and the construction of socialism."[23]

In his capacity as union solidarity committee president, Javier Navarro began working with the MIR-led student federation to identify and survey potential sites. Years later, Héctor Jego, then a first-year engineering student and MIR militant, recalled, "We studied areas in Concepción that were uninhabited, and discovered that Fundo Macera was not being used at all. It wasn't ever clear how [Carlos Mac-era Dellarosa] had obtained it."[24] The unpopularity of local businessman and land-owner Carlos Macera coupled with the ambiguous legal status of the land, which the Ministry of Housing and Urbanism (MINVU) announced it planned to acquire, made it an ideal choice for a land takeover.[25]

During warm summer days in early 1970, residents who lived along Avenida Golondrinas in the working-class neighborhood Hualpencillo might have noticed that the field across the road had become a popular place for soccer games. But these were not typical neighborhood pickup games (*pichangas*). On the field, union leaders played alongside representatives of pobladores, political groups, and university students. Yet for the players, the game was "secondary to the real pur-pose for their visits." Along with jerseys and balls, their equipment included "measuring tapes, small hammers, and tiny colored stakes." Play was frequently suspended "to meticulously measure the field, as if these players were obsessive rule followers intent on complying with regulations."[26] On other days, low-flying airplanes hired by students passed over the field, but the residents of Hualpencillo did not think much of the games or the airplanes.

The reconnaissance surveying trips and the aerial photographs enabled stu-dents to assist social leaders in determining "how we would distribute the families on the land." The MIR drew on the expertise of engineering and architecture stu-dents at the University of Concepción to design infrastructure and housing plans. This meant that by the night of the land takeover, the organizers had architectural drawings for the homes and plans to create a housing cooperative with the assist-ance of construction workers. A rapid and orderly toma was essential for the camp's chance at survival in the face of police orders to prevent illegal land takeo-vers. Despite careful planning, Héctor Jego noted, "once word got out that there was an organized toma underway, more people arrived than we had planned for, but we managed to accommodate them and assigned everyone spaces during the night." While the solidarity committee had selected and transported some four hundred families, another two hundred joined in the moment, meaning the new settlement had approximately three thousand people. On the night of the land takeover, Héctor Jego joined other students to map out the neighborhood design, with space "for the school, the health clinic, and community administration." At noon the next day, the FEC truck with university students' donation of corrugated tin and other building materials arrived.[27]

Public demonstrations of solidarity from diverse social organizations and local politicians worked to pressure authorities for a quick resolution in favor of the squatters. Several Christian Democratic and Communist politicians interceded to request a definitive solution in support of Campamento Lenin from Governor Alfonso Urrejola.[28] Student federations and trade unions—organizations that carried cultural and social weight in the region—mobilized existing solidarity networks. At the University of Concepción, MIR students sought institutional backing for these actions not only among students and the MIR-controlled student federation but also directly from the Consejo Superior, the university's highest authority. On May 13, 1970, the Consejo Superior agreed to the FEC's request to donate the equivalent of three months of a worker's wages in food and medical supplies to Campamento Lenin.[29] University students organized public rallies in solidarity with "La Lenin"; trade unionists held two-hour work stoppages to protest the police barricades. The solidarity committee fashioned "a human chain that permanently stayed on Avenida Golondrinas in front of the toma," to prevent police retaliation.[30] In record time, just five days after the land takeover, on May 14, 1970, the police cordon was lifted.[31]

Now came the question of the land. As in other land takeovers, political parties offered legal assistance. In this case, a Trotskyist lawyer and founding member of the MIR, Pedro Enríquez Barra, stepped in to act as legal counsel to Campamento Lenin residents as they negotiated with government authorities. Enríquez was a well-known local figure who represented trade unions and, as FEC lawyer, frequently bailed protesting students out of jail. Governor Urrejola, a Christian Democrat, initially proposed a plan to disperse the families to surrounding neighborhoods. After convening a general assembly, Campamento Lenin pobladores publicly rejected the offer and the MIR lawyer took their case to the Ministry of Housing and Urbanism in Santiago.[32] Direct negotiations between camp leaders and the regional housing authorities produced an initial accord on May 14, which granted pobladores the right to stay on the occupied land, to build homes under the "self-construction" state program, and to create housing designs subject to ministry approval; pobladores, in turn, agreed that there would be no additional residents. Under the agreement, the government formally recognized Campamento Lenin as a "community," which meant residents could participate in government savings programs to build their own homes. While the MINVU would supervise construction efforts through periodic visits, pobladores retained the right to continue receiving technical assistance directly from University of Concepción students. "Carnival-like" happiness filled Campamento Lenin at the public signing of the accord.[33]

In the case of Campamento Lenin, the pobladores' interests and needs converged with the direct action politics advocated by the MIR to produce results in record time.[34] Within a week, occupants became residents of the legally recognized Población Lenin. With this significant legal victory, they were one step closer to attaining homes. Yet as camp leader Javier Navarro reminded residents, it was time to "move beyond the first stage."[35] In the shift from land takeover to community consolidation, the MIR-oriented leadership in Campamento Lenin offered a different approach from tomas patronized by other political groups.

"A DIFFERENT CHILE": SOCIALIST UTOPIA AND THE CONSTRUCTION OF CAMPAMENTO LENIN

The political climate surrounding the contested 1970 presidential campaign conditioned how local officials reacted to Campamento Lenin and how they perceived this challenge from below. The Christian Democrats (DC), in power both nationally and regionally, were already on the defensive following the 1969 Puerto Montt killings and wanted to avoid using force against pobladores lest it detract from their electoral chances in September. Despite the pressure, Concepción's DC governor vociferously opposed Campamento Lenin, which in his judgment was no ordinary land occupation. He immediately denounced it as "an act with clear political goals [which] constitutes an open challenge not only to authorities but also to the country's legal system." In particular, he warned that it would be "a new and improved version" of the MIR's controversial 26 de Enero población in Santiago "with legal and political structures outside the Chilean system and with their own justice and police force." He further asserted, "That is called sedition. It is absolutely unacceptable and must be prevented at all costs." Departing from common practice, he rejected any possibility of negotiating with the pobladores.[36] In response, Javier Navarro extended an invitation for visitors to see Campamento Lenin for themselves, noting, "I want them to feel as though they are in Chile, but in a different Chile."[37] What were the terms of this "different Chile," and what was the revolutionary vision for Campamento Lenin?

Less than twenty-four hours after staking a claim to the land by raising Chilean flags and makeshift tents, the new residents of Campamento Lenin gathered in the first of many open-air assemblies governed by participatory democracy. Similar to the assembly-based tradition of Concepción student politics, Campamento Lenin pobladores organized themselves collectively into a general assembly of several hundred pobladores that functioned as the highest community authority.[38] As an example of the democratization of relations within the camp, each poblador had an equal voice and vote. These horizontal practices reinforced a sense of autonomy to envision change within and beyond the Chilean state. On the night of the toma, pobladores elected camp leaders. As one construction worker poblador recalled, "It was easy to agree on community leaders because everyone already knew one another."[39] The president of the solidarity committee, Javier Navarro, won election as camp president, and union leaders joined him on the governing community board.

Yet the elections marked an important passing of the reins. While MIR students contributed technical expertise and physical presence on the night of the land takeover, the vision and the majority of planning fell to housing activists with more experience. Looking back on the experience some forty years later, Héctor Jego acknowledged:

> There were old union leaders and neighborhood activists who had aspirations to do something like this long before we were born. They already had an idea of what their goals would be after the toma. They came with the experience of having participated in other tomas, and knew how to organize a población and what people would need. As students, our life experience was minimal. Most of us were single and didn't have children. We thought we knew everything, but we were just kids, and so we often deferred to the more experienced ones.[40]

While Campamento Lenin remained associated with the MIR and the University of Concepción in the months ahead, the land takeover and subsequent community organizations were not primarily the product of university students or a single political party. Similarly, although the prominence of unionized workers differentiated Campamento Lenin's planning phase, once the employed men returned to work, it would be those left behind, principally women and young people, who worked alongside housing activists to keep the camp running.[41] "As union leaders we carried out the land takeover," welder Víctor Rebolledo explained, "but the process going forward was led by community leaders with experience."[42] After the elections, full-time activists like Javier Navarro had more leeway to implement a MIR-oriented vision for socialist communities.

Successful land takeovers required a high degree of internal organization. More organized camps were better able to present their demands to authorities, often mobilizing well-worn tropes of morally upstanding working-class families in need of assistance.[43] To that end, organizing committees and neighborhood councils frequently set residency criteria and sought to regulate personal behavior. The reality of squatting in precarious makeshift tents without running water, electricity, or plumbing made working together to carry out the day-to-day tasks a priority. Campamento Lenin was no exception. On the evening of the toma, Javier Navarro announced the organizing principles for Campamento Lenin, which included a ban on alcohol sales and a commitment to protecting women: "Female compañeras can move freely at all times without fear of being raped. Woe to he who dares attack a compañera, regardless of her age." There would be no theft, according to the principles, because "we have only one wealth to defend and that is our freedom of conscience and self-determination, which brought us to occupy these lands." Those who forgot that this was a revolutionary endeavor would face "revolutionary justice, beginning with their expulsion from this land."[44]

Navarro's language of revolution differentiated Campamento Lenin from other land takeovers. Drawing inspiration from Che Guevara's "Socialism and the New Man in Cuba" and his experience as a Catholic priest, Navarro often spoke of the need to live exemplary lives.[45] He acknowledged alcohol and delinquency as real problems, yet contended these could be overcome by collective investment in the individual: "The poblador does not drink because he wants to but rather because no one has motivated him to stop by offering the possibility to succeed. It is the defeat that makes him an addict."[46] Navarro criticized the criminalization of poverty and the police as the face of the state in shantytowns. Instead, he asserted, "we will punish those who misbehave," and, in a gesture to the MIR's political education model, "the punishment will be work in service to the community: to read books and to prepare presentations for meetings."[47] Navarro proposed a holistic approach to individual uplift through community engagement.

Campamento Lenin pobladores offered a particular take on what it meant to live in a self-identified socialist shantytown. Just days after the land takeover, pobladores followed up on Navarro's organizing principles by issuing their community's "eleven commandments," collectively determining the codes of conduct by which they would govern themselves. Some explicitly banned fighting, wife beating, gambling, drinking, and stealing; others regulated participation in camp life, including mandatory attendance at general assemblies, active service on patrols, and collaboration in securing outside support; and still others addressed the residency requirement—all sites must be actively inhabited—and specified expectations for the maintenance of clean and orderly properties. The sanctions ranged from mandated service on behalf of the community to expulsion by general assembly vote. Noncompliance with any of the rules could be reported to the militia leaders, who would investigate the matter.[48]

Within these guiding principles, pobladores embedded a revolutionary campaign of self-transformation. The general assemblies that formed the camp's governing body also functioned as spaces of consciousness-raising. During the first months of the camp's existence, construction worker Humberto Fernández recalled that daily morning assemblies "stressed the importance of values, the importance for a family to be fraternal and affectionate, to be a family without aggression against the compañera or the children."[49] He added that the afternoon solidarity groups from the university "always made allusions to the new behavior."[50] Javier Navarro reiterated how social relations would be guided by solidarity and reciprocity: "We will be different from the bourgeois, we will be humane. Together we will act as one man to defend our dignity and our future. This población will be an example of what the workers of our country can do."[51] Concretely, he added, "if a compañera cannot build her house, then her neighbor should build it for her." Years later Humberto Fernández explained, "You had to help this compañera, free of charge. They stressed this point. Normally the women who were heads of households were relatively young, so when they say, 'without charging,' well, you know what they're talking about."[52] Removing the expectation of sexual relations in exchange for assistance suggests one way in which pobladores began to question traditional gender relations in the process of building Campamento Lenin.

Through their actions, Campamento Lenin pobladores engaged with the central questions about housing struggles in twentieth-century Chile: What constituted basic needs? What obligations did the state have to provide them? What if the state did not provide them? In the gap between the state's willingness and capacity to meet citizens' basic needs, pobladores organized to solve their own problems. Many families justified their participation in illegal land takeovers as a last resort when all other means had been exhausted. Amanda Galindo Mardones, wife of a construction worker, conveyed her frustration: "We took these lands because we didn't have anywhere to live. I've been enrolled in the CORVI [Corporation for Housing] since December. They said they would give me a house right away, but they haven't. They make us waste our money and then they don't give us houses."[53] When women engaged in housing activism, they often presented their actions in class and gendered terms—as humble women acting out of necessity for the best interest of their families rather than a commitment to political ideology.

When faced with continued government inaction, many Chileans, like Amanda Galindo Mardones, took matters into their own hands and embraced revolutionary politics along the way. Standing in front of her tent, she declared, "I like socialism." When pressed if it was right to occupy land that did not belong to her, she paused and then replied, "Maybe. I don't know. The only thing I do know is that I don't have any place to live. Now at the very least I have a plot of land. The rest will follow."[54] For Chileans like Amanda Galindo Mardones, the "socialism" of Campamento Lenin seemed like a more promising route to acquiring a home than institutional mechanisms. The brand of grassroots "socialism" that she articulated did not see the abolition of private property in favor of state ownership as the end goal. Rather, she imagined a more equitable distribution of material resources. If capitalism promised greater inequality, socialism held out the possibility of a more just future in which she and her new neighbors would finally have homes of their own.

More than simply to satisfy their legitimate housing needs, Campamento Lenin pobladores worked to create the conditions for lives with dignity. They contended that even Chile's most humble citizens deserved access to the same rights enjoyed by other citizens: decent homes in a healthy and safe environment, steady work, and access to culture and education. Many of their self-generated solutions centered on quotidian, not utopic, needs. Yet fulfilling these rights promised a transformation of social relations. Their proposal to form housing and industrial cooperatives responded to the reality that over a quarter of the six hundred heads of households lacked secure employment.[55] In addition to a university student–run health clinic, plans included an elementary school, a nursery school, a day care center, and a cultural center. Women in particular saw the provision of child care as facilitating their ability to participate as equals in this new society. When Javier Navarro anticipated hosting the university orchestra, choir, and theater troupes, his vision of making high culture accessible closely coincided with the new mission of the University of Concepción and its "Cultural Diffusion" outreach program created in the wake of the university reform movement.[56] Campamento Lenin pobladores laid claim not only to land but also to the fulfillment of their social, cultural, and economic rights.

Campamento Lenin pobladores' desire for "a more perfect community" involved the expansion of services to marginal communities as well as the creation of more egalitarian social relations.[57] Javier Navarro argued for creating integrated, multi-class poblaciones "formed by workers, employees, intellectuals, [and] technicians," in which "the doctor attends to his fellow compañeros from the camp and the professor teaches the children of his camp." This sense of shared responsibility—that my neighbor's fate is also mine—found an echo in the physician Ernesto Herrera's decision to live in Campamento Lenin. A self-identified Marxist-Leninist, Dr. Herrera believed that "one day we will arrive at a system in which everyone has equal possibilities because the son of a drunk or the son of a thief will turn out just like their fathers unless they see, and are given, conditions to avoid it." For Herrera, the teleological path toward socialism held out the promise to break cycles of poverty and offered "everyone equal opportunities to develop themselves."[58] Like many other Chilean professionals during the Popular Unity, Herrera put his beliefs into practice. His actions eroded spatial and class hierarchies by creating integrated cross-class communities. Instead of waiting for the revolution to happen, pobladores and their allies took action to make it a reality. In the day-to-day experiences of creating a community, a new society could be built from the ground up, and it would lead the way in the socialist future.

POPULAR MILITIAS AND POLITICAL CONTROVERSIES

As in other MIR-associated shantytowns, popular militias became the basic building block of community life in Compamento Lenin. By the late 1960s, the reality of escalating police repression against pobladores made some measure of self-defense logical. Campamento Lenin was no exception. Within hours of occupying the land, police in riot gear, stationed every twenty meters around the camp's perimeter, cordoned off the pobladores from the outside world. Ostensibly under orders to prevent the arrival of additional squatters and building materials, the police also denied the entry of foodstuffs donated by unions and medical supplies donated by the FEC. University students improvised a temporary solution: when police were not looking, they surreptitiously threw packages of food from moving cars as they drove along the access road on the camp's eastern perimeter. Reports soon emerged of police beating pobladores as they tried to reenter the camp.[59]

Following the first general assembly, pobladores organized a provisional popular militia, or night patrol, to stand watch over the camp.[60] The leader of this group of twenty men, armed only with sticks, observed, "The men in this encampment cannot sleep. We must stand watch and defend the land. They killed them at Pampa Irigoin because they were asleep." His remarks, referring to the 1969 confrontation in Puerto Montt, suggest a memory of state violence against pobladores that inspired a self-defense response. In an echo of the MIR students' audacity in 1960s protests, Campamento Lenin pobladores adopted a confrontational stance, affirming their readiness to "respond with all our force."[61]

The term "popular militia" intentionally evoked the combative discipline associated with Cuban revolutionaries and generated controversy in the local media. As the harsh winter set in, heavy rains inundated the newly formed Campamento Lenin. A representative from the regional housing authority, Humberto Otárola (DC), seized the opportunity to pillory the camp's leadership, which he claimed had abandoned the camp. In a front page exposé headlined, "Inhumane Living Conditions in Población 'Lenin,'" he scoffed, "instead of 'Lenin' they should call it 'Camp Irresponsible.'"[62] His mocking critique extended to the "tragicomic" situation of the militias responsible for maintaining order in the camp: "They wear tight green jackets, black berets and have long hair. Their hair, it's outrageous." In this way, he sought to discredit the guards by linking them to countercultural trends marked by otherness.[63] The DC housing authority concluded, "Children aren't responsible for what their parents do. Nor are the modest people [of Campamento Lenin] guilty for what's happening because they were put up to it."[64] His critique centered on ridiculing the militias for their subversive appearance and infantilizing the residents as duped by irresponsible unions and political groups.

The pobladores responded. They asserted that the housing representative had never visited the camp.[65] In a signed declaration, they proclaimed their "unity in support of camp leadership and the unions who support us with full confidence in the justice of our efforts."[66] Acknowledging their hard living conditions—shared by most workers and peasants in Chile—they organized "to overcome them by our own means."[67] If the Christian Democratic authorities cast pobladores as passive subjects in need of protection by responsible leaders, the pobladores and their MIR student allies saw them as actors, capable of generating their own solutions.

Analysis of the often-hyperbolic press accounts that mocked the "berets and beards" sported by Campamento Lenin's militia further reveals a disconnect between the anxiety generated by the terms "popular militia" and "people's tribunal" and the reality of these programs on the ground.[68] While the militias talked about "controlling" the police presence, engineering student Héctor Jego acknowledged in retrospect that the militia existed to warn of the arrival of the police but could not keep them out. The people's tribunal was the same general assembly of pobladores invested with the authority to determine the expulsion of individuals who did not comply with the camp rules.[69] Javier Navarro defused public concern by framing the militias in a discourse of respectability and dignity: "We have organized compañeros pobladores to supervise sanitation and cleanliness, to stop the entry of alcohol, and, in general, to prevent domestic conflicts between residents. . . . We emphatically declare that we do not have knives or guns of any kind or size."[70] Further, he said that they did not have berets or long hair.[71]

Similar attacks continued in the weeks and months that followed as pobladores consolidated Campamento Lenin into a revolutionary shantytown. Accusations went beyond reacting to the MIR's exaggerated rhetoric and hyping the threat of a possible Popular Unity victory in September. Instead, the criticism levied by public officials at Campamento Lenin pobladores belied a deep unease about the prospect of taking seriously the capacity of Chile's most marginalized citizens to represent their own interests and to change their own lives. For example, Campamento Lenin pobladores had rejected the government's initial efforts to disperse them and consistently sought to negotiate the terms of their inclusion, including reaching a settlement to purchase the land. The pobladores' defiance weakened the state's ability to co-opt and control the pobladores' movement as the Christian Democrats had attempted to do throughout the late 1960s. This kind of grassroots autonomy and the disregard for private property generated fear among local elites.

With time, Campamento Lenin's militias evolved from night vigilance to perform much broader functions related to discipline, internal order, health, education, and communal cooking.[72] As the historian Mario Garcés has suggested, this evolution within MIR-affiliated shantytowns gave rise to new types of poblador-created community organization, which functioned as "micro-spaces of participation and local power."[73] While the newspapers emphasized the militia's "beards and berets," what stood out years later for the student-trainer Hecter Jego was women's "remarkable participation."[74] Communist activist Ana Sandoval, who had helped organize the initial 1970 land takeover, observed that women participated "in all the internal activities within the camp because the men left [and] the women stayed behind in the camp and made decisions along with the camp's leadership."[75] Longtime Campamento Lenin resident Rosa Jara Alegría put it succinctly: "The woman was the *miliciana*." Some forty years later, she recalled how Javier Navarro often referred to her as "his right arm, because where he went, I went too," noting with pride that in the población "they recognized me as a political person."[76] She elaborated on women's double shifts: "At night we kept watch and we worked in the day to give bread to the children." Alluding to the validation that came from revolutionary association, another pobladora added, "We were *milicianas populares* just like in Cuba, with red bandannas and the insignia of Ché."[77] These women's memories attest to what one scholar has defined as the "pleasure of agency" that accompanied these experiences of empowerment and activism.[78]

Women's newfound participation did not go unchallenged. Another longtime resident of Campamento Lenin affirmed the importance of the well-organized militias, yet recalled how "people made fun of the women members," teasing that they were only there to make out with boys. She added that more than one romance started during a patrol, suggesting that the militias became spaces of youth sociability.[79] Some militias were segregated by gender, with women-only patrols assigned "specialized tasks" that conformed to traditional gender divisions, such as administering the camp's water supply, distributing donations, assisting the medical students, and running the communal cooking station (*olla común*).[80] In the tense early days, Rosa Jara Alegría was afraid to slip through the police barricade to buy food and relieved when "those kids in the MIR brought us food to eat, and so we started the ollas comunes;" within a very short time they routinely fed as many as three hundred people daily.[81] This gendered activism reinforced women's roles as mothers and caregivers, but their contributions within the domestic space of the camp became validated in a new language of revolutionary transformation "just like in Cuba."

Pobladores saw self-organization and self-vigilance as critical to overcoming the insecurity of life on the urban periphery. Many longtime residents like Ida Subiabre recalled with approval how the militias interceded in cases of domestic violence, emphasizing the autonomy with which the community policed itself: "The leaders carried out justice right here, they didn't go looking for carabineros (national police), they did it on their own."[82] When a news story surfaced in June 1970, alleging that Campamento Lenin leaders had harassed women, pobladoras like Celinda Opazo and "other homemakers" came forward to defend their leaders, calling the accusations of beating women "absurd." Opazo told reporters, "The day of the flood, they were more worried about our children than we were. They have never catcalled us, not even once, and we women are home alone."[83] As a woman in Campamento Lenin, Celinda Opazo could now leave her house in the dark early-morning hours without being afraid.

While Campamento Lenin's vision of an "integrated community" included women, in some significant ways women continued to be subordinated to men, particularly in the sphere of formal politics. On the camp leadership board, only one of the seven members was a woman. Ida Subiabre, whose husband, Bernardo Cardenas, was a MIR militant, recalled how when the MIR students or camp leadership came to see him, "he sent me out of the house, so that I wouldn't hear anything. He didn't want me involved in those things."[84] Other testimonies reflect the "unequal uplift" offered by revolutionary politics.[85] Pobladoras actively participated at assemblies and remember nostalgically their unity as women, yet they retrospectively acknowledge that the MIR largely excluded women from political discussions in the camp.[86] Thus, while women gained significant empowerment through their participation in camp life, machismo was by no means eradicated in Campamento Lenin.[87]

Other displays of autonomy by Campamento Lenin leaders were pragmatic responses—often advocated by women—to living in marginal conditions. For example, residents maintained a fence with a regulated entry point, issuing identification cards to each poblador.[88] When an indignant Christian Democratic politician was denied permission to enter, he exclaimed, "Is this not Chilean territory? This is unthinkable!"[89] Camp leaders, like the worker Luis Astete, downplayed the fence as an attempt to create "a state within a state," pointing out that "whenever the police have wanted to patrol the interior of the camp, they come and speak with the leaders," who let them in.[90] The police confirmed that they had never been denied entry. Camp leaders clarified that women had requested the fence be reinforced at an assembly. They added, "We want to avoid what happened at the other [fundo] San Miguel toma, where all kinds of people came in and where the camp president himself sells wine from his bodega. We also don't want politicians of any kind to come here and create problems."[91] The fence became a way for pobladores to regulate access to and membership in their community—to decide who could visit and who could stay. Campamento Lenin's utopian vision of community could only be sustained if certain elements—drugs, alcohol, and politicians—were kept out.[92]

The pobladores' general assembly decision in early June 1970 to ban all political propaganda and campaigning within the camp's territory reflected the reality that Campamento Lenin was hotly contested electoral real estate. Following the confrontation with the former Christian Democratic governor, which had been preceded by visits from representatives of the Communist and Socialist Parties, pobladores made one thing clear: politicians, regardless of their party affiliation, were not welcome. Pobladores recognized that the electoral struggles would end on September 4 but that their problems would persist. Alluding to the truck filled with foodstuffs that the Christian Democrats had brought to the camp, one leader asserted, "We don't want them to buy consciences with gifts." As the anthropologist Edward Murphy has noted, housing rights "were supposed to transcend political interests and positions, as they were a part of the liberal contract of justice and fairness between citizens and the state."[93] Campamento Lenin's residents mobilized a broader discourse that cast the Chilean housing rights struggle as apolitical.

This total rejection of "politics" signaled Campamento Lenin's rupture with the status quo, particularly the patron-client relationships that political parties often established with pobladores. Typically, a political party's work in shantytowns was premised on the expectation that residents would support that party at election time. Far from denying that residents had political sympathies, the leaders argued that voting was a personal decision. By banning campaign activities inside the camp, pobladores sought to overcome any sectarianism that could potentially divide them. Like other shantytowns in Chile, Campamento Lenin was politically heterogeneous. The majority of residents identified as allendistas, some were independent, and others were active militants in the Popular Unity parties or the MIR. The Christian Democrats also had support, but most Campamento Lenin pobladores saw their struggle as larger than electoral politics. What they had accomplished through self-organization would be lost if it was co-opted by traditional political practices.

With the MIR, politics became more than competition for votes. It was here that the pobladores' rejection of politics and *politiquería* (political games) coincided with the MIR's revolutionary discourse. The Campamento Lenin pobladores, not only in the act of taking the land, but also in the community they created on it, enacted their own vision of socialism in the present marked by new relations of equality. Significantly, with the creation of militias and other community organizations, women and young people gained new opportunities to participate in camp life. The impact that this agency had on the pobladores is apparent in the words of one resident's reflections:

> Those university kids opened our eyes. They taught us that from birth each man has the right to electricity, water, land, to everything that is part of our national patrimony. And they told us that we should never ever feel like delinquents. Because we were demanding what the law had not given us but what belonged to us by our own right. It was the light at the end of the tunnel.... From that moment forward, I embraced an understanding of what it means to defend people's individual and collective interests and I joined the MIR.[94]

The MIR's emphasis on self-transformation, when combined with redistributive measures to alleviate poverty, enabled individuals to participate fully as equals in society. In the months following the takeover, Héctor Jego maintained that students acted in supporting roles, working with the popular militias to prevent internal conflicts but not interceding to resolve them since that authority rested with the general assembly of pobladores. The MIR students, however, were not completely disinterested in the outcome of the militias. As Jego noted, "Of the people who participated in the militia, some went on to form part of the MIR's pobladores front [Movimiento de Pobladores Revolucionarios, MPR]," and "others developed and integrated themselves into the MIR" as full militants.[95]

Volunteerism—complete dedication to a cause and putting their skills at the service of the poor—defined the actions of MIR students and others in this period. From the earliest days of Campamento Lenin's existence, Concepción university medical students provided free exams for all the women and children in the camp.[96] The visits even became part of the medical school's clinical rotations. The students' solidarity played a central role in generating public sympathy for the land takeover and its residents, which, in turn, helped consolidate the residents' right to the land. More than just material support, the students engaged in modeling a socialist society driven by integration into the community, with greater equity in social relations.

"OUR STRUGGLE DOES NOT END OR BEGIN WITH CAMPAMENTO LENIN"

The ripple effects of Campamento Lenin went far beyond the borders of the shantytown and put housing rights at the center of public debates in Concepción province. The memoirs of Helmut Frenz, pastor of the conservative German Lutheran community in Concepción, reveal how wealthier Chileans viewed land takeovers: "Among the members of my congregation, the indignation about the [Campamento Lenin] land takeover was great, and it went without saying [that it] could be interpreted as an example of the Allende presidency's future policies, if elected."[97] The local press and some Christian Democratic officials seized upon the land takeovers to spread fear that a Popular Unity victory in September would spell the end of the rule of law. For Frenz, the laws were clear and squatter-led occupations of private property violated them. Yet the initial land takeover had produced no injuries, and, despite the tension of the police cordon, relations between police and residents had been peaceful. In the preelection mind-set, violations of the right to private property became read as acts of violence.

As the fate of Campamento Lenin riveted the public's attention, support began to come from unexpected places. Frenz, whose parishioners had so vehemently opposed illegal land seizures, was one of Campamento Lenin's first outside visitors. He performed funeral services for a child after Catholic priests had turned the family away. Visiting during the cold, rainy winter, the harsh living conditions of the two thousand Campamento Lenin residents, the majority women and children, astonished him: "The earth had been converted into a swamp. . . . Those with real tents were among the privileged because they provided shelter from the elements but not the cold. Others had built a shelter with boards and corrugated metal roofs. But the majority lived in *ramadas,* sheltered only by branches [*ramas*] and plastic awnings." Frenz encountered a "different Chile" in Campamento Lenin from the one he and his congregation knew. In conditions such as these, it no longer seemed surprising that a small child died from a respiratory infection. The illegality of the land takeover and the political firestorm that accompanied it fell away as Frenz's Christianity compelled him to action: "Before this congregated misery, I didn't see any other option than to stand in solidarity with them."[98] Frenz soon convinced his congregation to assist the pobladores in the construction of a more permanent structure for the health clinic that could double as a refuge for children during the inclement winter months.[99]

The controversy surrounding Campamento Lenin and the MIR's propensity to attract press attention increased the visibility of poverty in Concepción province, particularly for those like Frenz who had initially viewed the problem in terms of the rule of law. The construction of the health clinic violated Chilean law since it was a permanent structure on land that did not legally belong to either the pobladores or the German Lutherans. Yet if the law made aiding the residents a crime, then the law must be disregarded. This shift from a legal framework to a moral one found broader resonance in Chilean society.[100]

As more and more people confronted the precarious reality faced by many Chileans, the experience changed them as it had changed Helmut Frenz. In the 1960s, a growing social conscience guided many MIR students as they set out to encounter "el pueblo" and gain legitimacy with workers. For example, engineering student Héctor Jego reflected how the disparities of Chilean society was the motivation for his budding political commitment: "We [in the MIR] saw that so large an inequality could not be; it wasn't reasonable. Principally, from my point of view, it was not Christian. God made everyone equal, and that there was such difference was not justifiable. From there to arrive at Marxism is just one more step. We had to change this; we could change this."[101] He found continuity between Christian teachings about the equality of man and the Marxist principles espoused by the MIR. Many Chileans at this time, like Javier Navarro, Helmut Frenz, and Héctor Jego, experienced acts of solidarity with pobladores as transformative. This confrontation with poverty expanded their social consciences and inspired greater commitment to struggles for social justice. For some, like Javier Navarro and Héctor Jego, the MIR's revolutionary politics increasingly seemed to represent the best avenue to achieve their goals of social equality.

The toma of Campamento Lenin in May 1970 became a focal point for the expansion of the MIR in Concepción province. MIR students heralded it as evidence of their commitment to build socialism through supporting pobladores' struggle for housing. In July 1970, FEC president Jorge "El Trosko" Fuentes (MIR) asserted students' right to engage in activism before the Consejo Superior, the University of Concepción's highest governing body. Fuentes made no apologies:

> We take responsibility for our participation in the land takeover and the construction of Campamento Lenin. We are proud of it, very proud. We participated in the preparation process for the land takeover and we will participate in many more. The tomas will continue because they do not depend on our will. The living conditions of the pobladores and the lack of housing are inherent problems in the social system in which we live. As students, we will work together with exploited social sectors. Our struggle does not end or begin with Campamento Lenin.

He connected housing activism to larger aspirations: "Our struggle has as its goal—and we will say it clearly—the destruction of the existing social order." Yet he was careful to qualify that as students "we will not make revolution alone. Students cannot do it. The great mass of workers, pobladores, indigenous peoples, and revolutionary intellectuals will do it, marching with firm steps towards socialism."[102]

During the run-up to the September 1970 presidential elections, popular mobilizations multiplied across Chile. Concepción province witnessed sixteen other land takeovers between May and August 1970; half of these were large-scale tomas with 150 families or more participating.[103] The timing was no accident. Concern that police repression would jeopardize Christian Democrats' chances at the polls led the Frei administration to favor negotiation over eviction. In the case of Concepción province, police intervened to prevent or dislodge just one of every eight takeovers.

The still clandestine MIR sought to capitalize on this effervescence with a coordinated strategy of simultaneous tomas. Drawing on their experiences preparing for the Campamento Lenin takeover in May 1970, MIR students and pobladores attempted to replicate them. In total, the MIR participated in organizing six additional illegal land takeovers. In August 1970, police thwarted an attempt to occupy Fundo Bellavista, a property belonging to the University of Concepción. As with Campamento Lenin, MIR students collaborated in identifying homeless people, organizing a housing committee, and selecting the day for the Fundo Bellavista toma.[104] Students also facilitated transportation and building materials. Among those arrested in the frustrated takeover attempt were sixteen university students "carrying documentation that identified them as members of the MIR." The politically conservative local newspaper, *El Sur,* printed the names, ages, addresses, and majors of the fourteen male and two female students arrested. As for the other 134 detainees, *El Sur* observed only that "the majority are workers, detained carrying tools and other materials, along with three trucks filled with construction materials."[105] Undoubtedly, the men were also accompanied by their families, as many of them testified. Yet, with the exception of two female students, the police only took men into custody.

The fact that the majority of the detained pobladores readily acknowledged their participation in the failed toma suggests that they, along with the wider Chilean society, recognized the legitimacy of housing demands. Accordingly, workers offered a gendered defense that as heads of households they had an obligation to provide for their families' needs. In doing so, they performed what Edward Murphy has called the "urban politics of propriety," where "claims for housing continued to be made based on assumptions about proper gender and familial roles."[106] The testimonies also shed light on the political calculus that pobladores made in deciding whether to participate in an illegal land takeover. As one man explained, "Since the opportunity presented itself now, I didn't think twice. I went to see if it would succeed."[107] Pobladores' decision to participate was, moreover, predicated on an assumption that a land takeover might foreseeably produce results, and it was a chance worth taking.[108] Campamento Lenin had become a potent symbol of the possibility for action.

Although police foiled the August 1970 occupation of Fundo Bellavista, three other simultaneous MIR-backed land takeovers that same night succeeded. Concepción MIR leader Bautista Van Schouwen declared "the land takeover as the only form to attain an immediate solution to the housing problem."[109] Following a general assembly, Campamento Lenin pobladores occupied "without violence" adjacent lands to accommodate more than three hundred families.[110] They immediately began building provisional houses to discourage police from attempting an eviction since "the pobladores have already settled the occupied land." Residents made clear, however, that no "outsider families" would be allowed to join; the new takeover represented an effort to alleviate overcrowding in the original territory.

The same night, more than fifteen miles away, in the coal mining community of Coronel, residents occupied their own half-built houses to protest construction delays. Under the government's "self-construction" system, future home owners were furnished with building designs and materials and, in exchange, provided labor and downpayment contributions. During the building phase, the houses were not assigned to individual families; only once the entire neighborhood was complete would families learn which home would be theirs. Despite starting construction in March 1970, the houses still lacked running water, electricity, and plumbing. Tired of waiting, poblador coal miners allied with the MIR decided to take matters into their own hands, peacefully occupying the houses. Within three days of the toma, the government ceded the houses to the occupants.[111] Rather than contest the Communist's Party's role in the unions, the MIR initially sought to organize coal miners through their dual identity as pobladores in need of housing.

The multiplication of land takeovers in the wake of Campamento Lenin reveals three sociopolitical trends in Chilean society. First, addressing poverty and housing needs had increasingly become recognized as legitimate by broad sectors of Chilean society. Second, the tactics of direct action—the illegal land takeovers—produced rapid results, particularly when the political process produced an opening. Third, pobladores' ability to organize themselves was crucial to this success, alongside students' ability to offer solidarity and material resources. In comparison to other Chilean cities, between 1970 and 1973, Concepción witnessed more organizing around housing rights and disproportionately more urban land takeovers, particularly in the adjacent suburbs like Talcahuano, Penco-Lirquén, and Chiguayante.[112]

Furthermore, by 1970, pobladores' struggle for decent housing had begun to redefine how Chileans thought about the relationship between state and society. Following the university reform, students gained representation within the university administration. From this vantage point, MIR students pushed university authorities to recognize the legitimacy of housing rights activism and student activism. As the student federation continued to sponsor land takeovers, the board of trustees was forced to respond, particularly when students targeted university-owned land. FEC president Jorge Fuentes contended that "the university's responsibility is to never take repressive measures against the homeless, not to evict them, or jail students."[113] One professor sympathetic to the MIR, acknowledging the national significance of the University of Concepción, called on his fellow board members "to recognize the legitimate right of the homeless to occupy land and to express our solidarity with these sectors."[114] In October 1970, the board unanimously "reaffirmed its confidence that the new government of Salvador Allende will find a solution" to the housing demands while simultaneously affirming "its confidence that the people themselves will in an organized fashion help build the new society to which we aspire."[115] This statement captures the broad spirit that in the wake of Allende's election embraced the possibilities of a top-down democratic transition to socialism and acknowledged the power of grassroots activism to move that project forward.

University authorities increasingly found themselves contending with the fall-out from student-poblador activism. The Consejo Superior's deliberations reveal the extent to which students, with support from segments of the faculty and administration, succeeded in reorienting the social mission of the university to the common good. In December 1970, Campamento Lenin pobladores occupied the opulent fourteen-bedroom, seven-bathroom plantation home (*casa patronal*) belonging to Carlos Macera and demanded that it become a hospital.[116] A year after the original land takeover, Macera offered to loan his house to the University of Concepción free of charge until the government had completed the legal expropriation. Not only was the local authority—the Talcahuano governor—in favor of this arrangement, but so were the Campamento Lenin pobladores. Edgardo Enríquez Frödden, father of MIR founders Miguel and Edgardo Enríquez and University of Concepción rector, met with representatives from Campamento Lenin who asked that the university take charge of the unoccupied houses and turn them into a day care center. University authorities suddenly found themselves debating the possibilities "for a series of activities of great interest for this university."[117] In conversations with Campamento Lenin leader Javier Navarro, university authorities initially proposed studying the possibility of providing dentistry, pediatric, and legal clinics, a nursery school and day care center, a cultural center, a worker-training center, and a soup kitchen. While pobladores developed the preliminary plan for the soup kitchen, different schools within the university evaluated the feasibility of the other projects. The collaboration between top university authorities and pobladores offers a glimpse into the kinds of cross-class solidarities that emerged in this moment. Campamento Lenin residents' vision for integrated communities seemed to be on strong footing as the university promised to offer greater access to society's most marginalized citizens.

RADICALIZATION AND CONTAINMENT
IN THE POBLADORES MOVEMENT

A year later, under the banner, "The struggle continues," Campamento Lenin pobladores commemorated the anniversary of the land takeover by hosting a regional congress for revolutionary pobladores. Camp residents defined their "fundamental task" as elevating "the combativeness of the masses" in order to integrate "their creative capacity into the tasks that will facilitate the installation of a socialist regime." Lest there be any doubt, in this socialist future, "the organized people will exercise political power." Twenty campamentos sent delegates. Discussion topics ranged from practical debates about housing construction materials to the role of pobladores in Chile's historic transition to socialism and revolutionary struggles, and to more utopian reflections on the creation of a socialist morality. Despite the MIR's organizing role and the keynote address by Víctor Toro, it was a politically pluralistic meeting with city councilmen and government housing representatives from the Socialist and Communist Parties.[118]

The Concepción congress marked a turning point in MIR-oriented housing struggles. Nine months into Allende's presidency, the national MIR reevaluated its confrontational approach to illegal land takeovers during the Frei administration. After meeting with the MIR's Central Committee in Santiago, Víctor Toro recalled, he was sent to Concepción to deliver the keynote speech outlining the MIR's new strategy, which exchanged confrontation for negotiation.[119] To underscore this point, Toro proclaimed, "Today the enemy of the pobladores is no longer the government, which previously used repression, it is the great consortiums of construction firms who delay construction and the Cámara Chilena de la Construcción."[120] In the face of bureaucratic delays in government housing offices, Toro countered that the pobladores offered the government an alternative solution in the form of work brigades of pobladores and the unemployed.

Downplaying the previous emphasis on illegal land takeovers, Toro instead proposed that only the extensive landholdings of the wealthy should be expropriated by the government or occupied by homeless pobladores. He explicitly discouraged occupying small or medium-sized lands belonging to anyone other than large landowners. Likewise, he spoke out against occupying houses and apartment complexes being built for other workers, alleging that "these measures are currently being exploited by the Christian Democrats in the hopes of confusing the public."[121] The revolutionary pobladores' congress had attracted a number of unionized workers, many without homes.[122] Within weeks of its conclusion, MIR regional secretary Bautista Van Schouwen informed Toro that fifteen new grassroots MIR bases, each composed of five people, had formed in places like Talcahuano and Coronel. Participants at the congress had taken seriously the instruction "to create bases of the MIR" and had done so "on their own initiative."[123] This autonomous expansion indicates both the magnitude of the housing need in the region and the growing appeal of the MIR's approach to housing rights.

A test of this new, tempered approach would come just a few months later. As Concepción province prepared for the much-anticipated visit of Cuban revolutionary leader Fidel Castro in November 1971, "a wave of tomas" swept through the sleepy fishing towns of Lirquén and Penco. From the coastal towns, the land takeovers spread throughout the province. In just two months, between November and December 1971, approximately two thousand families carried out seventy separate tomas in Lirquén, Penco, Talcahuano, San Pedro, and Chiguayante—a magnitude never seen before. Newspaper headlines diagnosed a "psychosis of tomas," and there was uproar on all sides. This spontaneous wave of tomas ran counter to the MIR's new policy of negotiation and cooperation with the Popular Unity government. Decades later Víctor Toro reflected, "I don't know what people understood [as the new approach] because afterwards they did the complete opposite."[124] Contrary to Toro's call for land takeovers of extensive landholdings, the majority of the seventy takeovers consisted of a dozen families occupying lands that were unsuitable for permanent housing projects: the grass in the median of the road, small vacant lots, the railroad pass way, the hills around the city. While MIR activists had connections to less than one-third of the new land takeovers, the MIR's previous organizing work had emboldened the poorest sectors of Chilean society to see themselves as individuals invested with rights within a larger collectivity.

As the MIR sought to become more than a party of students, it had started sending emissaries to the surrounding towns. For example, in 1969, two MIR students had approached fisherman Carlos Robles on the Penco beach. "That's how they started with me until I caught the bug of Marxism," Robles said. Like those in the MIR bases in Coronel and Tomé, Robles recalled how his political awakening combined analysis of Marxist texts with personal reflections:

> They would select a paragraph and ask, "What do you think about this?" And I had to explain what I understood. When Lenin talks about the organization of the cops, the armed forces, and all that, well, damn! I realized these crazy kids are right. They educated me. All I wanted was to know more and more, and afterwards we put that knowledge into practice, right here, with the land takeovers.

The political education Carlos Robles received as a sympathizer and later as a full-fledged militant in Chile's revolutionary Left expanded his worldview: "After I had a certain degree of awareness, I said, 'I was born for this.' And I took my side with the revolution."[125] Through his discussions with the MIR students, Robles began to see the obstacles he faced as part of larger problems in the existing social, political, and economic order. His family's need for adequate housing was something he himself could change. Less than two years later, he along with his family and neighbors acted on that long-held dream by carrying out a land takeover and building their homes and their community from the ground up. In November 1971, when Carlos Robles organized his family and neighbors, he did so both as a poblador in need of housing and as a political activist, in this case as a MIR militant.

These overlapping identities are key to understanding Robles's trajectory from illiterate fisherman to disciplined revolutionary. Similar to the MIR's expansion in working-class enclaves like Coronel and Tomé, it was everyday people like Carlos Robles who persuaded their friends and neighbors that illegal direct action was not only legitimate but also promised the possibility of immediately transforming their lives. As Robles became drawn into the MIR, he aided students in their quest to "collect sympathizers among salt of the earth people." He brought his new MIR friends to a meeting at a local sports club and, decades later, recalled how "we went into the assembly with the idea of doing a land takeover, but [first] we had to organize it and convince people." After people began seeing Robles around town with the two students, other fishermen approached him. They would ask, "hey, what is all this crap about?" He responded by explaining, "It's your duty. The duty of every one—of all of us—is to liberate ourselves. 'To free us from what?' The boss and Capital." Robles would "burn the midnight oil reading those books" from the students, so that he could explain it to his neighbors. In addition to book learning, he gained leadership experience, especially in the art of persuasion. Robles recalled believing that other political parties had weaker arguments; they would say, "No, you can't. Compañero Allende this and that," thus suggesting that part of the MIR's appeal rested in its outsider status and its willingness to back direct action.[126]

Yet convincing people to join was not easy. Robles and the MIR students faced another challenge: the deep respect many Chileans of all classes held for private property. Robles detailed the work of going door to door to explain the meaning of rights: "We had to speak to people, talk it over, because they respected private property. They'd say, 'If I go [to the toma], I'm a thief.' That's what we were working with. [We'd say,] 'No, it's your right.' All Chileans have a universal right to a roof over their heads."[127] Through his work in the MIR, Carlos Robles began to spread awareness of rights and advocate collective action as the best means to attain them.

By November 1971, this organizing work had begun to take root. On November 16, Robles and his mother, sister, and neighbors from Cerro Verde occupied land belonging to the Chilean Automotive Club. He justified their choice by explaining that "the Automotive Club members only used the grounds once a year in the summertime when they came to vacation, and the rest of the year there was only the groundskeeper living there." After the toma, pobladores named their camp "Carlos Condell," after the nineteenth-century Chilean hero from the War of the Pacific. "After a week," Robles explained, "we knew that they [the authorities] would not send in the special forces on us. We divided the lands between everyone and the people started with hammers and nails to build the población." The new residents also agreed on basic rules that would guide living in the community:

"We're all compañeros and good neighbors," "We have to fight for services like water," and "You have to wait your turn in line."[128] Although the rules regulating camp life appeared less elaborate than Campamento Lenin, they nonetheless suggest a degree of cohesion and collective decision making.

The toma of Carlos Condell was but one of many land takeovers that riveted Concepción province in late 1971. By early December, the situation was increasingly untenable for both local authorities and President Salvador Allende, who personally met with the MIR's top leadership in Santiago and requested that Víctor Toro step in and help resolve the situation to avoid further conflict. By that time, the MIR had established a presence and legitimacy within the pobladores movement. As one scholar observed, Popular Unity housing officials recognized the MIR's vital role, but a stalemate developed: "Officials neither forced the MIR to stop, nor did they tend to go out of their way to provide neighborhoods settled by the MIR with services and land titles, although there were important exceptions."[129] The task for the MIR was clear: give the tomas order and organization and prevent them from being exploited by the opposition, particularly the Christian Democrats, as had happened in Santiago. Víctor Toro recalled Allende telling them, "If the MIR strategy is to take underutilized urban lands belonging to large landowners, then fine, do this. But look at where they are squatting [in Concepción province]."[130] It is significant that by late 1971, President Allende turned to the MIR as an ally, capable of providing critical leadership. As the political party most closely linked to radicalized sectors, most in favor of immediate action, the MIR during the Popular Unity often, paradoxically, found itself moderating grassroots goals or mediating negotiations between Allende's government and an increasingly radicalized base.

With this charge, Toro set off for Concepción accompanied by Allende's security detail and the housing minister. Although Toro admitted that he "had always been in favor of tomas," what he saw in Concepción shocked him: "People had started to take everything and anything possible, up to and including the patios of houses." The many hills surrounding Concepción looked almost like a "military parade[,] with Chilean flags everywhere you looked." As he toured the province, Toro spoke only as a representative of the MIR because the collaboration between the MIR and the Popular Unity government was never publicly acknowledged. When Toro met with pobladores, he proposed reorganizing the smaller occupations into larger ones under MIR leadership with the condition that the government provide trucks and resources. Later on, the hope was that the government would create massive construction projects, building entirely new neighborhoods for several thousand residents of modest means. Significantly, Toro linked the defense of land takeovers to the defense of the Popular Unity government before a newly resurgent political opposition.[131]

Publicly, Toro denied that the MIR had instigated the wave of land takeovers, declaring that "the only party behind these tomas is the lack of housing."[132] The historical reality of poverty coupled with a severe housing shortage plagued the region for decades. Consecutive governments had failed to complete housing construction targets. By 1971, "the people woke up."[133] That the tomas coincided with Fidel Castro's arrival in the region likely provided an opening for pobladores to act, much as the 1970 presidential campaign had protected Campamento Lenin from police eviction.

Yet beyond the political expediency of timing, when Fidel arrived in Concepción he undoubtedly saw thousands of Chileans mobilized to demand a place in the city and in the revolutionary process. With a banner aloft proclaiming, "Fidel! Campamento Lenin welcomes you in the struggle!," residents eagerly awaited the Cuban leader's motorcade. Pobladoras like Rosa Jara Alegría recalled how they surrounded the car and insisted Fidel stop to learn about their revolutionary shantytown.[134] The MIR had invested considerable energy in consciousness-raising about the historical problems of housing, as well as spreading Campamento Lenin's message of empowerment through the May 1971 congress and other activities. By December 1971, consciousness-raising had an impact, although not in a form anticipated or controlled by the MIR.

In the wake of the 1971 tomas, the MIR scrambled to establish a presence in the new campamentos under the auspices of the Revolutionary Pobladores Movement (MPR) and the newly founded Comando Provincial de Pobladores sin Casa (Provincial Command of Homeless Pobladores). Although Víctor Toro spent several weeks in the region, the long-term task of implementing this approach and coordinating actions fell to local población leaders like Javier Navarro and to grassroots MIR militants like Carlos Robles. The accelerated pace of change challenged the MIR's capacity to give leadership and direction to the ascendant popular mobilization in the province. As in the coal zone and textile mills, local activists took the initiative in defining alternative forms of belonging and self-organization. The success of these initiatives hinged less on the MIR's overarching ability to provide a coherent ideological orientation than on how everyday people tapped into the MIR's organizational energy and technical expertise to acquire a home and a place within the revolution.

4

"Let the People Speak!"

Popular Democracy and the
Concepción People's Assemblies

On July 27, 1972, workers, students, pobladores, women, and peasants converged on the University of Concepción Theater for a People's Assembly. Although originally planned in homage to the Cuban Revolution, participants sought not arms but a greater voice in the revolutionary process.[1] After representatives from five political parties had spoken, the much talked about People's Assembly seemed to be little more than an event typical of the Chilean Left, "where people go and listen to political leaders present their opinions" and then disperse. Instead, chants of "Let the people speak!" rang out from the audience. "It was almost like being at a play and watching a set change take place," recalled Mario Garcés, who at the time was an anthropology student and MIR militant. "First, the leaders conferred among themselves behind the curtains, and then the MC reappeared and announced, 'Two microphones are being set up, we ask for compañeros to come forward in an orderly fashion to speak.' That's when the real People's Assembly began."[2] What transpired that night in Concepción illustrates the fraught potential of popular democracy within a revolutionary process.

Among those who came forward was Fernando Manque, a peasant union leader from the rural town of Hualqui, 12 miles from Concepción. More than forty years later, he could still feel the sensation of standing on stage struggling to find his voice: "I started by saying, 'We are convening this assembly—the first in the region—and I hope there are many more because this is how to know the reality of the pueblo. I am here tonight to tell you about peasants—the poorest of the poor—and about the reality of the countryside. We are here to propose that the most basic of needs of the poor [be met].'"[3] The son of rural workers, he had known poverty his entire life. He was just seventeen years old when rural workers elected him to represent their demands to create a peasant union. The power of Chile's landed elites had stretched back for centuries. The legalization of peasant unions occurred only in 1967 as part of Eduardo Frei's Agrarian Reform, nearly four decades after industrial workers had won the same rights. In a few short years, Fernando Manque had gained a tremendous amount of organizing experience; he worked with the Communist Party in the first union, then with the New Left Movimiento de Acción Popular Unitaria (MAPU; Popular Unitary Action Movement). Finally, he said, "the bug of the MIR bit me." In 1972, he was both a respected community and labor organizer in Hualqui and a militant in the MIR's Movimiento de Campesinos Revolucionarios (MCR; Revolutionary Peasant Movement).

Manque's multiple roles blurred the line between grassroots social leader and full-time political activist. In anticipation of the People's Assembly, he had met with his MCR-MIR contacts at the University of Concepción to go over his speech. Yet in the theater, it was not the MIR but the crowd that had lifted him off his feet and pushed him onto the stage. His individual experience reflects a larger tension in the relationship between social movements and political parties in 1970s Chile. In explaining the 1973 breakdown of democracy, the sociologist Manuel Antonio Garretón criticized Chilean political parties for ideologizing every space and failing to allow autonomous social movements to flourish.[4] The assumption at the time, of course, was that political parties were behind any event like the People's Assembly, manipulating individuals like Fernando Manque from off stage. This perspective correctly highlights how ideology often inhibited political parties from theorizing and validating innovations coming from grassroots initiatives. Yet its focus on political parties as the primary actors diminishes the significant agency of popular sectors. Fernando Manque was no puppet.

Far from the theater of conflict that played out in the national press and between national political parties, this chapter offers an interpretation from below of the Concepción People's Assembly. Contrary to depictions at the time and since, the People's Assembly was not the act of a single party—the MIR—or of a few rogue regional political leaders. Rather, it was driven and made possible by the strategic work of coalitional grassroots movements. The spontaneous May 1972 assembly had set a precedent for the formal July People's Assembly by demonstrating the ability of grassroots activists to articulate their own political ideas and to demand something other than politics as usual—even from the leftist parties with which they were allied. Despite close ties with radicalized grassroots movements, the MIR did not escape the same rigid internal hierarchies and top-down control that plagued other political parties. Faced with rank-and-file demands, regional political leaders convened the July People's Assembly as a space for grassroots participation in the revolutionary process.

Demonstrating the momentous challenges of popular democracy, the Concepción People's Assembly opened a space for several hundred grassroots leaders and party activists to debate Chile's future. It simultaneously underscored a "stead-fast commitment to defend the Popular Unity government" and propelled the question of popular power—the idea that everyday Chileans should have a say in the direction of the revolution—to the forefront of national debate.[5] President Allende promised that, unlike under previous governments, state force would not be used to repress. Protected and emboldened by the institutional "revolution from above," grassroots movements mobilized in ways that simultaneously pressured the government and demonstrated their capacity to solve their own problems. This rapid expansion of grassroots agency appeared poised to challenge the status quo.

As Chileans from diverse walks of life seized the opportunity to carry out what they thought the revolution should be, their actions often centered on transforming their daily lives. These accumulated experiences of collective action gave rise to the Concepción People's Assembly, which sought to scale up local practices of direct democracy in places like Campamento Lenin and the University of Concepción into a regional space where an organized citizenry could articulate its own goals. For some, popular democracy appeared to be an unruly mob challenging the foundations of the state. For others, it represented democracy in its truest sense.

Collective action by a united Left defined Concepción's radicalism during the Allende years. Despite the MIR's positioning of itself outside Allende's government, it succeeded in becoming a key political actor in Concepción because of its cooperation with four parties in the Popular Unity coalition: the Socialist Party (PS), the Popular Unitary Action Movement (MAPU), the Radical Party (PR), and the Izquierda Cristiana (IC; Christian Left). Coordination between regional leaders, in fact, mirrored preexisting collaboration across party lines in the bases.[6] Between May and July 1972, Concepción offered the nation evidence of this accrued social power and its possibilities: first, in the impromptu assembly and mass mobilization on May 12 and later in the official, self-proclaimed People's Assembly convened on July 27 by 140 grassroots social organizations: 60 unions, 31 shantytowns, 27 mother's centers, 16 student federations, and 6 peasant organizations.[7] The power of this assembly rested in its representativeness. As a radical democratic project from below, the Concepción People's Assembly signified the projection onto the national scale of a regional alternative to Allende's centrally planned revolution.

This display of popular sovereignty did not happen just anywhere or everywhere in Chile. On the basis of local movements, it became possible for leftist organizations to converge in Concepción in a way that was not possible nationally. In mid-1972, regional leaders highlighted how Concepción's "particular combination of political and social forces favorable to the Revolution" placed it at the vanguard.[8] Within the contingencies of the moment, grassroots activists clamored to respond to an anti-Allende opposition they increasingly perceived as seditious and pushed their political leaders to embrace new forms of organizing that would give them greater autonomy and greater power.

As a region with deep historical ties to the Old Left (Communists and Social-ists) and a rapidly expanding New Left (the MIR, MAPU, IC), Concepción could send a message to the nation that the Chilean people were prepared to defend Allende's government and the revolutionary process in the streets. As the historian Camilo Trumper argues, the momentary "seizing [of] city spaces" created "site[s] of democratic political practice, contest, and exchange." The struggle "to win the battle for the streets" (*a ganar la calle*) was not just about preventing one group from marching; it was also, on a much deeper level, about generating "new modes of political expression" centered on the exercise of popular sovereignty.[9]

A national political backlash quickly suppressed the assembly's revolutionary possibilities.[10] Conservative newspapers like *El Mercurio* immediately labeled the People's Assembly a seditious attempt to create a parallel power premised on the destruction of the Chilean Congress and demanded President Allende respond.[11] The more moderate Communist Party had refused to endorse the People's Assem-bly, denouncing it as a "divisionary" ploy by the "ultra-left," meaning the MIR.[12] The national MIR leadership gladly accepted credit for this revolutionary advance, despite the fact that a regional alliance between the MIR and the left wing of the Popular Unity had organized the July 27 event. Just days after its celebration, fear-ing greater diatribes from the Right, President Allende publicly dismissed the Concepción assembly and asserted his control over the Popular Unity coalition and the course of the Chilean revolutionary process.[13]

Subsequent scholarly treatments have produced a second layer of silencing around the Concepción People's Assembly. Pointing to the subsequent suspension of the August 1972 People's Assembly, scholars dismiss the July 27 assembly as mere propaganda with minimal political impact.[14] Located within a Cold War frame-work, most accounts of the Popular Unity years emphasize ideological conflict and privilege political parties as the primary actors. Thus, the Concepción People's Assembly is relegated to a footnote illustrating the internecine conflicts within the Chilean Left that plagued Allende's ability to govern.[15]

This perspective obscures how the autonomy of diverse local movements shaped the trajectory of Chile's revolutionary process. In examining the dynamics of revolution and counterrevolution that defined Latin America's twentieth cen-tury, the historian Greg Grandin offers a different interpretive lens that privileges open contingencies over ideology: "It is the imperative of maneuvering through the intricacies of immediate insurgent politics and confronting real opposition that determines action, rather than an insistence on holding true to ideological dogma."[16] This view replaces a restrospective lens tinged by Allende's overthrow with an open-ended sense of historicity in which the indeterminacy of any given moment meant that people acted without knowing the future.[17]

As an experiment in popular sovereignty, the Concepción People's Assembly was abandoned because of how deeply it challenged the Chilean political system.

An authoritarian tradition underwrote the much-lauded stability of Chile's democracy.[18] Even in 1972, the agency of popular classes—their ability to think, act, and decide—was unimaginable to most. Across the twentieth century successive democratic administrations, including the Frei government (1964–70) and the Popular Unity government (1970–73), extended rights and recognition to a growing number of groups. Yet the unprecedented levels of popular mobilization in the 1960s and into the early 1970s posed a significant challenge to this status quo.[19] Despite the calls by centrist and leftist political parties for mass participation in the 1960s and 1970s, they continued to act largely *on behalf of* and *in the name of* those they hoped to mobilize. Political parties cast "the masses" in the role of chorus— acquiescent political props whose function was to listen to speeches and to applaud the decisions of political elites.[20] In Concepción, on the night of July 27, 1972, the chorus rebelled.[21]

"A GANAR LA CALLE": THE COUNTERREVOLUTION COMES TO CONCEPCIÓN, MAY 1972

By mid-1972, Chile's revolution seemed at a crossroads. In his first year in office, Allende had made tremendous strides toward socializing the economy. But as the opposition-controlled National Congress repeatedly blocked Allende's legislative agenda, the Popular Unity's project for a phased, institutional transition to socialism by 1976 risked stalling. Determined to stop any further advances, a recalcitrant opposition began to challenge Allende's policies in the streets.[22] As the centerpiece of the opposition's new "mass strategy," the March of the Pots and Pans in December 1971 appropriated the same organizing strategies that had been a mainstay of the Chilean Left. Elite right-wing women guarded by the openly fascist shock troops from Patria y Libertad [Fatherland and Freedom] marched through Santiago banging pots and pans in symbolic protest of the hardships imposed by Allende's government.[23] At the time, however, no shortages existed, nor had the government implemented rationing. Moreover, as women from Santiago's relatively prosperous *barrio alto,* they were largely insulated from adversity. Yet never before had the dominant class's hold on power been so contested. These actions marked a significant historical departure: for the first time, elite conservative women took to the streets to demonstrate their dissatisfaction with government policies. The timing was no accident. It coincided with the end of Cuban leader Fidel Castro's nearly monthlong stay in Chile, from November 10 to December 4, 1971.

While Fidel's visit reinvigorated anti-Allende organizing in Santiago, to the south in Concepción province, it coincided with a renewed wave of urban land invasions. Just as they had done during the 1970 presidential campaign, pobladores in Concepción province seized the political opening presented by the Cuban revolutionary's visit to assert their right to a home and a space in the city. More than one Campamento Che Guevara and Campamento Fidel Castro appeared in November and December 1971, when nearly eleven thousand men, women, and children carried out seventy separate land takeovers. Both the scale and accelerated pace of housing activism in Concepción outstripped other urban areas.[24] President Allende requested that the MIR recall housing activist Víctor Toro from Havana and send him directly to Concepción.[25] If anyone could effectively rein in the land invasions, it was Toro and the nascent Movimiento de Pobladores Revolucionarios (MPR; Revolutionary Pobladores Movement), a tacit acknowledgment of the MIR's growing legitimacy among Chile's urban poor in their struggle to acquire decent housing.

Allende's request reflects the complicated relationship of collaboration and competition between the MIR and the Popular Unity government. Despite Allende's overtures in the form of ministerial appointments, national MIR leaders refused to join the governing Popular Unity coalition in 1970. Instead, they opted to provide critical support while maintaining an independent, more radical position that endorsed class conflict and promoted direct democracy.[26] Allende remained firmly committed to a more moderate political strategy premised on building Left and Center-Left electoral coalitions. Of all the Popular Unity parties, the Communist Party was the most disciplined and faithful to Allende's cross-class strategy. These differences over ideology and strategy sometimes brought the MIR and the Communist Party into open conflict. For example, in December 1970 members of the Communist Ramona Parra Brigade shot and killed MIR student Arnoldo Ríos at the University of Concepción. High-level negotiations diffused tensions and avoided further violence.[27] Periodically during his presidency Allende initiated talks with national MIR leaders; Fidel Castro even brokered one round during his visit in December 1971.[28] Against this context of tense but not necessarily antagonistic relations between the Communist Party and the MIR, the Chilean Left confronted a resurgent opposition.

If Castro's visit prompted right-wing women to march in Santiago, for conservatives in Concepción the boisterous Cuban leader embodied the very overturning of social mores and disregard for private property that over ten thousand local residents materialized in the 1971 wave of land takeovers. Taking their cues from Santiago, regional opposition parties, which had remained largely silent during Allende's first year in office, announced plans for a "Democracy March" in Concepción on May 12.[29] Just as the March of the Pots and Pans capped Fidel Castro's extended stay, the Democracy March coincided with the United Nations Conference on Trade and Development (UNCTAD III) meetings in Santiago. While Concepción would be the staging ground for this rally, the intended audience was national. If the Popular Unity government refused to authorize the march, the opposition could claim their democratic rights were threatened. This preemptive rhetorical assault on Allende's government marked a tactical shift by his opponents.[30]

Leftists in Concepción wasted no time in responding. As early as January 1972, the Concepción Revolutionary Workers Front warned that "all workers who pride themselves in being revolutionaries and who are willing to defend the stability and program of the people's government" should be prepared to adopt "a confrontational attitude against fascism and the parties that welcome it."[31] On the heels of coal miner Jorge García's victory in Coronel union elections, the MIR's labor front contended that the front lines would no longer be the union hall but the streets. Before an audience in the coal zone, MIR general secretary Miguel Enríquez contended it was time for the Left to go on the offensive, because the Right "has already made up its mind to defeat the Popular Unity government, to repress the workers, and to restore power to the bosses and [U.S.] imperialism."[32] Now in response to the opposition's plans to march in May 1972, the FTR and Popular Unity leaders in Concepción made separate plans to rally supporters.[33] In addition, local construction workers had called for a May 12 work stoppage so that their twelve thousand members could attend a meeting on the University of Concepción campus, where they would vote for the ratification of a single provincewide union, integrating blue- and white-collar workers. Considered by many to be a revolutionary advance, the *sindicato único* would give blue-collar workers a permanent majority.[34] Afterwards, construction workers along with students planned to march on the city.

The conflicts over competing May 12 marches in Concepción had national repercussions. From the perspective of the Allende government, the top priority was to maintain public order. The Popular Unity strategy was premised on a cross-class alliance, and Allende still hoped to negotiate a truce with the Christian Democrats. Initially, the regional Popular Unity, including the Communist Party, agreed to combine forces with the MIR and hold a single countermarch.[35] Yet two days ahead of time, the Allende government interceded and cancelled the Left's march, citing fears of street confrontations between pro- and anti-government forces.[36] In permitting the opposition march while suspending the UP and MIR march, Allende sought to signal to domestic and international audiences that his government respected democratic dissent. The regional Communist Party immediately acceded to Allende's request, but the other four Popular Unity parties (Socialists, MAPU, IC, and Radicals)—announced that they, along with the MIR, would mobilize as planned.[37]

By 1972, it appeared to many on the Left that forces opposed to Allende increasingly were flirting with fascism. Regional political leaders pointed to mounting evidence of the Chilean opposition's "seditious attempts . . . to hand Chile over to U.S. imperialism by means of a dictatorship": the October 1970 assassination of Chilean army general René Schneider, the anti-Allende propaganda campaigns of terror, and the recently publicized meetings between the U.S. corporation International Telephone and Telegraph and the Central Intelligence Agency to channel funds to Allende's opponents. In a joint statement by what would become known as "the Group of Five," the MIR and four UP parties warned that the opposition's "hypocritical slogans of 'democracy and freedom' obscure their dark class interests and their reactionary resentment against the program of the UP government and against the people's mobilizations."[38] All the parties in Allende's Popular Unity coalition—except the Communist Party—joined the MIR in supporting the determination of workers, pobladores, and students to demonstrate that in Concepción the streets belonged to the Left.

The perception of an opposition actively moving toward counterrevolution combined with the Left's greater strength in numbers made action appear both urgent and possible. The feeling on the ground, according to then regional MIR leader Enzo La Mura, was that the Left in Concepción was in a position to stop the opposition in its tracks.[39] As a bastion of the Chilean Left, striking miners and their families had for decades marched on Concepción from the coal zone, as had textile workers from Tomé. The streets of the city had long been the primary arena of contestation between police and university students fighting for university reform in the late 1960s. Textile workers in Tomé and coal miners in Coronel, along with a dozen other unions, took out a full-page newspaper ad calling for a May 12 countermarch. The Concepción student federation (FEC) and the newly created Provincial Command of Pobladores joined them. At the last minute, the regional branch of the national labor federation (CUT) also endorsed the march, despite opposition from its PC president.[40] Speaking for the labor federation, PS leaders stated that the CUT must be on "the barricades with the working class." "We call on all the combative workers to support their government." The CUT leaders emphasized, "Our position is not one of provocation, we will only defend what has already been attained at the cost of so many past struggles."[41]

The Left in Concepción—both regional party leaders and grassroots activists—interpreted the anti-Allende march as open class warfare "by the exploiters" who sought to regain power lost under the Popular Unity government. The Left's countermarch, in effect, became symbolically important as a show of force. The ten-thousand-strong countermarch on May 12 and the open forum that preceded it on the University of Concepción campus heralded the strength of grassroots social organizations and the regional political alliances that would give rise, just weeks later, to the realization of the July People's Assembly in Concepción.

"THE STREETS BELONG TO THE PEOPLE":
THE FIRST PEOPLE'S ASSEMBLY, MAY 12, 1972

When Concepción residents opened *El Sur* on May 12, they found two full-page political ads. "Today the Patria Marches," announced one, accompanied by hand-drawn images of a large Chilean flag waving above marching men and women dressed in collared shirts and jackets.[42] The other image depicted a campesino and a worker striding confidently and combatively forward carrying sticks. The headline implored: "We call on the people to occupy the streets of Concepción and to stop the outrage and provocations by fascist groups like Patria y Libertad, the Christian Democrats, and the National Party."[43] In addition to endorsements by diverse organizations of workers (18), students (2), pobladores (2), and peasants (1), the Socialists, Radicals, MAPU, Christian Left, and MIR added their support. The same image circulated through Concepción as a noon hour handbill on May 12, confirming that the afternoon march was on.[44]

Behind the scenes on May 12, President Allende issued a request to suspend all marches, including the previously authorized opposition march.[45] Yet anti-Allende marchers rallied as planned to voice their discontent with his administration's "sectarianism, misgovernment, incapacity, food shortages, and inefficiency."[46] Across town, on the University of Concepción campus, leftist political parties regrouped their militants.[47] Citing evidence that Patria y Libertad had planned violence, university student leaders conveyed the government's decision to suspend marches by both sides.[48] Student leaders proposed that the thousands of leftist sympathizers already gathered should rally on campus until they received confirmation that opposition parties had indeed called off their march. More and more columns of workers and students converged on the campus, filling the central esplanade connecting the iconic bell tower to the gateway arch.[49]

In the ensuing improvised rally–which would become known as "the first People's Assembly"—dozens of people spoke over the course of three and a half hours from the raised cement stage in the center of the University of Concepción campus.[50] This was the same site of innumerable debates during the university reform movement, and where Salvador Allende had debated MIR leaders in June 1971 and where in November 1971 Fidel Castro had addressed students.[51] The first to speak on May 12 was provincial labor federation leader Heriberto Krumm (PS), who had adjourned the construction workers meeting by urging them to head to the forum.[52] Then a series of student federation leaders took the microphone. Fernando Robles (MAPU), for example, criticized the government's decision to suspend the marches. Communist student Antonio Leal then celebrated the Allende government's achievements. Martín Hernández (MIR) echoed Robles on the need to confront the reaction at every turn, an implicit criticism of the UP government's conciliatory posture. Construction worker Vicente García emphasized the importance of worker-student alliances, noting that workers had much to learn from students and that students in turn had much to learn from workers. García concluded by inviting attendees to march on the city center and demonstrate the workers' revolutionary force. Next came Luís Astete, an FTR leader from the Sigdo Koppers union, one of the unions that had organized the Campamento Lenin land takeover two years earlier. As a Campamento Lenin resident, Astete called for ending leftist sectarianism and affirmed workers' readiness to join with the students in a show of unity. Yet he cautioned, "Participation isn't just done with words." Celebrating Concepción "as Chile's red city," the FTR leader asserted that the workers must show the power of the people.[53]

The May 12 rally represented a quintessential bottom-up response.[54] Nearly four decades later, then high school student federation president Marcial Muñoz (FER) did not remember his own speech but rather the number and diversity of speakers: "In my memory there were fifty-three speakers altogether: workers, pobladores, peasants, students, FTR. People spoke in the name of the MIR and for the other parties." Those approaching the open microphone were not party leaders or well-known public figures "but people who were leaders in their neighborhoods, poblaciones, or campamentos."[55] This open microphone was, in many regards, spontaneous—an ad hoc plan in response to the last-minute cancellation of the marches. Yet it drew on the tradition of direct, participatory democracy in University of Concepción student politics, where open assemblies decided collective resolutions. It also followed the model of assemblies in the bases—where pobladores, for example, debated a course of action in their shantytown and where the most persuasive speakers often carried the day.

Although the open forum drew on the region's assembly-based political culture, its scale was unprecedented. The sheer number of leftist sympathizers astonished the young Marcial Muñoz:

The campus was completely full of workers, pobladores and students. What's more, they arrived organized in what we called back then the *masa armada* [people in arms]. The coal miners arrived with their helmets and headlamps on, carrying sticks of dynamite; the pobladores came with their spears and slingshots. People marched from Talcahuano and came by train from Lota and Coronel, marching in columns ten across. It was an awesome sight to behold.[56]

Indeed, estimates put the May 12 attendance at over twenty thousand, making it one of the largest rallies in Concepción's history.[57] Empowering to students and some leftists, the image of coal miners with dynamite and pobladores with spears undoubtedly stoked the opposition's fury.

"WE TOOK THE CITY":
THE MARCH ON CONCEPCIÓN, MAY 12, 1972

In Concepción, the events on May 12 simultaneously responded to the emboldened, recalcitrant Right and challenged leftist party leaders to redistribute political power to the bases. Participants that day witnessed grassroots radicalism as reflected in FTR leader and Campamento Lenin resident Luis Astete's declaration that "participation isn't just done with words."[58] High school federation president Marcial Muñoz asserted that demonstrators wanted to send a message to the Right that they could not occupy the streets of Concepción. "In Santiago it was another story," he said, "but in Concepción, no, impossible." Before the awe-inspiring crowd that had turned out on campus, Muñoz sensed that "the political leaders, including the MIR, were afraid that we would try to go to the city center."[59] As the afternoon wore on, tensions came to a head between party leaders trying to contain the rally within the campus and grassroots sectors ready for street confrontations. When Luis Astete tried to lead a march down Diagonal Avenue toward the city center, MIR leaders intervened to stop him.[60] Despite being outside the Popular Unity coalition, the MIR often acted as a government intermediary to rein in an increasingly radicalized base. Eventually, after negotiating with police, regional leaders diverted the march down Víctor Lamas Street.[61] Yet Muñoz detected their apprehension: "The [leftist] political leaders never thought, never imagined, that the response to their call to mobilize would be answered by so many people. The level of organization of the workers and the pobladores was so great that the political leaders were a bit overwhelmed."[62] The "never-ending march" stretched for thirteen city blocks, running parallel to the downtown and the opposition's march, which had also taken to the streets.[63]

On May 12, revolution in Concepción was lived as a kind of liberation in which the region's poor and dispossessed occupied the city center and overturned social hierarchies. This convergence of workers, pobladores, and students generated a sense of empowerment that changed how individuals perceived the strength of the Left and expanded imaginable horizons. Some of those in attendance, like high school student and member of the MIR's FER, Álvaro Riffo, had arrived prepared: "We had handkerchiefs, gas masks, slingshots, and sticks." His inventory suggests the Left's "masa armada" was equipped for street skirmishes but lacked both the training and the weaponry to confront the professional armed forces. His brigade detoured from the leader-led march down Víctor Lamas and broke police barricades to confront "the fascists in the plaza." Riffo exulted in the rush of leftists into the plaza, the dispersal of the opposition, and the retreat of the police. "Concepción's city center was completely taken," he exclaimed. "I mean, we took the city! It was a fiesta!"[64] The advancing revolutionary tide appeared invincible that day.

In local memory, the day's events remain a touchstone of the Left's accumulated social power in Concepción. Decades later, Marcial Muñoz conveyed his wonder at witnessing such a large turnout: "It was an awesome sight, really just incredible. [You could even imagine someone saying,] 'Let's take the city, expel the cops, and invade the few military barracks,' and in the euphoria of the moment it would seem feasible."[65] Many participants evoke May 12 as "lo máximo"—the "greatest expression of popular action and unity in Concepción during the Allende years"— and the corresponding sensation of opening that empowered people to act.[66] What that action would be was up for debate. But the Left's revolutionary potential was visible to the bases, the regional leaders, the opposition, and President Allende.

"THE CHILEAN PEOPLE ARE NOT PUPPETS":
LESSONS OF MAY 12 FOR THE LEFT IN CONCEPCIÓN

Divergent interpretations of what happened in Concepción on May 12 and what it signified for Chile's revolutionary process brought the regional MIR and the left wing of the Popular Unity into direct conflict with the Communist Party and, by extension, the national Popular Unity coalition. In the immediate aftermath, the Group of Five (MIR, PS, MAPU, PR, IC) reiterated the goals of the May 12 mobilization as preventing the opposition from taking the streets and demonstrating mass support for the Allende government.[67] But they also wanted the government to answer for police brutality. On the evening of May 12, protesters learned that police attacked the remaining groups in the plaza, beating one leftist high school student to death and injuring sixty others. The martyrdom of Eladio Caamaño convulsed the province. Students again faced repression during the funeral march that culminated in a public viewing in the university's art museum, which had also held the *velatorios* for the MIR "martyrs" Arnoldo Ríos (December 1970) and Luciano Cruz (April 1971).[68] While the right-wing Patria y Libertad had injured several police officers, state repression had only been directed against leftist activists.[69]

Departing from a previous modus vivendi of nonagression with the MIR negotiated after the December 1970 shooting of MIR student Arnoldo Ríos, the Communist Party blamed the MIR for the May 12 mobilization and resulting violence. In contrast to the relative autonomy displayed by the Group of Five, the Communist Party was strictly governed by positions taken by their national leaders. Local and national PC leaders dismissed May 12 as "a stunt" by the MIR and vowed that "with President Allende and the Popular Unity program, we will defeat the provocations of the ultra-Right and the ultra-Left."[70] In the weeks ahead, the Communist Party launched a national campaign with the same slogan. This outspoken criticism directed at the MIR in 1972 responded, in part, to the potential consolidation of a more radical tendency within the bases of Chilean society and increasingly within the Popular Unity coalition itself.[71] For the remainder of May, the regional Popular Unity leaders ceased their weekly meetings with PC leaders, and relations between them remained strained.[72]

While tension with the Communist Party had fractured the regional Popular Unity leadership, the push for greater unity across the Left in Concepción continued unabated. It was often aided by personal relationships. Between May and July 1972, regional party secretaries Rafael Merino (PS), Eduardo Aquevedo (MAPU), Joaquín Undarraga (IC), Manuel Vergara (MIR), and Pedro Enríquez Barra (MIR) met frequently.[73] They were bound by ties to the University of Concepción, and in some cases, by family.[74] Longtime lawyer for the student federation (FEC) Pedro Enríquez Barra had known Eduardo Aquevedo since his days as an outspoken Christian Democratic student leader during the university reform movement.[75]

The MAPU and Christian Left leaders, moreover, had all been Christian Demo-crats in the late 1960s. In 1972, Aquevedo began teaching at the University of Con-cepción sociology institute, where many prominent local MIR intellectuals also taught, including Fernando Mires and Néstor D'Alessio. Across campus, Rafael Merino taught philosophy, and Joaquín Undarraga taught economics. Many other regional political leaders, including Manuel Vergara (MIR) and Ricardo Bozzo (MAPU), were university students at the time. This mix of current and former UdeC students and faculty within the ranks of regional party leaderships sustained friendships across party lines. The prominence of the MIR and its influence within the university carried over to regional politics. MIR lawyer Pedro Enríquez Barra emphasized that this political harmony "only existed at the regional level. Nation-ally, this kind of relationship [between the MIR and the Popular Unity left wing] existed, but it was much less intense, whereas [here] in Concepción, it was practi-cally an alternative to the Popular Unity."[76] Viewed from Santiago, the emergence of a regional political alliance between the Popular Unity and the MIR threatened to undermine the cohesion of Allende's national coalition.

Simultaneously, in mid-1972, the opposition continued, undeterred from plans to destabilize Allende's government. On the one hand, the anti-Allende movement continued to exert pressure with street demonstrations, actively seeking violent confrontations that would create a sense of chaos. In the Congress, opposition pol-iticians undermined Allende's ability to govern by blocking new legislation, defund-ing approved laws, and, starting in mid-1972, impeaching his cabinet members. Faced with the powerful display of grassroots agency in Concepción, elite sectors turned to familiar tropes: "The reactionaries have always disavowed these popular expressions, characterizing them as banditry. Or, as they used to say openly, but now remark [only] in private, 'the people are rebelling' [el pueblo está alzado]."[77]

In anticipation of another opposition march authorized for May 24, regional leaders in Concepción decided against calling their supporters to the streets. Instead, the left-wing Popular Unity (PS, MAPU, IC) and the MIR distilled the lessons of May 12 into an eight-page "Concepción Manifesto" that was dissemi-nated nationally. Foreshadowing the July People's Assembly, regional leaders emphasized that the most important aspect of May 12 was not the massive march, the street skirmishes, or even the police brutality that left Eladio Caamaño dead but rather the open assembly, which represented "something magnificent and new in national politics," despite being "the incident that was most covered up after the fact." The assembly brought together thousands of workers, pobladores, and stu-dents who listened with rapt attention and enthusiasm to thirty-five speakers. During "this self-convened assembly, the people of Concepción decided to defend actively the stability of the government and the continuation of the revolutionary process."[78] Before this peaceful and powerful display of popular political agency, Joaquín Undarraga acknowledged, "As political leaders, we have received an eloquent and productive lesson that the Chilean people are not puppets: they have their own consciousness and they have moved beyond the strongman stage. They do not follow leaders, but ideas." He added, "Their advance is no longer controlled from above."[79] This acknowledgment of popular sectors' consciousness would increasingly put the regional leaders in conflict with their national counterparts.

The impromtu May People's Assembly on the University of Concepción campus demonstrated not just grassroots movements' willingness to mobilize but also, and more important, their capacity to express their desires publicly, collectively, and democratically. In an affirmation of popular sovereignty, the regional leaders asserted, "Never has there been a more democratic form of representation. No parliamentary arrangement, nor any summons could be more effective and more authentic than this assembled multitude, [where] there was belief in unity and unity in belief."[80] By late May 1972, regional Popular Unity and MIR leaders, with the exception of the Communists, appeared ready to grant grassroots organizations a more active role with real decision-making powers. If the parties did not cede some of their power, the bases would take it.

In the May 12 assembly, regional leaders saw a new mechanism for self-expression and participation that could be a model for the country. In recognition of grassroots demands, regional leaders warned that popular democracy would not be tamed by "an institutionalism that was created to repress it," but rather the tremendous energy and poential must be channeled "in the direction of class struggle and shap[ed] through new institutional forms that lay the foundation for revolutionary power."[81] Galvanized by events in Concepción, party leaders believed confrontation was inevitable and argued that the Left should create new kinds of institutions that could effectively counter the Right's entrenched economic and political power. Yet the regional Left's new offensive-driven strategy was not—as the conservative press claimed—conceived as a campaign of violence. An embrace of class struggle was implicit in the Concepción Manifesto, yet neither arming workers nor organizing them into the Russian Revolution's soviets figured anywhere in the document. Despite the almost perfunctory Marxist rhetoric about "crushing their class enemies," the Concepción Manifesto concluded with a platform of surprisingly moderate measures centered on strengthening grassroots organizations and promoting participatory democracy:

· Encouraging worker participation in the state-run factories by granting workers more decision-making power and control over administrative bodies.
· Installing workers' control in private industries.
· Ensuring real participation of the pobladores in the leadership of housing agencies.
· Granting effective decision-making capabilities to the peasant councils, giving them the necessary material resources.

- Uniting popular organizations into Consejos Comunales de Trabajadores [Workers' Councils within a given territory, or *comuna*], whose bases will hold assemblies to resolve matters of immediate concern for workers, including control of foodstuffs through the price control boards (JAP), [and in matters of] education, health, etc.[82]

These measures centered on building popular power through deepening spaces for participation and granting greater control over matters of material interest to people's everyday lives. Going forward, both the MIR and the Socialists endorsed the creation of workers' councils that would unite within a territory "workers, pobladores, campesinos, and students and grant them decision-making powers."[83] As new revolutionary organizations, the workers' councils appeared as the first step to institutionalizing decentralized local power. The Concepción Manifesto coalesced a set of ideas that had been circulating under the rubric of popular power into a concrete plan of action.

"A NEW POWER STRUCTURE BUILT UP FROM THE GRASSROOTS": CROSSROADS ON THE PEACEFUL ROAD TO SOCIALISM, JUNE 1972

As a novel political proposal, Chile's peaceful path to socialism moved into uncharted territory. Allende's election marked the culmination of the decades-long strategy by the Communists and Socialists to take power by engaging the system and occupying the state. Now that the Old Left controlled the executive branch, would it succeed in using existing state institutions to transition Chile to socialism? In May 1972, events in Concepción, particularly the use of police force, demonstrated a fundamental tension within the Popular Unity strategy: the Chilean state had not been built to channel popular interests but rather, as the Group of Five warned, "to perpetuate the interests of the bourgeoisie."[84]

The Concepción Manifesto and the regional alliance between the MIR and the Popular Unity left wing had national repercussions. The Communist Party immediately demanded that the national Popular Unity coalition hold a closed-door meeting to evaluate the Allende government's future economic, political, and social strategies. At the June meeting, President Allende and the Communist Party affirmed their commitment to a strategy centered on consolidating economic gains, building cross-class alliances, and negotiating political compromises, particularly with the Christian Democrats. To do so, they contended, required greater worker discipline and limited participation. By contrast, the Socialists and MAPU urged Allende to trust the initiative of workers, expand worker participation, and back growing grassroots militancy. As the historian Peter Winn explains, the left-wing sectors within the Popular Unity coalition called for Allende's government to "scrap its original strategy, place itself at the head of the revolution from below, and rely on its creativity and dynamism to see the revolutionary process through the coming crisis."[85] The more moderate position carried the day. As a result, Allende suspended formal talks with the MIR and requested that Cuba stop military assistance to the MIR.[86] The national Popular Unity coalition formally censured regional party leaders in Concepción for the manifesto and made overtures to the Christian Democrats.[87]

Yet faced with a Christian Democratic Party more eager to impeach than negotiate, Allende's conciliatory strategy seemed doomed to fail. As allegiances veered from center to right, Christian Democrats broke off negotiations with the Popular Unity and opted to throw their support behind an antidemocratic, increasingly authoritarian anti-Allende movement.[88] Continued congressional intransigence further constrained the government's ability to carry out the Popular Unity program. In early July, the opposition-controlled Congress impeached the minister of the interior, Hernán del Canto (PS), a popular labor leader. The Right lacked the two-thirds majority in Congress to impeach the president, but they had a quorum to impeach his entire cabinet. Minister del Canto was the first of many top Popular Unity government officials removed from office. The foreclosing of the Popular Unity's moderate option emboldened more radical sectors on the Left, who increasingly looked for an alternative strategy to ensure the revolution's continued expansion.[89]

It was, once again, in Concepción where a new experiment in participatory grassroots democracy took place. In June and July 1972, regional leaders debated the possibilities for convening a People's Assembly.[90] Grassroots activists and party leaders drew inspiration from the Popular Unity program's promise to democratize society through a "new power structure ...built up from the grassroots."[91] Allende's campaign platform outlined plans for a new political constitution premised on "institutionalizing the inclusion of the pueblo into state power." It promised to replace the existing two-chamber Congress with a single-chamber "People's Assembly as the national expression of popular sovereignty," aimed at ensuring "respect for the will of the majority."[92] The People's Assembly would also function at the local and regional levels. In 1971, the Socialist Party, the MIR, and the FTR had renewed calls to create a People's Assembly.[93] The national FTR campaign program envisioned a People's Assembly as "the true expression of the will of the exploited majority, by granting power to the workers and campesinos," to censure and recall elected representatives.[94] Yet throughout the first year and half of Allende's presidency, these ideas remained tasks for an undefined future moment in the revolutionary process.

According to MAPU regional secretary Eduardo Aquevedo, he first proposed organizing a Concepción People's Assembly to other political leaders. Reflecting back on the political climate of mid-1972, he recognized the intense conflict within the Left, "but those of us in Concepción tried to implement a unified approach of a revolutionary front, but without directly calling it a revolutionary front. So we said, 'Look, let's organize a People's Assembly.'" The regional secretaries of the Socialist Party, the MIR, the MAPU, the labor federation (CUT), and, significantly, the Communist Party, all initially agreed.[95] MIR regional leader Pedro Enríquez Barra explained the idea emerged out of conversations with the Socialists, noting that in Concepción it was possible to organize a People's Assembly because of the "enormous density of leftist supporters." These plans annoyed national leaders, including Allende, "who was absolutely opposed to it because he said it detracted from the strength of the Left and didn't lead to an alternative solution." But as Pedro Enríquez underscored, the People's Assembly "was a regional thing."[96]

While nationally the MIR continued to criticize the Communist Party, the Group of Five leaders in Concepción, including the MIR, remained committed to building a revolutionary alliance across the Left. In practice, this meant securing the participation of regional labor federation leaders, PC leaders, and the rank and file.[97] The obstacle, recalled MAPU leader Eduardo Aquevedo, was convincing the Communist Party that the People's Assembly was not intended as a challenge to Allende's government but rather as a show of support. Aquevedo contended, "The Communist Party's social base, especially its union base, was in favor of participating." Many PC union leaders viewed the People's Assembly as a positive initiative; among the regional party leaders, there were also some in favor.[98] Despite multiple meetings with the MAPU in late July, regional PC leaders refused to endorse the People's Assembly, warning that a rally with twenty thousand people "would lead to chaos; no one will understand anything."[99] As in May, according to Aquevedo, the Communist Party did participate in the People's Assembly "in a semi-visible way through their mass fronts, so as not to lose face with their base, while at the same time obeying instructions from Santiago."[100] Pressured by grassroots demands in May, political leaders made arrangements to convene a People's Assembly as part of the regional revolutionary process.

"THE REVOLUTIONARY PROCESS WILL GO FORWARD!": CALL TO ASSEMBLE, CONCEPCIÓN, JULY 1972

At this critical juncture in the revolutionary process, the central question was how to institutionalize popular power beyond street demonstrations. The People's Assembly appeared to offer the possibility of deepening Chilean democracy by creating a more representative, participatory alternative. Parallel to the behind-the-scenes negotiations between regional party leaders, social organizations in Concepción declared their intention to organize a People's Assembly. For example, on July 19, 1972, unionized workers at *El Sur* newspaper argued that "the laws of the people, the laws that benefit the workers, must be made by workers themselves," and concluded that it was time "to get the People's Assembly that is contemplated in the Popular Unity government program up and running." Delegates would be drawn from the labor federation (CUT), unions, peasant councils, student federations, and pobladores' organizations. Noting that the process would happen first "by province, and then nationally," the workers affirmed that "this is the way to strengthen the government and to advance the revolution in our country."[101] These participatory bodies would channel grassroots creative energy into a power that could stop the counterrevolution in its tracks and, even more broadly, transform the dynamics of power in Chile.

In assemblies across the province and in paid newspaper advertisements, diverse sectors articulated their vision for this new form of power.[102] Labor leaders referred to people's assemblies in the plural, suggesting they conceived of them as decentralized local spaces for discussion within the bases rather than as a singular People's Assembly that would immediately replace the existing national Congress. CUT leader Oscar González offered a radical affirmation of grassroots agency that critiqued bourgeois laws. In new institutions, "true laws will be created to reflect workers' real needs. In dialogue, workers, miners, peasants, and fishermen will analyze their own problems and transmit them to their leaders in the [national People's] Assembly, who will then be responsible for finding appropriate solutions with truly effective laws." A coal union leader, González envisioned local people articulating their own needs more clearly than elected officials could. Faced with the current stalemate marked by congressional intransigence in Santiago, González contended, "With the formation of the People's Assemblies we are saying NO to the bourgeois Parliament! We are saying to these gentlemen that with or without the law, the revolutionary process in Chile will go forward!"[103]

As with the May 12 mobilization, Socialist leaders in the provincial labor federation played an important role in legitimating the July People's Assembly.[104] After the hotly contested CUT elections in late May, an alliance between the radical left (PS, MAPU, MIR) in Concepción had consolidated a narrow majority in the provincial CUT.[105] On July 22, Heriberto Krumm (PS), speaking on behalf of the labor federation leadership, proudly proclaimed that "once again, the workers of Concepción have put themselves at the vanguard of the [revolutionary] process. . . . Starting July 27 the People's Assemblies are happening, [and] with them the workers in this province are giving another example of their combativeness."[106] Although the Communist labor federation president Juan Bravo refused publicly to sign on, the labor federation's collective endorsement offered the local Communist Party a way to save face with workers while simultaneously following national party directives.

The following day full-page invitations to the People's Assembly appeared in the local press. Adorned with the same May 12 image of the worker and peasant armed with sticks, the July 23 declaration called for the people of Concepción province to assemble on July 27 and "to discuss, analyze, and denounce, directly and democratically, the Parliament and its counterrrevolutionary character" and, in addition, to celebrate the Cuban Revolution's 26 of July anniversary. While the open invitation was addressed to the masses, it explicitly named the grassroots organizations whose leaders or elected delegates must attend. These included "unions, administrative boards, production committees, workplace vigiliance groups, neighborhood councils, pobladores' committees, campamento commit-tees, peasant councils, agrarian reform centers and settlements, peasant unions, student governments, professional and technical organizations, artisan organiza-tions, small and medium businessowners and industrialists, and in general, all leaders of popular and mass organizations."[107] This comprehensive list—ranging from peasants to industrialists—powerfully illustrated the breadth and diversity of the people's revolutionary coalition envisioned by the planners of the People's Assembly.

As a respected community organizer and Revolutionary Peasant Movement (MCR) militant, Fernando Manque anticipated that he would likely be tapped to speak at the People's Assembly. Like the coal miners in Coronel and the textile workers in Tomé, peasants affiliated with the MIR fought for union democracy based on more horizontal relationships, where rank-and-file members took an active role in generating solutions, rather than the typical delegation of responsi-bilities to union bosses.[108] Like the Revolutionary Workers Front (FTR), the organ-izing tactics of its peasant counterpart combined bread and butter issues with a commitment to collective transformation in the present: "More pay meant noth-ing if it was not accompanied by a social consciousness. As the MCR, we volun-teered our time and all our effort so that we could create this better life, this better country for all." Much like Campamento Lenin pobladores, Fernando Manque had helped carry out two 1971 land takeovers for homeless agricultural workers.[109] Despite his impressive organizing résumé, he recalled both his enthusiasm and anxiety: "I had experience in the land takeover [in Hualqui], in the peasant union, and in organizing peasants all over [the province], but I didn't have any experience of speaking before hundreds or thousands of people." He added, "I knew what was coming and wanted to coordinate" with political leaders in the MIR.[110]

Soon after the invitation appeared, Manque's MCR-MIR contacts in the Uni-versity of Concepción informed him, "You are going to speak in the theater for the People's Assembly. There will be pobladores, peasants, workers, students—all sec-tors of society. The sharpest Socialists in Concepción will be there, and so will the MAPU, the Christian Left, everyone." He agreed enthusiastically, with an attitude of "alright, let's do it!" The MIR student leaders laid out the stakes and the antici-pated audiences: "If you're prepared, it's going to go well. We don't want to give the impression that we're improvising because the President will be listening. He'll say that we don't have any real support and that we're just waving flags and pretend-ing." The MIR chose him because "you are from the countryside. Many people will say that guy is not authentic, that the MIR just put a poncho on him." The MIR students' rationale about both symbolism and representation seemed logical to Manque, who recognized that despite all his organizing work, he had never spoken before a crowd of more than a few dozen peasants.[111]

Regional political leaders convened the July People's Assembly to showcase grassroots agency, and the expectation was that grassroots leaders would speak as they had in May but in a more organized format with national implications. The MIR and other political parties took steps to ensure their local leaders arrived prepared. Fernando Manque emphasized decades later that the MIR did not put words in his mouth but rather worked with local leaders, and this gave him the confidence to express himself. In addition to proposing concrete changes to the existing agrarian reform, Manque listed broader demands: "Freedom for peasants—for education, for health, for technology, for the possibility to be more than we are [de ser más]."[112] His experience underscores the close relationship between grassroots social organizations and political parties in 1970s Chile. This was not always a hierarchical relationship. Political militants listened to local people, validated their concerns, encouraged their participation, and fostered the ability to act using the inner strength they already possessed. The invitation to participate at the People's Assembly set in motion Fernando Manque's efforts to craft the content of his speech in close collaboration with MCR-MIR student activists.

Nationally, the conservative press sounded the alarms with sensational headlines such as "To Supplant Congress, People's Assembly formed in Concepción!"[113] In response, regional MIR leaders emphasized that behind attempts to descredit the People's Assembly was a deep-seated fear of grassroots agency: "In this historic moment in Concepción province when the social organizations and political parties of the people want to express themselves, to deliberate, to exchange experiences, and to resolve their principal problems, the reaction hurls insults everywhere."[114] A furious opposition was natural, the MIR observed, because "when the pueblo speaks by itself and for itself, the people begin to be power."[115] While the organizers undoubtedly hoped that sooner rather than later President Allende would move forward with plans for a new constitution and a more representative assembly, they never believed that on July 27, 1972, grassroots organizations in Concepción would oust the existing national congress. Rather, the goal of the Concepción event was to strengthen decentralized local power through greater coordination and to project a vision of power in which workers and grassroots sectors had a mechanism for their voices to be heard.

Just as Campamento Lenin pobladores had rushed to greet Fidel Castro, leftist activists across Concepción linked support for the Cuban Revolution with their efforts to build new forms of popular power. On the 26 of July anniversary, prominent local unions, including the textile mills in Tomé and Chiguayante, the petrochemical plant in Talcahuano, the unified union at the Huachipato steel mill, the paper mill in Arauco, and the bottling factory in Concepción's Costanera, took out paid newspaper ads proclaiming hemispheric solidarity: "With Cuba, for Our Revolution!"[116] Adorned with images of Fidel Castro and Che Guevara, textile workers from Tomé's three mills (FIAP, Oveja, and Bellavista) and Chiguayante's Caupolicán mill declared, "We will also triumph! We will continue fighting until Chile is the second liberated territory in America."[117] Other organizations went a step further, explicitly identifying the July 27 People's Assembly as a vital step forward in the Chilean Revolution. The University of Concepción's top administrative board, democratized by the university reform to include student representatives, celebrated the regional and transnational unity of the Left, acknowledged the legitimacy of the Concepción People's Assembly as rooted in Chile's tradition of popular mobilization, and affirmed their unshakeable support for the Allende government.[118] The Consejo Superior's celebration of grassroots movements' desire for self-expression was not hollow. The following day, under the simple title, "List of Organizations Endorsing the People's Assembly," the names of the 140 grassroots organizations filled an entire newspaper page.[119] In Concepción province, the defense of the Allende government and the acceleration of the revolutionary process did not appear as mutually exclusive ends.

"A MOMENT OF TRUE POPULAR EXPRESSION": THE JULY 27 PEOPLE'S ASSEMBLY

The scale of the People's Assembly and the regional stage it provided for grassroots leaders marked a departure. It promised an opportunity to debate Chile's future openly and democratically. Initially, public announcements made clear that "since it is a people's assembly, there will not be any special speakers; members of the audience will speak."[120] Many had taken seriously the open call and began preparing speeches in consultation with party leaders. They included local schoolteacher Lily Rivas, who by 1972 was one of the most visible women in the Concepción Revolutionary Workers Front (FTR).[121]

Lily Rivas was no political novice. Hailing from a family of Radical Party politicians in southern Chile, she rebelled against family tradition by joining the Socialist Party in Concepción. In 1964, she left the PS along with her close friends Bautista Van Schouwen and Miguel Enríquez and other Socialist Youth dissidents to form the Vanguardia Revolucionaria Marxista (VRM), which merged the following year with the newly formed MIR. She gained local notoriety after being briefly imprisoned in connection to the 1969 kidnapping of journalist Hernán Osses. After Allende's election and the MIR's decision to prioritize mass fronts, Rivas became an organizer for the FTR and ran for a seat on the provincial labor federation. As an educator, Rivas had earned the respect of her fellow teachers as an outspoken advocate of educational reform, encouraging greater student and parent participation in high school administration. Her efforts to awaken a feminist consciousness in her female students by calling attention to gender disparities frequently ended in conflict with school authorities, but her popularity soared among students. On the morning of July 27, Rivas recalled a member of her MIR base showing up at her classroom imploring her, "Lily, there's an assembly tonight and we need someone to speak for the FTR in Concepción, and that someone is you."[122] He left her with some talking points. Given the original plan to have social leaders speak, the regional MIR had taken steps to ensure that representatives from its mass fronts, including people like Fernando Manque and Lily Rivas, would arrive at the assembly prepared.

However, on the evening of the People's Assembly, as people were already arriving in the downtown theater, the Popular Unity and the MIR leaders failed to reach an agreement over the format. At the last minute, in place of social organizations, they decided that each of the five political parties would designate a representative to speak in two rounds of discussion. On these new terms, political leaders inaugurated the Concepción's People's Assembly on July 27.[123] By all accounts, the five formal speeches centered on "laying out each group's political orientations and views on people's assemblies" and celebrating the Cuban Revolution.[124] Some of the designated political speakers, like a MAPU union leader from the coal zone, renewed appeals for unity across the Left: "Even if we disagree about some points, we cannot lose sight of what is truly important: this rich experience, this experience of discussion within the masses must be repeated." He concluded optimistically that "these people's assemblies are the beginning of a new stage" of protagonism for popular sectors.[125]

Yet for many of those present, the leaders' formal speeches fell far short of the anticipated People's Assembly and its promise for grassroots leadership. The memory of the May 12 assembly's spontaneity and participation set an important precedent that raised expectations. As the first round of speeches ended, Mario Garcés, an anthropology student, recalled, "No one got up. A rumor started to circulate that the people will speak. Soon this started to be chanted by different groups scattered through the theater, we must have been 3,000 or 4,000 people, and in the end, almost all of us were standing up, shouting: "Let the people speak! Let the people speak!"[126] MAPU leaders told reporters that the public pressure had begun with "FTR compañeros who approached the stage," leading the chants.[127] Not an orchestrated takeover, the FTR chant emerged organically as the right slogan in the right moment.[128] By altering the format and blocking direct participation, political parties silenced the very voices the event had planned to showcase. The desire and belief that grassroots activists could speak for themselves reverberated in the thousands of voices who made the slogan their own.

When the political leaders announced open microphones, the People's Assembly was transformed into what its name and original intent suggested. The

Concepción People's Assembly was one of the few times during a public event that people could take center stage and voice their desires and find them validated by others. This transformation from a typical political event into an open assembly marked a point of inflection for Chile's revolutionary process. Sitting in the audience that night, as the speeches stretched well past midnight, Mario Garcés remembered being "enveloped in a cloud of smoke, cheers, and much applause, [as] people began to get up on stage and take the microphone: all the diversity of the pueblo. They spoke in their own language, sharing their experiences, pointing out the deficiencies that they saw, and proposing how to create better coordination and how to promote a politics of alliance."[129] Student federation president Manuel Rodríguez (PS), who at the time was on stage presiding over the event, would later confess that despite the MAPU and PS initiative to convene a People's Assembly, on the night of July 27, "in fact, it was the MIR's grassroots leaders who took control of the assembly."[130]

The open assembly format enabled leaders from the MIR's mass fronts to excel. Just as in the era of the university reform in Concepción and in meetings of pobladores to organize land invasions, the MIR would compensate for its small numbers with well-prepared, outspoken social leaders. The fiery local union leader and Campamento Lenin resident Luis Astete (FTR) was one of the first speakers to come forward. Peasant union leader Fernando Manque was in awe of Astete, who was legendary for "his rapid-fire speech. He was one of the best speakers in the region, really without equal for how well he could raise and lower his voice and bring the audience along with him." Standing there, Manque drew "inspiration from him." After Astete, another Campamento Lenin resident spoke, followed by a university student, and afterward Manque recalled "lots and lots more people spoke, ordinary folks, and they began to be heard, and it stuck with you. Then I saw a compañero from the FTR in Hualqui up on stage and he saw me down below. I felt hands grabbing me, pushing me, and I was lifted onto the stage." Once there, time seemed to stand still. More than forty years later, Manque remembered his prepared speech, but "then just on my own I went on to propose that the government carry out closed-door expropriations for farms that were 45 hectares, not just 90 and above." He expanded on the need for "education, health care, transportation, and basic foodstuffs in the countryside." He spoke of what people felt at the time and of what "needed to be proposed and struggled for until equality and unity are attained and the possibility for a better world becomes a reality." It was only a speech of seven or eight minutes, but to Fernando Manque it felt like a lifetime.[131] The personal impact of the speech did in fact last a lifetime.

As Lily Rivas entered the overcapacity theater on the night of July 27, the sensation that greeted her was of stepping into "a beating heart that swelled and contracted" with the energy in the room. She was a capable leader and a gifted public speaker. She was also a disciplined MIR militant, who looked at the party's talking points but spoke of what she knew. As an educator, she understood that success hinged on her ability to engage the audience: "All of us who went up, each one had to argue for such and such thing at a certain time. But you always had to wait and see if you would be allowed to speak or not, because if you said things that did not have wide support, the audience would silence you with jeers and shouts." Rivas noted that the assembly tradition was present, with "a constant running dialogue between the person on stage speaking and the assembled public."[132] While no definitive historical record survives of the thirty-some unannounced speakers at the People's Assembly, Lily Rivas's and Fernando Manque's experiences suggest that many of those who came forward were well-known grassroots leaders with prior political formation within leftist political parties and mass fronts.[133]

The majority of the speakers affirmed a desire to accelerate the revolutionary process. They called for "going on the offensive to stop the actions of the Right" and at the same time voiced their "unwavering commitment to defend the Popular Unity government and to continue advancing without compromise."[134] Newspaper accounts tended to emphasize the more radical interventions. One reported that "some speakers proposed the necessity of destroying the Parliament and creating popular militias."[135] FEC president Manuel Rodríguez noted years later, "Whoever wanted to speak, spoke without screening or censure. Of course, this created space for hotheads to make wild proposals that went beyond public opinion." He lamented that "without fail, someone would get up and say, 'I propose we distribute arms. If the Popular Unity parties will not, then we will find out where they are,' which basically amounted to a call to storm the barracks."[136] As it unfolded in the contingencies of the moment, the Concepción People's Assembly opened a regional space for direct expression without top-down mediation by the political parties. From a carefully planned event to showcase the strength of the Left, the political organizers had, perhaps, not adequately accounted for how the region's radical political culture, centered on open democratic participation, could challenge the prewritten proposals presented in the opening round.[137] In the moment, the chant "Let the people speak" and the dialogue between grassroots leaders—many of whom like Lily Rivas, Luis Astete, and Fernando Manque were also political militants—and the several thousand workers, students, pobladores, and peasants in attendance transformed the People's Assembly into a more participatory affair.

In converting the event into an open assembly where anyone could speak, Concepción residents not only broke free of party oversight but also asserted popular sovereignty within the revolutionary process. Fernando Manque emphasized how the people's assemblies had appeared as "the only setup in which the pueblo was participating in the process." Behind them was "the idea that the people had power—popular power—that the people decided their own destiny, decided how to do things, and that not everything came down from above, that the people as they advanced began to create their own initiatives, and that as the revolutionary

process advanced, the people would do more and more." Like many other participants, Manque underscored that the Concepción People's Assembly and its proposals were "not against the Popular Unity government" but rather sought to persuade government leaders that they "had to go faster, that the method should be
different, that you had to go forward another way."[138]

The intensity of the Concepción People's Assembly was lived by participants as
a kind of unity, what Émile Durkheim would call "collective effervescence." Scholars of social movements have recognized the importance of appealing to people's
emotions as a strategy for successful organizing.[139] By claiming the right to speak,
the assembled public appeared to have outstaged the careful planning by the
regional political leaders. "For me," Mario Garcés reflected, "the People's Assembly
was a fiesta, a kind of catharsis in which the pueblo took center stage and offered
their perceptions, their dreams, their desires, their criticisms . . . No one moved,
no one left. And that's how we lived [the People's Assembly], with great happiness,
as a tremendous fiesta because it was a moment of true popular expression."[140] A
sensation of possibility buoyed participants as they took to the streets afterwards.
As Garcés concluded, "We left the theater that night marching, joyful, shouting as
we went. [We were] happy, above all, with a sense that the Popular Unity was taking another path [*tomaba otro rumbo*] and that we could create something different, more participatory." People became credentialed as political agents by their
participation in this revolutionary moment. The triumph of the People's Assembly,
lived by grassroots activists as an opening onto an uncharted path of greater protagonism, would endure in their memories, shaping their lives in inchoate but
unmistakable ways.

The People's Assembly in Concepción was a vital attempt to create new mechanisms for citizen participation within an unfolding revolutionary process. As an
act of popular democracy, the People's Assembly questioned the idea that only
political parties and national leaders should direct the course of change. A national
backlash effectively silenced repetition of this question—foreclosing both the formal regional alliances between Popular Unity parties and the MIR and the creation of a regional space for deliberative exchange among social organizations and
political parties. As grassroots activists in Concepción struggled to make sense of
the polemical debate over the People's Assembly, they seized a different message:
go forward. Rather than see this culminating, climactic moment as merely deriva-
tive of national debates within the Popular Unity coalition over ideology and strategy, the People's Assembly in Concepción was the outcome of and the prologue to
a local revolutionary process.

5

"Building Their Own Power"

Grassroots Response to
the October Bosses' Lockout

On the morning of January 13, 1973, a group of angry workers, housewives, and students marched across Coronel's central plaza. Their objective lay just beyond: Panadería El Progreso, the town's largest bakery. In recent weeks, the quality of bread sold at the establishment had precipitously declined. Local authorities knew about the situation but did nothing.[1] Rumors circulated that the owner, Antonio Sánchez, made two kinds of bread: a high-quality white bread for sale in the provincial capital, Concepción, and a dark bread of lesser quality for coal miners and their families. Some said he undercooked the daily bread to make it weigh more; others claimed he altered the recipe to hoard flour and profit on the black market.[2] Among the group that day was nineteen-year old Hugo Monsalves, a coal miner's son and a medical student, the only one of his eleven siblings to study at the University of Concepción. At 11:00 that morning, Monsalves joined other members of the MIR and its Revolutionary Workers Front (FTR), as well as members of the Socialist Party. They were not full-time political activists, outside agitators, or even the parties' local leaders but grassroots activists and residents of Coronel's sprawling working-class neighborhoods like Villa Mora and Camilo Olavarría. Monsalves explained years later, "Our objective was to commandeer the bakery truck going to Concepción to sell the high-quality bread. We planned to distribute [the bread] throughout Coronel."[3]

The bakery owner, however, had learned of the plot and took the precaution of sending a police officer in the truck's cab. With the plan foiled, Monsalves explained, "we continued marching into Coronel and decided then and there to take over the bakery."[4] Another mirista present that day, Aníbal Cáceres, remembered that it was "señora Luz Madariaga who said, 'Let's go for the bread!', and so we left. The old ladies seized the chance and went to take the bakery."[5] For some participants, perhaps the memory lingered of the owner's broken promise to let women bake bread in his clay ovens.[6] For Cáceres, it was, above all, an action carried out by local people: "They say it was the MIR who did it, but it wasn't. It was a group of people from Camilo Olavarría, [who] marching into town took over the bakery. Afterwards the MIR along with the Socialists ran the bakery, but they arrived after it was already taken."[7] As a collective action by local people the bakery takeover illustrates the extent to which revolutionary fervor came from below, fueled in part by women as consumers.[8]

By noon, the takeover was complete. Panadería El Progreso had been rechristened Panadería El Pueblo—the People's Bakery.[9] The posters that plastered the outside walls announced the action as "a corrective measure" applied to force the owner into improving the quality of bread for popular consumption.[10] A reporter from Concepción's conservative daily, *El Sur,* interviewed one of the occupants, who like pobladores after a land takeover deployed a gendered defense, declaring, "We are all fathers of families or single men with responsibilities at home." He added that they were motivated by women's complaints about the bad quality of bread. Their intention, he explained, was for the bakery to make one bread of equal kind and quality: "good for everyone" (*bueno para todos*).[11]

Starting in early 1972, access to foodstuffs and basic consumer goods was the front line of revolutionary struggle in Chile. Economic transformation was central to the Popular Unity's strategy to transition to socialism by means of constitutional democracy. In his first year in office, President Allende nationalized Chile's major industries, including Concepción province's coal mines and textile mills, and expropriated over one hundred factories. The government's redistribution policies meant real wages increased along with the working class's buying power. Many Chileans could buy consumer products, like refrigerators, for the first time. Following the logic of Keynesian economics, the Popular Unity government assumed that increased consumer demand would stimulate a corresponding increase in production. Yet the UP government only controlled parts of the economy, not all of it. This reality left it vulnerable.

The economy became the realm in which the Chilean opposition and the U.S. government sought to destabilize Allende's government. As early as September 1970, less than two weeks after Allende's election, President Richard Nixon ordered his top advisors to devise a plan to "make the economy scream."[12] The U.S. government implemented an "invisible blockade"—a covert economic boycott of Chile, pressuring international lending organizations to cut off foreign loans and ending U.S. economic aid that had flowed so freely under the Alliance for Progress to the Frei administration (1964–70). With Allende in office, U.S. military aid and direct contact with the Chilean Armed Forces increased. These covert U.S. government policies sought to polarize Chilean society, particularly by generating hardships for the middle class that would push them toward the conservative opposition. Although cutting off economic aid might seem abstract, it started to create the sense that society was falling apart.

With the end goal of bringing the economy to a standstill, Chilean economic elites, backed by the Central Intelligence Agency, organized a massive work stoppage known as the "Bosses' Lockout" (Paro Patronal) in October 1972. Their strategy hinged on making a play for the middle class and the political Center—the Christian Democrats. Despite the government's expropriation of key industries, the primary transportation and distribution routes that served Chile's distant geography remained in the hands of the opposition. Workers in state-owned factories put in longer hours to produce new products that never reached the shelves. Contrary to their economic interests, the Chilean opposition opted to forgo profits rather than produce to meet increased working-class consumer demand. Owners and shopkeepers created artificial scarcity by hoarding goods in warehouses, where they could be sold on the black market at higher prices. When right-wing women first marched through Santiago in December 1971, banging pots and pans in protest of Fidel Castro's visit and Allende's government, few shortages actually existed in Chile.

By April 1972, however, shortages of foodstuffs and other basic goods had become a reality. In response, the Popular Unity government adopted a rationing system of local neighborhood supply and price control boards, known by the acronym JAP (Juntas de Abastecimiento y Precios). The opposition seized on Allende's decision to ration to accuse him of turning Chileans into communists. The JAPs grew in number and significance during the Bosses' Lockout and became key grassroots organizations in the battle over the right to basic consumer goods.

Across Chile, new manifestations of popular power emerged to defend the embattled Popular Unity government. In Concepción province, the grassroots response to the Bosses' Lockout took the form of dispersed local actions, like the Coronel bakery takeover. While massive assemblies and street demonstrations in May and July 1972 had served as focal points, the contest was no longer in the streets of Concepción but closer to home. Owner lockouts threatened workplaces, shopkeepers closed their doors, and neighborhoods suffered without basic goods. During the October lockout, unions began collaborating with community organizations to demonstrate how collective organization could turn back the insurrection of the dominant classes. Drawing on the empowerment and precedent for participation in the People's Assembly, many grassroots activists within the MIR worked to fortify the price control boards and other social organizations that could directly resolve immediate problems of continuing production and maintaining access to basic foodstuffs.

As in the Coronel bakery takeover, the initiative came from below. It was not ideological coherence or vanguardism that motivated grassroots activists. Over time the revolutionary party—the vanguard—that so many activists believed was the essential ingredient for any revolution was increasingly at odds with the diffuse everyday revolutions in Chilean society that the MIR itself had promoted in Concepción. Instead, grassroots activists' vision of revolution centered on democratizing local power relations and improving ordinary citizens' quality of life. The defense of the revolutionary process and the effort to build socialism in Chile increasingly became understood locally as enacting equality and redistributive justice in the present.

"WE WILL NEVER GO BACK":
THE ROAD FORWARD, JULY–OCTOBER 1972

Immediately following the People's Assembly, the legal face of the counterrevolution appeared in Concepción. On July 27, 1972, the Third Circuit Court in Concepción declared illegal the Popular Unity government's May 1971 requisition of the Caupolicán textile mill in Chiguayante and ruled the state had five days to return the mill to its former owners, the textile magnate Yarur family. The ruling formed part of the opposition's strategy to use the courts to challenge Allende's expansion of the public sector. It sparked a new flash point between the will of the people and the existing institutional order.

The expediency of mobilizing to defend the expropriated factory produced a unified class response that superseded party lines: workers from the Popular Unity, including the Communists, now marched alongside Christian Democrats and the MIR. In doing so, they demonstrated the possibility of successful coalitional organizing in the aftermath of the People's Assembly and in the midst of a Right-directed backlash. Just as the province had mobilized to defend the university reform and to show solidarity with the struggles of Campamento Lenin pobladores, support for Chiguayante textile workers poured in from unions and student organizations.[13] On the night of July 27, Concepción's central plaza housed the overflow crowds from the People's Assembly. The following afternoon it filled again with Caupolicán workers, who marched eleven kilometers from Chiguayante. Gathered in front of the regional government, textile workers petitioned Communist governor Vladimir Chávez to reject using force against the workers and to ignore the judicial orders.[14] The workers expressed their "unanimous decision to not return a single state-owned (APS) industry to former owners."[15] In contrast to the national Christian Democrats, local DC labor leaders backed the Popular Unity government's efforts to create a socialized state sector. Provincial labor federation (CUT) leader and Christian Democrat Ramón Reyes openly called for the laws to be modified "because today they exist to serve a small bourgeois minority and to repress the workers."[16] Class unity over party affiliation continued in the days ahead.

The Popular Unity government quickly allocated resources to the public prosecutor to fight the ruling to return the mill.[17] By the end of July, as Governor Chávez faced the possibility of being held in contempt for failing to comply with the court order, workers across the province converged in a massive rally at the Caupolicán union headquarters. Tomé textile workers alone filled seven train cars.[18] Socialist union leader at Caupolicán, Gabriel Muñoz, announced that as "the workers who run this company, we will not hand it over for any reason. We will defend it whatever the costs." Since its nationalization in May 1971, the Caupolicán mill increased production, "exceeding even the most optimistic calculations."[19] Local textile federation president Jaime Quintano celebrated that this "new experience is producing good results," adding, "We will never go back."[20] Eventually the Allende government interceded to block the return of Caupolicán to the Yarur family.[21]

The collaboration across party lines to defend Caupolicán appeared a natural outgrowth of the leftist unity and grassroots agency that had led to the People's Assembly. The response from the Popular Unity government was immediate, yet not initially critical. Student federation (FEC) president Manuel Rodríguez, at the time an important national Socialist Youth leader, received a call the next morning. Preparing for a reprimand, he was surprised that Allende was curious and supportive: "I told him about the principles that motivated us, [admitting] that I wasn't sure if we had achieved our goal. And then Allende said, 'Manuel, revolutionaries do not always achieve their objectives, but we will not know whether or not they can if they never dare to try.'"[22] His recollection indicates that Allende sought information directly from regional organizers, who briefed him on how events had unfolded in Concepción.

Yet, within days of celebrating the July 27 People's Assembly in Concepción, a national political backlash contained the possibility of its repetition in Concepción and elsewhere and undercut grassroots initiative.[23] Faced with political fallout within his governing coalition and the increasingly vitriolic criticisms by the rightwing media, Allende distanced himself from the People's Assembly by publicly condemning it.[24] Contrary to the tone of his phone call with Rodríguez, the president dismissed the assembly's significance and asserted his control over the Popular Unity coalition and the course of the Chilean revolutionary process.[25] Contending he could only serve the workers by protecting the current government structure, Allende put to rest any discussion that the National Congress would be replaced by a more representative body.[26]

Tensions within the national Popular Unity coalition that had been temporarily smoothed over by the June 1972 meeting flared again. Even if the Communist Party and Allende likely did not accept the opposition media's claims that the Concepción People's Assembly intended to replace the Congress, the MIR's participation posed a problem for the national Popular Unity coalition. A few days after the July 27 People's Assembly, a delegation composed of the top Popular Unity leaders arrived in Concepción. Their purpose, according to regional MAPU leader, Eduardo Aquevedo, was "to force us—the Socialists, the Communists, everyone—to stop this [initiative] for the people's assemblies with the MIR. [The MIR's presence was the problem because] it established a new political alliance that didn't exist at the national level—where it was the Popular Unity separated from the MIR—here in Concepción it was the Popular Unity plus the MIR."[27]

After a night of drinking and eating mussels in nearby Lirquén, the national delegation presented their case against the Concepción People's Assembly and its grassroots character. They warned that because of distorted depictions, the assembly was a "serious political error" that provoked "the Right and the military[, giving them] a pretext to talk about the creation of a revolutionary political bloc [*polo revolucionario*] that threatened the institutionalism of the country and the moderate politics of the Popular Unity." The government leaders added that it was also wrong because "it inflated the MIR and promoted the idea of a new alliance beyond the Popular Unity."[28] The threat, added Aquevedo, was for the regional parties to stop or face national intervention. The regional leadership reiterated that they had no "intention of making the People's Assembly permanent." Rejecting total capitulation, Aquevedo added, "We left open the possibility of meeting [with the MIR] if the political conditions in the country and region warranted it. So we said yes and no at the same time."[29] They agreed to cancel the assembly they intended to hold in August. Rather than engage the challenges posed by its grassroots supporters, national Popular Unity leaders chose to hold regional leaders responsible. Despite criticisms of the People's Assembly as something it had not been in practice—an attempt at dual power—the regional UP leaders acquiesced and did not defend the event they had organized.[30]

Initially, the Group of Five political parties worked together to write an analysis of all formal and spontaneous proposals made at the People's Assembly; but the national Popular Unity coalition blocked the publication of this document. At the time, failure to produce a consensus around the concrete tasks coming out of the People's Assembly was cited as evidence of the event's failure and its limited impact. Instead, only the regional MIR circulated a clear proposal. They advocated (1) preparing the province for a national strike to protest "the reactionary majority in Congress, which aims to return the factories to the exploiters and stop the advances of workers"; (2) combating speculation and hoarding with price freezing and combating rising cost of living with bonuses for the lowest wage earner and control over millionaires' salaries; and (3) creating workers' assemblies and councils "in the struggles for health, education, public transport, housing, and against delinquency."[31] In this sense, the vision for the People's Assembly advanced by the MIR in Concepción was not a parallel congress but rather "a democratic initiative that promotes mass organizations in the bases."[32] Again, the Concepción MIR affirmed its commitment to the direct empowerment of local people.[33]

The novelty and scale of the Concepción People's Assembly shielded it from public criticism by national MIR leaders.[34] They celebrated the People's Assembly as evidence of a new phase in the revolutionary process in which the MIR—as the self-proclaimed vanguard—would presumably take the lead.[35] In an attempt to shape public opinion first in Concepción province and then nationally, the MIR widely circulated MIR regional secretary Manuel Vergara's July 27 speech, "El pueblo comenzó a ser poder."[36] Vergara argued that the People's Assembly "is, without doubt, a revolutionary act, whose protagonist is the most legitimate subject: the people themselves, disagreeing, deliberating, doing. That is, compañeros, beginning to be power."[37] General secretary Miguel Enríquez echoed these sentiments, emphasizing the autonomous capacity of workers' councils (Consejos Comunales de Trabajadores): "The people do not need anyone to govern on their behalf [por él y para él]; rather the people, on their own, have the means to control the bureaucratic apparatus and can, on their own, govern themselves and choose their own path."[38] In such moments, the MIR offered a radical critique of the existing political system. This alternative vision of power rooted in decentralized participatory democracy attracted many supporters to the MIR, yet it also existed in constant tension with the MIR's own notion of its role as a vanguard party.

At various times, the national MIR leadership extrapolated meanings from the People's Assembly based more on their Leninist ideology than on the reality of events in Concepción.[39] Skeptics emerged among MIR leaders in Santiago and Concepción who questioned just what kind of advance the People's Assembly represented and for whom. This skepticism increasingly hinged on the definition of the polo revolucionario—whether it was conceived as a grassroots alliance across the Left or as a formal political alliance that would stand outside the Popular Unity coalition. National leaders backed the initiative only to the extent that it was a power play to put the MIR firmly at the head of the new revolutionary alliance. Similarly, some of the MIR student leaders at the University of Concepción adopted a more hard-line stance that favored radicalization and promoted the idea of the MIR as a vanguard party of trained cadres.[40] The point of contention, explained Concepción FER leader, Álvaro Riffo, hinged less on how much energy to invest in the MIR's relatively minimal military capabilities than on "what attitude to take towards the government, if we should be more [or less] permissive with the Popular Unity—who would be summoned and who would be the summoner?"[41] The People's Assembly opened a point of contention between the national MIR leadership and the Concepción regional leadership over strategy that continued unresolved in the year ahead.[42]

Despite the emergence of these dissenting views, there was little space within the MIR's hierarchical internal party structure for open discussion. Since the national leadership's criticism "was never made explicit" to its bases, critiques of the People's Assembly circulated only as rumors, generating more uncertainty for the MIR's rank and file in Concepción province.[43] For grassroots activists and midlevel militants like Mario Garcés, disbelief set in when what they saw "as a great accomplishment, this celebration . . . that had something of an epic feel to it . . . began to be contained by a tremendous political critique, a series of denouncements against the Assembly that, for me, were very troubling."[44]

The Concepción People's Assembly provoked controversy over the meaning and implications of creating popular power. Yet as this rallying cry reverberated through revolutionary circles in Chile, the idea remained broad enough to encompass a range of understandings: from the local grassroots organizing to the eventual creation of a parallel governmental power to a proletarian state.[45] In practice, what popular power looked like and came to signify for many leftist supporters was often distant from the Marxist ideology guiding political parties' definitions.

Despite the effort of national Popular Unity parties to prevent a Popular Unity-MIR alliance in Concepción, joint actions among leftist parties continued largely unabated. By late August 1972, when rightist parties and the Christian Democrats called for another national Hunger March, the regional MIR and the regional Popular Unity, including the Communists, publicly affirmed their determination "that we will never let [the opposition] march" in the streets of Concepción and announced plans to occupy city streets. Unlike in May when the Communist Party eschewed participation in the mass demonstration, by August the regional PC leadership asserted that "this is not an opposition march, which we respect, but one of organized fascism."[46] The participation of the Communist Party signaled how conditions had changed in a short time. Soon the stakes would be raised beyond political street demonstrations, when a new phase of the counterrevolution emerged in the October Bosses' Lockout.

"WE HAVE TO TAKE A STAND": GRASSROOTS RESPONSE TO THE BOSSES' LOCKOUT, OCTOBER 1972

A strike initiated by truck company owners in the remote southern province of Aysén in October 1972 soon spread across the country, threatening to bring the Chilean economy to a standstill. This was not a coincidence. It had been more than a year in the making as Chilean business elites made a play for the middle class.[47] In the late 1960s, as the Frei administration's agrarian reforms threatened their class interests, Chilean economic elites began to open up their traditionally closed organizations—the National Agricultural Society, the Society for Industrial Development, the Chamber of Commerce—to smaller merchants, shopkeepers, farmers, and manufacturers. While the *gremio* (guild) movement remained elite controlled, middle-class leaders acted as the visible face during the Bosses' Lockout, lending weight to the opposition's claim that popular sectors rejected Allende's Marxist agenda.[48]

As the Bosses' Lockout threatened to paralyze the country, the Left debated strategies that would enable effective responses. Winn characterized Allende's "revolution from above" as remaining "on the defensive, always a step behind its antagonists, parrying opposition thrusts but unable to contain the spreading strike or mobilize a counteroffensive that could transform the crisis into a revolutionary breakthrough." After the July People's Assembly in Concepción, the national Popular Unity leaders reprimanded their regional leaderships and reasserted the primacy of a top-down, Santiago-led revolutionary process. As a consequence, the imperative to await instructions from Santiago slowed the response of the regional Popular Unity and provincial labor federation leadership at critical junctures. In the absence of political leadership, Winn asserts, "it was the revolution from below that took up the torch, interpreting the CUT's calls for vigilance as a license for direct revolutionary action."[49]

Despite its position outside the Popular Unity government, the MIR also lagged behind. The Central Committee in Santiago issued general slogans—"Create Popular Power"—but offered little practical guidance on a plan of action. Regional secretary Manuel Vergara suggested the MIR should occupy Concepción's streets carrying MIR flags. For Enzo La Mura and other members of the MIR's Regional Committee, this proposal missed the point: "We were quick-tongued—as a legacy of our student protest days [in Concepción]—so we responded, 'We aren't evangelicals preaching on the street corner. We have to take a stand.'"[50]

The anti-Allende Bosses' Lockout appeared to confirm what many in Concepción province believed back in May and July: the opposition was about more than Allende. While political leaders debated what to do, La Mura reflected, "the more spontaneous response from people [in the bases] was to go out and open the businesses that closed." The Left had to prevent the Right from having its way, and in Concepción they had the strength to take a stand. MIR regional leaders once again appeared to be taking their cues from the grassroots and adjusted the party's priorities accordingly. La Mura's side contended that "the legitimacy of [the MIR] rested in helping to organize actions that would stop the effects of the strike—forcing [drivers] to keep the buses on the streets, pressuring shop keepers to open stores, or directly opening them [if they refused]." With the slogan "Mobilize to stop," his side won the debate.[51]

The October Bosses' Lockout galvanized grassroots activists, who without clear guidance from above acted on their own to ensure access to basic goods, to keep factories running, and to open stores. Across Concepción province, workers, social organizations, and political parties organized to combat the effects of disrupted distribution chains. Workers began to sell products directly from their factories.[52] FTR union leader Jorge García celebrated the collective resolve of Coronel residents to keep shops open and transport moving, adding, "As workers, we cannot allow you to make the poor go hungry. We are ready to go out and run every business that closes and to seize every truck stopped in the zone."[53] García spoke with confidence because he spoke from Chile's well-organized coal zone.

During October and November 1972, different grassroots initiatives emerged to fight speculation by distributing goods directly through unions and government agencies. These centered on workers controlling the products of their labor. For example, workers at Tomé's Oveja mill insisted the company store sell its products locally.[54] At the four large textile mills—Oveja, FIAP, Bellavista in Tomé, and Caupolicán in Chiguayante—workers issued a joint statement in late October on behalf of textile workers, their unions, and the companies affirming worker control over the "distribution of the products from the social sector."[55] They announced plans to open additional stores in Concepción and to sign new agreements and contracts with unions, neighborhood supply and price boards, mothers' centers, and community councils of workers and peasants. On the two-year anniversary of the Popular Unity government, textile workers published a notice affirming their commitment to seeing that products go directly "from the hands of the worker to the hands of the people."[56] The workers came to the defense of a local businessman, Juan Carvajal López, whose downtown Concepción outlet for Tomé textiles was vandalized by three hundred anti-Allende protesters after he refused to close.[57] In other instances, workers collaborated with government agencies, like the nationalized distribution chain, Dirección de Industria y Comercio (DIRINCO), to facilitate continued access to basic goods. When a third of the businesses in downtown Tomé closed in early November 1972, for example, a group of textile workers accompanied DIRINCO personnel to notify shopkeepers to reopen their doors.[58]

When bourgeois lawyers, engineers, and physicians announced they would walk off the job in compliance with the lockouts sponsored by their professional associations, students and faculty from the University of Concepción organized to replace them. Just as medical students and engineers had provided medical checkups and logistical support to shantytowns like Campamento Lenin, students and leftist professionals organized to ensure hospitals and clinics would remain staffed, with regular hours.[59] As in Santiago, the determination by grassroots sectors to mobilize and immediately confront the strike proved critical to reversing its course.

In Concepción, the response to the Bosses' Lockout generated new forms of organizing—including among journalists—that highlighted both the possibility for people's direct expression and the mounting tension over who had the right to determine the course of revolutionary change. On October 17, 1972, workers at *El Sur* went on strike after the conservative editor refused to publish a paid insert opposing the Bosses' Lockout by a local construction workers' union. During the thirty-eight-day strike, *El Sur* workers occupied their workplace and revived the self-published paper *El Surazo* as a form of worker direct expression. Over the next two weeks, workers and pobladores produced *El Surazo*'s content. In a direct action that challenged the opposition-controlled media's role in promoting the Bosses' Lockout, *El Surazo* sought to harness the power of mass communication for the workers. Although the Revolutionary Workers Front members figured prominently among the striking workers—most publicly, FTR journalist Gabriel Sanhueza served as editor of *El Surazo*— the paper steadfastly refused to become "an organ of any party" and maintained that it was "a paper of the Left, whose pages were open to any revolutionary expression that contributes to unity."[60] As in the defense of the Chiguayante textile mill, worker-based grassroots unity carried the day.

Despite widespread local support for *El Surazo*, the effort to create a worker's cooperative and an autonomous platform for worker self-expression ultimately failed. The newspaper workers' strike ended with the firing of Sanhueza and sixteen others and the imprisonment of the strike leaders on charges of theft of materials. Respected local MIR leader Pedro Enríquez Barra acted as lawyer for the workers facing prosecution. In retrospect, Enríquez Barra saw the "absence of official backing from the Popular Unity government" as a key element.[61] He explained, "This could have been a great movement that ended with what the workers wanted, which was to create a workers' cooperative that would take over and run the newspaper." He recounted efforts by the union leaders to negotiate with the government: "We were called once to Santiago for an interview with Allende [and] the minister of the interior. . . . Allende took the position before all of us gathered there that the government adhered to the institutional legality of the constitution that recognized the right to private property, and so the government hoped that this would be resolved by direct conversations. Period. There was never help."[62]

The fate of *El Surazo* speaks to the larger tension within revolutionary Chile between the autonomy of grassroots action and political party control. In Concepción, the local Popular Unity authorities and the provincial labor federation promised to seek a solution for *El Sur* workers on the condition that the paper become an official Popular Unity paper. The MIR labor lawyer recalled the general sense of discouragement, "because the idea was that the newspapers' own workers would continue publishing *El Surazo* on their own." The strikers concluded this "was not good for anything because the workers would have given up everything they had fought for." Enríquez Barra's reflections indicate that the short-lived *El Surazo* experience during the Bosses' Lockout marked an example of the Popular Unity government reining in the revolution from below and explicitly stifling workers' power in favor of respecting private property.

At the start of the October Bosses' Lockout, the Allende government declared a state of emergency in a number of provinces and turned to the armed forces to restore order.[63] President Allende initiated the practice of appointing a *jefe de plaza*— a local military commanding officer—to replace the civilian governor. In Concepción, the jefe de plaza reported "absolute calm" across the province. Both contemporaneous newspaper reports and oral histories concur that the Bosses' Lockout had comparatively less impact in Concepción province than the rest of the country. The disruption of public transportation was less severe than in Santiago; outside urban Concepción, in the coal zone, for example, services continued regularly.

For the most part, moreover, businesses across the province did not join the strike en masse. Newspaper coverage noted isolated closings around Concepción's downtown, particularly large department stores. Yet in the surrounding neighborhoods businesses remained open, which meant the majority of Concepción's population was not seriously affected by immediate food shortages.[64] In the outlying industrial towns in the province, in Tomé, Penco, Coronel, and Lota, newspapers affirmed that the shops opened normally.[65] In Santiago, anti-Allende students and women occupied the streets banging pots and pans in protest. These public protests were largely absent in Concepción province.[66] Thus, while the CIA-backed Bosses' Lockout wreaked havoc in Santiago and produced a serious crisis for Allende's government—eventually resolved by bringing three military officers into his cabinet—in places like Coronel "the reactionaries' strike did not exist."[67]

Although grassroots organizing succeeded in mitigating the lockout's impact in Concepción province, it did not completely deter counterrevolutionary violence. On October 23, 1972, a suspicious fire at the Caupolicán textile mill left half of it inoperable.[68] The act of arson erased any doubts about whether the counterrevolution was real. It confirmed for many leftist supporters in Concepción province that opposition forces, having failed to reverse the requisition in the courts, now turned to extralegal avenues. As FTR union leader Esnaldo Sanhueza explained, the Caupolicán mill had functioned normally throughout the strike with government-owned CORFO trucks and assistance from military personal. The weaving section targeted by the fire had increased production of a popular fabric used for flour sacks in high demand at nearby mills. "This was no accident," Sanhueza affirmed, pointing out that someone had shut off the water at the plant Sunday afternoon, slowing attempts to put out the fire that broke out after midnight. Looking to the future, he asserted that the union had to expand its focus beyond union matters and serve the broader public. He highlighted decisions to let the distribution chain DIRINCO operate out of the Caupolićan workers' union building and to "protect the small shopkeepers who want to work" as examples of how workers, including FTR members, saw greater collaboration with government agencies as part of a collective effort to combat the Bosses' Lockout.[69]

The sabotage of the Caupolicán mill in Chiguayante was a stark reminder of the need for greater vigilance and cross-sector coordination. Concepción PS leaders called for their base to create self-defense committees in every neighborhood and factory and to organize coordinating commands (*comandos coordinadores*) across sectors to resolve problems related to food and transportation. Above all, these coordinating committees should "prepare for the defense of the revolutionary process."[70] By October 23, comuna-wide coordinating committees (*comités coordinadores comunales*) had been created in Chiguayante, Penco, Concepción, Tomé, and Talcahuano. Committee members were selected at open general assemblies, "where anyone who wanted could contribute their opinion and become informed" and "everyone could elect their leader."[71] The emergence of coordinating committees in Concepción province again represented a grassroots initiative in which the MIR and the Popular Unity parties, including the Communists, worked together. In the Chiguayante coordinating committee, for example, FTR textile union leader Esnaldo Sanhueza worked with unions, neighborhood councils, mothers' centers, price control boards, sports clubs, cultural centers, and student groups. He affirmed that workers gained strength through solidarity with other community organizations.[72]

Throughout this period, the scope of the newly formed coordinating committees remained broadly defined as (1) "coordinating the struggles of workers, pobladores, and students"; (2) "obtaining concrete solutions for the pobladores most in need"; and (3) "forming bases for the eventual creation, in the right moment, of a comunawide workers' council." To accomplish this, they set up work commissions to explore matters ranging from those directly related to the strike, such as vigilance, transporation, and price control to longer-term questions of social, economic, and cultural rights related to education, culture, health, and housing.[73] Significantly, *Diario Color* mentioned no political party affiliations in its coverage of the newly elected leadership board for Chiguayante's Coordinating Committee.[74] The MIR, PS, and MAPU had all endorsed this type of integrated community organizations at the People's Assembly and, later, in the early days of the October lockout.[75]

As efforts expanded around Concepción to defend the Popular Unity government, everyday citizens became the eyes and ears for identifying hoarding and other more serious actions. Self-defense and vigilance took on greater significance after the sabotage of the Caupolicán mill. These measures focused on protecting neighborhoods and industries from rightist aggression, particularly that of the openly fascist Patria y Libertad's paramilitary shock troops. By necessity, leftist parties prepared their members for street skirmishes. Meanwhile, local people engaged in community self-regulation. For example, women members of the Barrio Norte coordinating committee in Concepción reported to the labor federation that there were fifteen trucks hidden in the neighborhood, loaded with goods for the black market. Thanks to the women's efforts, the trucks were "requisitioned and put to work."[76] Going forward, the provincewide mobilization to stop the October lockout affirmed the idea that everyday people possessed the authority to denounce and regulate essential functions within their communities. It would be the local rationing boards, better known by their acronym JAP, which more than any other organization dominated in this role.

"FIGHTING AGAINST SPECULATORS AND FOOD SHORTAGES": THE JAPS AS NEIGHBORHOOD ORGANIZATIONS FOR POPULAR PARTICIPATION

In the face of the Bosses' Lockout, the Concepción MIR eventually decided that it would actively back grassroots sectors that wanted to mobilize, including through Popular Unity government initiatives like the JAPs.[77] During the October lockout, these local price control boards expanded rapidly across the province: from 76 in March 1972 to 114 by January 1973.[78] In Concepción's Barrio Norte and Costanera neighborhood, in Tomé, Penco, Lirquén, and Coronel, local people who had joined the MIR played a critical role in the expansion and functioning of the JAPs by working to give them a degree of legitimacy within the community as spaces of democratic participation.[79]

As unions became more active in community organizing during the Bosses' Lockout, FTR members advocated for greater collaboration with the JAPs. In the coal zone, FTR leader Jorge García informed El Rebelde in late October 1972 that "workers have thrown themselves into the creation of sufficient numbers of JAPs to ensure the people's control over the food supply."[80] García's comments reflect the reality that, in the wake of the Bosses' Lockout, consumption became the front line of conflict. With the formation of coordinating committees in Concepción province's five industrial centers—Tomé, Talcahuano, Penco, Chiguayante, and Concepción—unions began to work with neighborhood associations, like the Juntas de Vecinos, mother's centers, and the JAPs. As initiatives created by the Frei administration (DC), the Juntas de Vecinos and mothers' centers were institutionalized organizations with clear guidelines for their formation and legalization. During the Bosses' Lockout, the JAPs surpassed these older community associations as the primary organization regulating and rationing access to food.

Although few shopkeepers supported the strike and public transportation was soon restored in Concepción province, the disruption of distribution routes in the Bosses' Lockout coupled with hoarding and soaring prices on the black market eventually started to produce shortages in the coal zone. These shortages hit hard because coal miners—now working for a nationalized industry—were earning decent wages and could acquire products previously unaffordable. Shortly after taking office in December 1970, President Allende nationalized the Lota and Coronel coal mines and the Bellavista-Tomé textile mill. With higher employment rates and increased wages, "people really [had] greater purchasing power [that] was expressed in most quotidian things." Former Communist congressman representing Tomé, Iván Quintana, highlighted greater access to products like Nescafé, powdered milk, and toilet paper.[81] Coronel resident and then MIR militant Aníbal Cáceres summarized the contradiction produced by the 1972 shortages: "People had money, but there wasn't anything to buy, so speculation began. And that's when the JAP appeared, fighting against speculators and against food shortages."[82]

To address these problems, JAPs concentrated on ensuring local food distribution and curbing black market profiteering within a local territory. While decentralized JAPs were a government initiative, the task of getting them up and running fell to local activists like students Aníbal Cáceres and Hugo Monsalves and coal miner Tito Carrillo. Cáceres characterized the JAP in Coronel's Camilo Olavarría neighborhood as relatively autonomous, noting, "We came up with the organization ourselves."[83] Each block elected a delegate—"someone known on the block for being honest"—and delegates collectively carried out a neighborhood census and distributed rationing cards according to family size. Camilo Olavarría resident Lautaro López noticed changes in his neighbors as they took on more responsibilities within the JAP: "People gained experience and learned how to share in their neighborhood. That a pobladora learned to say how many kilos of flour each neighbor was entitled to and not keep the largest portion for herself, well that's an important lesson."[84]

Unlike in Santiago, where the Communist Party dominated the price control boards, the MIR in Concepción actively participated in the JAPs, often taking on leadership roles. This was true despite the Communist Party's hegemony in the coal zone. As a struggle located in neighborhoods—barrios populares and poblaciones—these were areas where the MIR's local base had traditionally excelled at organizing. As Aníbal Cáceres explained decades later, in Coronel "almost all the JAP was MIR. Why? Because the miristas had organizing experience."[85] Through the JAPs, MIR activists defended the participatory democratic practices so central to their earlier union and shantytown organizing and gained election to and often ended up leading local JAPs.[86] For example, in Coronel, MIR members critiqued the corrupt practices of the Communist Party and gained the support of residents. In Hugo Monsalves's Villa Mora neighborhood, Communists organized the first JAP without holding open elections. With clear contempt, he stated that the Communists "began to distribute things only between PC militants and not to the entire population." During a meeting of the Junta de Vecinos, he remembered charging that "their JAP didn't represent anyone but themselves." In response, the assembly "voted to dissolve the first Communist-run JAP and elect a new committee on the spot. A MIR compañero was elected president. When it came time for the delegates to be named someone nominated me as 'the *joven* [youth] who spoke up.' Well, I didn't have any other choice than to say yes, and so I joined the JAP."[87] As they set about the task of organizing the JAP in Villa Mora, they made ration cards, and "people agreed to them because what little there was had to be shared among everyone."[88] As the experiences of Hugo Monsalves and Aníbal Cáceres suggest, by 1972 the MIR in Concepción province had become synonymous among locals with the defense of transparency and participation.

The reputation of MIR militants as having revolutionary ethics also contributed to members' election to the JAP. For Lautaro López, controlling distribution in a given area granted a large degree of power to JAP leaders who needed to have a strong sense of justice: "If there had not been a guiding role from a party with a revolutionary or social ethic, this could have gone in any direction." He contended that "in various JAPs led by Communists the leaders committed abuses, and this began to discredit the JAP in many neighborhoods in Coronel." Yet local activists in the JAP also mobilized, "making a great effort to control" the abuses by holding open forums for the public to denounce irregularities.[89] Coal miner Tito Carrillo explained the application of MIR ethics in the system of distribution, explaining that "cigarettes would only be sold to those who smoked, not to those who didn't." "Sure it sounds controlling," he admitted, "but well, people began to take advantage [*chorrear*], so the MIR ran things in such a way that everyone had [access to what they needed]. The JAP controlled this and gave each family their can of milk."[90] According to Carrillo, "Never before and never since did people drink so much milk. People had milk, cans of it, powdered milk, condensed milk, and Nescafe, everything. They never had it before because they couldn't afford it, and never since because they didn't have access to these things."[91] Contrary to the dominant memories of scarcity and long lines in Santiago, Carrillo's reflections indicate how these times of shortages are often remembered as times of plenty when JAP regulation facilitated access to consumer goods.

In addition to the regulation of food rationing, the mirista ethic was expressed in direct actions that the JAP took to secure additional supplies. Aníbal Cáceres recounted how his MIR base commandeered potato trucks to ensure fair distribution in Coronel. "We would be on the lookout for the trucks passing through town in the middle of night to sell the potatoes in Concepción for more money, and here we were without potatoes," he explained. "We grabbed the trucks and got my brother who was a government official to certify them as stolen property. Then we took them into Coronel neighborhoods and divided the sacks of potatoes among the corner stores." Cáceres did not see this as giving away the potatoes: "We sold them, and the owner got the money. That's what was done, and the people were in agreement with the JAP; otherwise, they'd charge you an arm and a leg."[92] The story of the requisitioned potato trucks illustrates how direct actions—sometimes illegal ones—began to occur and how the law was circumvented in the name of ensuring equitable access. The story is less an experience of chaotic lawlessness than one of creative resolution of the real problems posed by politically manipulated scarcity. It conveys a sense of moral obligation to continue producing and providing for workers, who, more than ever before, could afford to feed their families.

As the JAPs expanded neighborhood by neighborhood in Coronel, Aníbal Cáceres explained, "we began to meet at the citywide level where we had the famous assemblies of the JAP Comunal."[93] The JAP Comunal began as an instance of coordination between the JAP leaders in different neighborhoods, but soon, with the slogan, "The JAP informs the people," the umbrella organization began holding open assemblies in the coal miner's union hall, which regularly drew crowds of several hundred. Daniel López, who ten years earlier had held the VRM meetings in his living room and by 1973 identified with the MIR, was JAP Comunal president. Lautaro López recalled how his father, Daniel López, "perhaps influenced by his Trotskyist tradition," reinforced an assembly-based tradition.[94] The elder López often remarked that it was no longer enough for five leaders to meet but time to "bring together the hundreds of people engaged in the same work." At assemblies, it was "no longer only the leaders who speak, but anyone who wants to can take the floor." In this form of direct democracy, the JAP Comunal achieved such high levels of participation, representativeness, and legitimacy in Coronel that "even the Chief of Police ordered his men to affiliate with the JAP and he himself participated in the JAP Comunal's leadership board."[95] It was the growth of the Coronel JAP Comunal that led to the discovery of the irregularities at Panadería El Progreso.

"PRODUCING WITHOUT THE BOSS": THE PEOPLE'S BAKERY TAKEOVER, JANUARY 1973

After the takeover, the occupants turned the business over to the Coronel-wide Juntas de Abastecimiento y Precios (JAP Comunal), under the leadership of Daniel López.[96] His son, MIR student Lautaro López, described how the bakery was run by an alliance of bakers, local residents, the MIR, and the Socialists, and noted, "They even established a working understanding with the police chief, who came to speak to my father directly and told him not to worry because the police were not going to repress the action."[97] As the bakery takeover in Coronel illustrates, local people acted on their own and sought political backing afterwards, much like pobladores carrying out illegal land takeovers.

When irregularities threatened production, the challenge was to keep the bakery running. "You take power not when you stop production but when you are capable of producing without a boss," explained Enzo La Mura, then head of the MIR in the coal zone. He added, "They got the flour directly from the mill without any trouble, and Coronel never lacked for good bread those days."[98] Aníbal Cáceres noted that the distribution of bread improved tremendously: "Bread began to arrive in neighborhoods where it hadn't been [before and] people were grateful, especially in the poorest neighborhoods. They were happy because we brought bread in and sold it."[99] Although local Communist leaders, including Coronel's mayor and governor, opposed the bakery occupation, citing the Popular Unity government's policy of maintaining alliances with small and mid-sized business owners, there were limits to how far they could oppose an action that had popular support. Even PC union leader Juan Alarcón, who felt that the bakery owner, Antonio Sánchez, had been unfairly targeted, was pressed into lending his truck for bakery deliveries. "I had a little second-hand truck, and the people in the MIR couldn't find anything better than to come to me to get bread from this poor guy's bakery," he remembered. "They wanted to nationalize his bakery, nationalize everything including peanut vendors—but I had to go. I was an authority here, a union leader, and I couldn't say no." Still ambivalent about the action decades later, he concluded, "But they shouldn't have been doing what they were doing."[100] The reluctant participation of Juan Alarcón along with the police chief's decision to send an officer to guard the occupied bakery suggest the degree of legitimacy that the bakery takeover enjoyed within the local community, as well as the costs of opposing it.[101]

While the JAP Comunal ran the bakery, the money earned from producing and selling the bread was returned to Antonio Sánchez, and after several weeks so was the bakery.[102] "The quality of bread improved because," according to Aníbal Cáceres, "Sánchez knew a [social] force existed that was ready to pressure, inspect, and watch him." In line with the JAP's mission to denounce and regulate—and to invest everyday citizens with that capacity—the bakery takeover, in the end, functioned "as a warning."[103] It was one in which the predominant action was not of taking but, as Lautaro López suggested, of sharing their daily bread. Reflecting on the lessons derived from the bakery occupation, Lautaro observed that "the people ensured an equitable distribution of bread, which is a symbol of sharing, and this was done with justice and with bread of good quality . . . well, I think it's a good example of what is possible when the people themselves, guided by a sense of justice, are the ones running society."[104]

Beyond the real necessity of food shortages, often artificially produced by hoarding, what did the bakery symbolize for Coronel's residents? In a small industrial town like Coronel where "the bourgeoisie hardly existed," owners of small and medium-sized businesses were perceived as representatives of the business class.[105] Thus, Panadería El Progreso was a site of local power over the well-being of ordinary people and a symbol of the exclusion of the coal miners and their families. By taking over the bakery, participants inverted local power relations and challenged businessmen like Antonio Sánchez to produce "good bread for everyone."[106] The takeover was not an example of top-down state socialism but rather a grassroots action that ensured just and equitable access in a market economy in which social justice mattered more than private profits.

Far from an ideologically driven vision for socialist change, local activists envisioned a socialist future in practical terms: bread, work, and freedom. The 1973 Coronel bakery takeover represents one example of the diverse everyday revolutions in the Chilean countryside and in universities, shantytowns, and factory towns across the country. The memories of participants convey a sense of being protagonists acting autonomously to resolve immediate problems. This was about more than affordable bread: it was the collective "no" to the powerful and the personal liberation of participating in something larger than the individual. "I remember asking my father," Lautaro López reflected, "what would Chile be like if what we are doing now—sharing bread—was done elsewhere?"[107] Forty years later, the bakery takeover persists in local memory as a means of imagining alternative futures.

The experience of running the people's bakery held important lessons for Coronel residents about the power of direct participation and collective action. The successful bakery takeover also appeared to advance the principles celebrated by the Concepción People's Assemblies, which prioritized creating autonomous spaces for local participatory democracy to flourish over a narrow focus on occupying the state. In this sense, the MIR's grassroots organizing work was fundamentally about stimulating greater inclusion for those sectors traditionally outside of politics (pobladores and peasants) as well as defending participation and ensuring greater decision-making powers for sectors with longer political traditions (industrial workers and students).

MIR mass politics during the Popular Unity period have often been stigmatized as exceeding rational limits. Juan Alarcón's retelling of the story of his truck being pressed into service for bread deliveries evokes an image of the MIR taking everything; even the peanut vendor's private property was not safe. Contrary to this portrayal, the bakery takeover illustrates how grassroots activists interpreted the MIR's message not as state ownership but as greater participation for popular sectors. Unlike other revolutionary left groups in Chile, including the Partido Comunista Revolucionario (PCR) and the Vanguardia Organizada del Pueblo (VOP), the MIR did not only function as an antisystem movement during the Popular Unity period. The People's Assembly and the bakery takeover demonstrate that the MIR's strength in Concepción came from working with other leftist political parties within Allende's coalition.

Over time, however, the MIR's ability as an organization to synthesize, process, and learn from the everyday revolutions happening in the bases was often short-circuited by its hierarchical party structure. MIR leaders "even at the regional level," reflected Lautaro López, "did not value" the experiences of the Coronel bakery takeover and the JAP Comunal; no mention of the bakery ever appeared in the MIR's national paper, *El Rebelde*. Just like the People's Assembly, which had seemed to many participants a successful demonstration of all the principles they believed the MIR embodied, the bakery takeover did not find support from above.[108] In 1973, as grassroots mobilization continued at a fevered pace, disillusionment started to set in for many activists as their efforts increasingly appeared insufficient to stem the rising counterrevolutionary tide.

6

"Living within a Special World"

The Unraveling Revolution and the Limits of the Vanguard

The 1972 move to Santiago marked a liminal transition for Alejandro Alarcón, a Tomé textile worker turned national MIR labor candidate. MIR leaders had taken a special interest in Alarcón, selecting him as the party's figurehead for the Revolutionary Workers Front (FTR). His nomination for 1972 national labor federation (CUT) president catapulted Alarcón onto the national stage. From this privileged vantage point, the young labor leader gained access to a world unimaginable to those he left behind. As he campaigned for the CUT presidency, he said, "the MIR gave me the best teachers, the greatest political minds and intellectuals." University of Concepción professors Fernando Mires, Néstor D'Alessio, and Luis Vitale, to name a few, tutored him privately.

Decades later, Alarcón reflected on the widening distance between the MIR's national leadership and its grassroots base as a major factor in the MIR's diminishing success. He noted that "you view politics differently when you are in the factory," as opposed to the Marxist theory that dominated leftist political circles. "If the working class had penetrated the interior of the party and become part of its structure," he observed, the MIR "would have had another dynamic and different forms of discussion and decision making. It would have changed its character and the lens through which the party viewed the pressing issues of the moment." The failure of the MIR to merge more effectively with the working class left Alarcón disillusioned by mid-1973, a sentiment he never publicly expressed at the time.[1]

From its start in 1965 as a movement to unify Chile's heterogeneous revolutionary Left, the MIR was subject to two competing tendencies: a participatory, assembly-based movement and the impetus to form a vanguard party. Alongside the apparent success of its mass politics in the early 1970s, the MIR's top leaders continued to pursue their vision of an elite revolutionary vanguard. Over time, the plurality of voices and ideological differences within the MIR diminished in favor of a single party line established by the Santiago-based MIR Comisión Política (CP; Political Commission).[2] Throughout the Popular Unity years, the primary responsibility for establishing the MIR's ideological positions and its political strategy belonged to just five CP members: Miguel Enríquez, Andrés Pascal Allende, Nelson Gutiérrez, Edgardo Enríquez, and Bautista Van Schouwen. This concentration of power in the hands of an elite core of young national leaders produced overconfidence in their ability to read society and to diagnose its needs correctly with historical examples and theoretical models. Faced with growing political crisis and economic dislocation, the national MIR leadership in Santiago proclaimed that a revolutionary breakthrough was at hand and called on its supporters to launch a popular and revolutionary counteroffensive. The MIR became more rhetorically committed to an armed defense of the revolution, while actual military preparations remained limited. Using Marxist-Leninist theory to explain reality, the MIR's leaders predicted that the heightened polarization and intensified class struggle in Chile would favor the workers. Yet Chile in 1973 was not Russia in 1917. This inability to read society—the very pueblo the MIR sought to mobilize—proved paralyzing and polarizing for the MIR's leadership in late 1973.

As national MIR leaders retreated into theory-driven analyses of revolutionary stages, the MIR in Concepción remained attentive to the situation as it unfolded on the ground. The close, if at times conflicting, relationship between working-class militants and sympathizers and the Concepción university-educated MIR leadership sheds light on why some regional leaders developed a dissenting view of Chile's revolutionary process. Tempering the optimistic declarations by national MIR leaders, these University of Concepción professors and students contended that the Right was gaining ground and reasserting its class power. At different times in 1973, this regional group advocated behind the scenes for the MIR to rally behind an embattled President Allende and his Popular Unity coalition. Although nationally relations between Allende's government and the radical Left (the MIR, left-wing Socialists, and the MAPU) became increasingly strained in 1973, this rupture never happened in Concepción province.[3] During 1973, the Concepción MIR continued drawing closer to the Popular Unity, and grassroots activists affiliated with the MIR continued to see their role as defending Allende's government.[4]

Between 1972 and 1973, leftist grassroots activists in Concepción continued to enact their vision of the revolution. Yet their vision diverged more and more from both the Popular Unity project for a phased centrally planned revolution and the MIR's understanding of socialism rooted in Marxist-Leninist theory. In the first half of 1973, the MIR in Concepción grew exponentially at the grassroots, attracting more followers and expanding its organizational capacities. Despite the fevered pace of mobilization, it increasingly appeared insufficient. The creation of local spaces of power and grassroots participation did not find a corresponding echo on the national scale. The everyday revolutions, manifested in the day-to-day struggles to build community and redistribute material resources, now appeared divorced from the national political theater.

Power was still rooted in Santiago and was still firmly in the hands of the military and business elites, tacitly supported by the U.S. government. After the October Bosses' Lockout, the new battleground in the campaign to unseat Allende became the March 1973 congressional elections. After anti-Allende forces failed to gain the requisite votes to impeach the president, many on the Right, increasingly joined by conservative Christian Democrats, turned to a military solution. In late June 1973, the Allende government staved off a failed coup attempt, known as the Tanquetazo. As was the case in the Bosses' Lockout, grassroots sectors again mobilized to defend the constitutional government. Yet the enormity of the national crisis appeared well beyond grassroots control. Faced with a conjuncture of forces they had little power to stop, how did leftist militants navigate these turbulent months? As militants in Concepción experienced the tensions and internal contradictions within the MIR and Chile's unraveling revolution, their story is one of disillusionment and sadness as people struggled in the face of adverse conditions and unequal forces. Frustrated by their inability to reverse the onslaught of the counterrevolution, nonetheless, they hoped that continued organizing and sacrifice might well make a difference.

The MIR's rigid internal hierarchy came into conflict with the defining feature of radical popular movements: participatory democratic practices and a corresponding sense of grassroots agency. In Concepción, where the MIR functioned as a mass party, its limitations as an ideologically driven vanguard became increasingly visible. In the year ahead, these conflicts would have consequences for the MIR's overall capacity to mobilize its social bases, to provide effective leadership, and to navigate Chile's mounting political crisis.

In Concepción province prior to the September 11, 1973, military coup, the competing tendencies—between hierarchical internal party structures and horizontal grassroots practices—collided. The MIR's national leadership proved unwilling to confront directly internal disagreements over the changing political situation in Chile and the adequacy of its strategy and military preparations for a potential coup. The MIR's closed party structure inhibited the consideration of alternative strategies and more honest assessments of the MIR's real capacity on the ground to resist a coup. While Concepción leaders appeared to perceive these limitations, they too never fully articulated or implemented a viable alternative. Instead, internal divisions produced a crisis within the regional leadership. The vanguard dissolved at the very moment it was most needed. As a result, even the Concepción MIR was unprepared for the coup they had long predicted was coming.[5]

THE CONTRADICTIONS OF POWER:
THE CENTRAL COMMITTEE, JANUARY–JUNE 1973

As Concepción leaders spent more time in Santiago, they witnessed a more authoritarian MIR than the one they knew at home. The trajectories of prominent Concepción MIR leaders like Alejandro Alarcón and Enzo La Mura uncover the internal tensions lived by MIR militants as they confronted their party's deeply undemocratic political culture. Their experiences in Santiago in 1972 and 1973 shed light on the contradictions of power that gripped the MIR from within.

After finishing with a dismal 2% of the national vote in the May 1972 CUT elections, Alejandro Alarcón remained in Santiago as a member of the MIR's union commission. From this vantage point, he "was occasionally invited to the Political Commission meetings," where he "witnessed how the MIR's Political Commission worked."[6] As Alarcón reflected decades later, "When I came to live in Santiago, that's when the first problems appeared and my perception of the MIR changed completely."[7] In Santiago, Alarcón came to "see the MIR leaders from the inside" and to know "their excesses, their deliriums, their ambitions for power, and above all their ambitions to be protagonists and to order people around." He attributed these failings to their "petit-bourgeois attitudes," but he also felt that these negative qualities were part of national politics and the elite political class as a whole.

Despite feeling uncomfortable with what he saw, the corrosive effect of power also enveloped Alarcón and for a time inhibited him from speaking out. Looking back, he admitted the experience "made me lose myself. I could have articulated these reflections much sooner, but one way or another I repressed these discoveries because I was living within a special world." It seems that he was "walking on air without seeing reality because power, from what I could see, had tremendous advantages in terms of access to people, to food, to material things, to women." While he saw these things then, it was only "with the passage of time, I can acknowledge them now." It was Alarcón's compañeros in Tomé who eventually grounded him: "The *viejos* [old-timers] in Tomé would say things that made me reflect about their relationship to the party, the congress that never happened, the party that never 'proletarianized'; people at the grassroots quickly perceived these issues, but they never had any decision-making power."[8] Even at the local and regional levels, workers were virtually absent from leadership positions, held mostly by former and current university students.

As a founder of the Leftist University Student Movement (MUI) and champion of university reform, Enzo La Mura typified the trajectory of a Concepción student turned professional revolutionary. Yet as he straddled the regional and national MIR leaderships, La Mura tried to square what he heard in Santiago with what he saw working with unions in Concepción. When La Mura attended the forty-eight-person

Central Committee meetings, he found something quite different from the open assemblies and endless debates that marked his earlier contact with Miguel Enríquez and the other CP members during their student days fighting for university reform. By 1973, La Mura reflected, "the Political Commission had accumulated such a degree of power to create the party line and everything else that in reality the Central Committee meetings were like a lecture class." Someone from the Political Commission would read the political report—the key document establishing the MIR's current assessment and policy objectives—and the rest of the CC members would "take notes, just like in class; there was no discussion. The final conclusions for future actions were already written."[9] Despite being the largest and most representative governing body within the MIR, the Central Committee began ratifying rather than questioning the Political Commission's views.

In the absence of official mechanisms, such as a party congress with elected delegates, to resolve internal debates, MIR leaders at all levels relied on cultivated loyalty, side groups of supporters, and back channels to maintain their power. The Central Committee in Santiago unilaterally appointed new committee members starting in 1969. For example, following a conflict with regional MIR leaders over the 1972 University of Concepción student federation elections, the national leadership expanded the Concepción MIR's representation on the Central Committee. On one level these promotions promised to give Concepción a greater voice in the national organization. In practice, however, the expanded presence of Concepción members gave the Political Commission tighter vigilance over dissenting voices.[10] At key moments, these loyal supporters opposed the independent views espoused by Concepción regional secretary Manuel Vergara and the university professors close to him.

In February 1973, MIR general secretary Miguel Enríquez arrived in Concepción to preside over a national conference. In a closed meeting held at the UdeC sociology institute, Enríquez faced little opposition as he presented the Political Commission's assessment of the country's current situation and the MIR's corresponding strategy for 1973.[11] Centered on the creation of a polo revolucionario, it sought to wrest control of mass movements and the revolutionary process from the "reformist" Popular Unity leadership. As Political Commission member Andrés Pascal Allende explained, "The general opinion within the MIR favored a policy aimed at regrouping revolutionary sectors by advancing agreements with the Socialist Party, the Christian Left, and the MAPU-Garretón faction. This alliance was in the process of being formed [in 1973], but it was never fully realized."[12] In essence, this strategy sought to scale up the party collaboration behind the Concepción People's Assembly to create a more permanent national revolutionary alliance that would act as a counterweight to the more moderate leftist sectors who favored negotiating with the Christian Democrats.

By most accounts, Enríquez's brilliance and theoretical acumen was unrivaled. One MIR student militant recounted the first time he heard Enríquez debate in a forum: "What most impressed me was Miguel's intelligence, his quickness of thought. In a debate with Trotskyists, Socialists, various groups, of course, Miguel was the fastest speaker, the most brilliant, the most lucid, and the most consistent with his relentless rationality. And so he seemed to me a respectable leader."[13] Looking back on this inability to challenge the top leadership, Concepción MIR militant Martín Hernández reflected, "[If] we, as younger militants, had a different opinion, we did not have the argumentative capacity to refute them. They could deploy such a battery of arguments that, in the end, we kept quiet and embraced" their position. He lamented, "We always ended up agreeing, because in the end, they always convinced us. They won not by votes but with arguments."[14] The MIR's internal political culture, where those who could cite the most Marxist theory won the ideological debate, had its roots in the University of Concepción student movement.[15] It is fitting perhaps that some of the only individuals willing to challenge the Political Commission members were their former professors in Concepción.

After Miguel Enríquez left Concepción in February 1973, sociology professor Fernando Mires openly contradicted the Political Commission proposals. The reality of being in the provinces required MIR regional leaders to keep looking at society and what was happening in the bases. Grassroots experiences and innovations in Concepción province—a region disproportionately populated by workers and students—shaped how a sector of the MIR's regional leadership read the rapidly changing situation on the ground. Less interested in leadership of the revolutionary process, Mires and his colleague Néstor D'Alessio looked at the national situation from outside Santiago and concluded that the national MIR leaders' optimistic assessments were erroneous. The balance of power put the Left in an inherently defensive—not offensive—position before a powerful and resurgent Right that was leading an increasingly violent counterrevolution.[16] The logical conclusion was that the MIR should join forces with the Popular Unity coalition. This sparked a heated argument among regional MIR leaders.[17]

The possibility of joining the Popular Unity was not a new question. Yet national MIR leaders had repeatedly rejected the ministerial appointments offered by President Allende and the invitation to join the Popular Unity coalition. Fidel Castro initiated a rapprochement between the MIR and the Popular Unity between December 1971 and January 1972, and another round started in April before being broken off by the national Popular Unity following the May 1972 Concepción Manifesto issued by the left wing of the regional Popular Unity (Socialists, MAPU, and Christian Left) and the MIR. During Central Committee meetings, however, Concepción regional secretary Manuel Vergara "always came out openly in favor of accepting Allende's offers. His views were not a secret."[18] Starting in late 1972, a minority of MIR regional leaders, principally Vergara and his closest advisors, Mires and D'Alessio, advocated behind the scenes for a more solid alliance with the Popular Unity, a policy they never articulated openly or succeeded in implementing.[19]

When Mires did broach the possibility in February 1973, Enzo La Mura and Martín Hernández interceded to refute him. Reflecting on his feelings at the time, La Mura explained that he still believed then "it was possible [for revolutionary sectors] to break through," that repelling an "attack from the Right was still winnable."[20] The MIR's strategy "to co-opt" regional leaders like La Mura, by bringing them into the national leadership, appeared to have paid off. Although La Mura had at times been critical of the national leadership's interference in 1972 FEC elections, he remained a disciplined MIR militant and dutifully advocated for Miguel Enríquez's policies in Concepción and, shockingly, reported Vergara's dissenting position to his superiors in Santiago.

The MIR's lack of internal democracy had repercussions. When critical voices emerged at key junctures—like Fernando Mires in February 1973—the initial response from loyal militants was to silence them by toeing the official party line. In hindsight La Mura reflected, "The problem was that in 1973 we were facing a serious situation in Chile and we did not have any mechanism to discuss it."[21] The Political Commission members faced minimal resistance, which reinforced confidence in their ideological projections. There was "an absolute prohibition to debate or to propose the need for a Plan B," admitted La Mura, "because Plan A was always 'go on the offensive.'"[22] Throughout 1973, the MIR's Political Commission espoused overly optimistic assessments of Chile's political situation. The self-fashioning as a vanguard became self-confirming: for national leaders, it appeared inevitable that the MIR would assume its vanguard status over the revolutionary process. This same lack of internal democracy circumscribed the national MIR's ability to read the changing social and political situation in Chile and to learn from varied local experiences that offered lessons different from those visible in Santiago.

"PEOPLE FELT THEY WERE A PART OF SOMETHING": EVERYDAY REVOLUTIONS IN CONCEPCIÓN, JANUARY–JUNE 1973

Deepening divisions between national and regional MIR leaders marked the first half of 1973, yet at the grassroots in Concepción province this same period was one of expansive growth for the party. Isolated from power struggles in Santiago, grassroots activists and midlevel leaders dedicated their energies to building the party, improving its organizational capacity, and sustaining the diverse forms of social mobilization that had sprung up across the Left during the October Bosses' Lockout. From their vantage point, immersed in organizing and implementing the MIR's mass politics, revolution still seemed possible.

The MIR's relevance as a political actor in Concepción province derived from its relationship to the Left, not its isolation from it. In Concepción, the MIR had proportionally more influence than in the rest of the country. When the Left marched in Concepción, the MIR and its supporters easily made up a third of the participants. "How you experienced the MIR here [in Concepción] was less as a Leninist party like in Santiago and more like a mass party," reflected MIR student Álvaro Riffo.[23] Similarly, student leader Martín Hernández, who like La Mura and Alarcón moved between the regional and national leadership, admitted that "some sectors of the MIR were more authoritarian than others. In Santiago, the MIR was tremendously authoritarian, internal relations were more hierarchical, and the [leadership] tended to utilize its mass fronts." Hernández drew a contrast between the political practices promoted by regional MIR leaderships and the "fight to the death for political leadership" that was driving the national MIR. In the provinces, the MIR "operated with much more flexibility [and] people felt they were a part of something. They would go to meetings and debate; it was possible to participate."[24] At the grassroots the MIR attracted more and more supporters through 1973, but it did so as an ally of the Popular Unity.

Following the Bosses' Lockout, the country turned its attention to the upcoming March 1973 congressional elections. During 1972, opposition parties started to gain ground in high schools and universities, often through new alliances between the Christian Democrats and the hard-right National Party and emergent new-right gremial movement.[25] This alliance foreshadowed the formation of the Confederación Democrática (CODE, Democratic Confederation) for the March elections, in which the opposition parties vowed to attain the two-thirds majority in the Senate necessary to impeach Allende.[26] For its part, the Popular Unity government sought to rally its bases and secure a majority mandate for continued reforms. Martín Hernández recalled the attitude at the time: "Everyone saw the necessity for the Popular Unity government to have greater freedom of action, which, according to the UP's own proposal, would come after achieving a good performance at the polls." Consistent with Chile's pluralistic democratic traditions, it made sense to all sides that elections would be a referendum on the revolutionary process.

The MIR's national leadership carefully weighed its options.[27] In a reversal of its boycott of the 1970 presidential election, the MIR recognized that "the political class struggle for the time being would happen through the electoral campaigns."[28] Rather than run independent candidates, the MIR opted to offer "conditional support for Popular Unity candidates" deemed sufficiently revolutionary.[29] General secretary Miguel Enríquez's candid assessment was that running MIR candidates would seem like a "divisionary tactic" within the Left, and, more important, "the masses will not vote for us."[30] The MIR leadership reiterated that its top priority remained deepening "direct democracy ... to continue building through the coordinating committees new forms of power that in the future will form the coun-terweight to parliamentarians."[31]

During the early months of 1973, the MIR's main party structure in the city of Concepción—GPM-1 led by Carlos Rioseco—threw itself into organizing the cam-paign for the MIR-endorsed Christian Left candidate. Rioseco was the same UdeC student who years earlier had recruited poblador fisherman Carlos Robles into the MIR. By 1973, he had put aside his dentistry studies to dedicate all his time to the MIR as a professional revolutionary paid by the party.[32] "The campaign allowed us to traverse the city and get to know the areas assigned to us," explained Mario Garcés, who at the time was a second-year anthropology student and served as Rioseco's second in command. GPM-1 covered Concepción's working-class neigh-borhoods surrounding the railroad tracks—Costanera and Pedro de Valdivia—as well as the sprawling Barrio Norte, with numerous light industries, just north of the city center. Nestled between these sectors on the road to Talcahuano were a number of new campamentos, the products of land takeovers in 1970 and 1971. With fewer than twenty full-fledged MIR militants, the organic structure of GPM-1 was still relatively small. "In the process of gathering people for campaign events," Garcés reflected, "we began to reorganize existing MIR bases" and establish new contacts in the area.[33]

While Chileans looked to the polls for a resolution to the political stalemate, both sides could claim victory in the March elections.[34] In absolute numbers the right-wing opposition won 55.6% of the vote but failed to secure the two-thirds majority in Congress needed to impeach Allende. The Popular Unity picked up seats in Congress, garnering 44% of the vote. Despite economic turmoil and grow-ing unrest in the streets, support for Allende's government went from 36% when he was elected in September 1970 to 44% in March 1973. The turnout was down from a high point of 50% in the March 1971 mayoral elections but still revealed a remark-able level of support from Chile's poor majority for the changes carried out in the previous two years. As a demonstration of the Left's continued social and political strength in Concepción province, the Popular Unity had gained five of the nine congressional (*diputado*) seats.[35]

At a press conference, Miguel Enríquez proclaimed that the March elections "on balance produced excellent results" for the MIR, particularly because cam-paigning had facilitated the "enormous diffusion of revolutionary ideas."[36] In Con-cepción there was truth to this assertion. Despite the failure to elect the MIR-backed Christian Left candidate, the MIR emerged from the campaign with more local supporters and an improved party organization. Through extensive grass-roots organizing, the MIR in the University of Concepción used the election to build the party.[37] When Martín Hernandez arrived in Concepción in November 1972, the membership of the campus-based GPM-2 totaled only 80 in a student body of nearly 10,000.[38] Hernández recalled that "from these 80 people, we recruited over 60 more in a matter of months—the grassroots work was tremendously productive." Similarly, from an initial 20 militants, GPM-1 in the city center had grown by mid-1973 to 89 members.[39] GPM-1 leaders drew on the new MIR bases created during the campaign to subdivide their territory into four sectors—Costanera, Madesal, Barrio Norte, and Centro—each with new leaders and coordinators, which produced a more efficient and effective party structure in Concepción. MIR activists filled the leadership boards on key community organizations in these working-class neighborhoods, including four price control boards (JAPs) and three neighborhood councils (juntas de vecinos).[40] In addition, just as in Coronel, a MIR activist served as president of the citywide JAP for Concepción.

In mid-1973, Mario Garcés led a column of pobladores and workers from Barrio Norte as they marched on the city center. He recalled looking over his shoulder "and seeing people marching several blocks deep, the city's poor and humble people, and in that moment I felt happy."[41] The MIR's social organizing work had yielded visible results: "The mobilization of large sectors of the populace—400, 500 people or more—all with MIR, MPR and FTR flags." Garcés reflected, "I can remember thinking to myself then, 'If this is not a revolution, then it is surely something close to it.'"[42] Indeed, the level of consciousness and ability to mobilize broad swaths of the population had reached unprecedented levels. By 1973, previously marginalized groups laying claim to expanded rights had changed Chilean society.

"THE DAYS AHEAD WILL BE DECISIVE": THE TANQUETAZO DRESS REHEARSAL FOR A COUP, JUNE 29, 1973

Although many had looked to the March 1973 congressional elections as a way out of Chile's growing political crisis, the path instead appeared on June 29, 1973, in the form of a military uprising by Santiago's Tacna regiment. As tanks rolled down Santiago's streets, leftist activists mobilized across Chile to defend workplaces and neighborhoods as they had during the Bosses' Lockout in October 1972. The FTR and other MIR fronts in Concepción province again immediately responded.

Yet in a repetition of October, prominent Popular Unity leaders in Concepción opted to await instructions from Santiago on how to proceed. Early on June 29, Barrio Norte resident and FTR member Manuel Torres headed to the provincial labor federation (CUT) headquarters in downtown Concepción, looking for a local journalist, Ricardo Torres, FTR representative in the CUT. After learning the journalist had already departed with Socialist representative Heriberto Krumm to visit factories, Torres turned to the CUT president, Juan Bautista Bravo, who was watching Santiago events on television, and exclaimed, "Compañero! From what you can see [on TV] we have enough information. I think the information about our province is in the industrial belts and you should be there." When Bravo answered that the

CUT leaders had already left, the frustrated FTR member asserted that as provincial labor federation president, he "should be down there with all his political team."[43] Yet Bravo, Communist union leader turned general manager at the Schwager coal mines in Coronel, waited before issuing any calls to mobilize.

In contrast, MIR leaders in Concepción (GPM-1) responded immediately to news of the military uprising by visiting the factories in Costanera and Barrio Norte. They did so on their own initiative, without waiting for a party directive. Carlos Rioseco and his second in command, Mario Garcés, "offered encouragement to the union leaders to stay firm, to occupy the factories, and to coordinate with the CUT."[44] Within hours, General Carlos Prats and forces loyal to the government had successfully put down the anti-Allende rebellion in Santiago.[45] As MIR militants in Concepción, Garcés reflected, "We felt good. Our union leaders had been prepared and the response was quick." Yet he added, "The response was essentially centered on creating assemblies, occupying the factories, and maintaining communication between the unions and our militants"; it was not about "putting up barricades in the streets" or generating other forms of defense.[46] At that point in time, the MIR's mass politics operated according to the logic that the demonstration of the people's willpower—to occupy factories and to keep the country running—would be a sufficient deterrent to the counterrevolution.

Despite the rapid mobilization in Concepción province, the failed coup attempt made clear that still greater coordination was needed. Locally, the FTR and the MIR played a central role in generating instances of popular power in their more familiar Santiago form: *cordones industriales,* or industrial belts, linking smaller factories in a given sector with the nationalized, larger industries. "The FTR started the whole mobilization of unions after the Tanquetazo," recalled Manuel Torres, noting his surprise that even "in unions where only two or three leaders participated [regularly in FTR meetings], all of sudden FTR banners appeared with all the compañeros marching behind them."[47] Using contacts established during the March electoral campaigns, the MIR in GPM-1 worked with their union leaders to establish connections between nearby unions in the Costanera and Barrio Norte neighborhoods.[48]

In early July, the Concepción CUT called on workers to occupy their factories as "a measure of security and vigilance" to prevent sabotage.[49] Two weeks after the Tanquetazo, Concepción province had six cordones industriales, created and run under the auspices of the provincial CUT.[50] CUT delegate Juan Moncada repeatedly informed reporters that the cordones "are not parallel organizations [to the government], nor are they armed."[51] Instead, he contended that "the only weapon workers have used to defend their interests when they are forced to by their exploiters" is greater organization and unity.[52] On their own initiative, the local MIR began to form connections between unions and neighborhood organizations, enacting the MIR's broader vision for *comandos comunales* that joined unions and all popular organizations in a given territory.[53]

The rapidly changing political situation did not alter the national MIR leader-ship's conviction that "the correlation of forces favors the workers," offering as evidence their expanded organizational capacities.[54] In a July 7, 1973, radio address, MIR general secretary Miguel Enriquez proclaimed, "The working class and the pueblo have put their political leaderships on notice: the struggle has left the hallways of Congress behind and does not allow for retreats or concessions. It is here and now when the vanguards, the leaders, and the parties will be tested in a trial by fire."[55] Enríquez warned MIR supporters that "the days ahead will be decisive," and urged workers "to consolidate their conquests and attain new ones, to demand a revolutionary and determined leadership, [and] to reject the retreat of vacillating leaders."[56] The days ahead, however, presented new obstacles. Even as grassroots MIR activists worked to build new autonomous grassroots organizations, including cordones industriales, coordinating committees, and comandos comunales, these efforts in Concepción province remained in the preliminary stages between July and September 1973. They proved no match for an emboldened counterrevolution that moved closer to a military solution.

Acting on the advice of General Carlos Prats, President Allende ratified the opposition-sponsored arms control law, which gave the Chilean Armed Forces the discretionary authority to search and seize weapons from the general population. Peter Winn has argued that the application of the law served the dual purpose of intimidating Allende supporters and acclimating conscript soldiers—often drawn from poor sectors—to the abuse of fellow citizens.[57] Following the failed coup attempt in June 1973, the armed forces began to apply the law, carrying out raids in factories and working-class neighborhoods across Chile. They found few arms, but the savagery of their actions, directed almost exclusively at leftist supporters, raised concern across the Left. By late July, provincial CUT president Juan Bautista Bravo requested meetings with Governor Fernando Alvárez (PC) and General Washington Carrasco Fernández and Rear Admiral Jorge Paredes Wetzel, commanding officers of Concepción's Third Army Division and Talcahuano's Second Navy Zone, respectively. Bravo conveyed the CUT's "concern over the procedures used to search industries," citing the navy's particularly violent treatment. He protested "the methods used and their lack of respect for workers."[58] In tandem with expanded grassroots organizing, local people affiliated with the MIR in Concepción province experienced new forms of targeted repression in the coming months.

"THE REVOLUTIONARY AND POPULAR COUNTEROFFENSIVE," JUNE–JULY 1973

When the opposition strategy to unseat Allende at the polls failed in March 1973, the MIR warned that the dominant class would seek to defeat Allende and Chile's popular movements by force. In response, the MIR's general secretary declared that the moment for the Popular Unity's peaceful transition to socialism had passed. It was now time "to launch a revolutionary and popular counteroffensive."[59] The path would not be easy. Before a packed audience in Santiago's Teatro Caupolicán in July 1973, Miguel Enríquez asserted, "Compañeros, we are in one of the most important and difficult moments of the workers' struggle. Going forward history will open the paths to victory or defeat." He urged that "the people must prepare themselves to resist, to fight, and to win."[60]

As part of the MIR's new national strategy to open a revolutionary counteroffensive, the Central Committee sent members from the Fuerza Central (Central Force), the MIR's clandestine military wing, to Concepción in mid-1973 to design a military strategy for the region. Among this group was Héctor Jego, the engineering student who had aided the toma and creation of Campamento Lenin in May 1970.[61] Reflecting back on his return to Concepción, Jego explained that in the MIR "we knew that at some point the reaction would carry out a coup against the Popular Unity government, and we had to be prepared to resist this coup and defeat it. In the process of preparing, we looked for ways to build strength."[62] True to the MIR's propensity for internal studies, the Fuerza Central compiled copious amounts of information on "points of interest, centers of power, military activity, [and] the preparation [MIR] members would have" in Concepción.[63] As a long-time frontier, Concepción had always had a substantial military presence. In 1973, the Third Army Division was garrisoned inside the city, blocks from the University of Concepción, at the Chacabuco barracks, and the Second Navy Zone was headquartered in Talcahuano's port.[64]

In early July, the local opposition press obtained copies of the MIR's secret study.[65] On July 8, 1973, El Sur ran a front-page exposé on "Operación Comando," chronicling the 120-page report on the MIR's organizational and military capacity in Concepción province.[66] According to Héctor Jego, who had helped to write it, the report represented "a fairly precise definition of what we wanted to do."[67] Although El Sur's "discovery of a vast plan by extremists" made for sensational headlines, the actual information it contained revealed the limited extent of the MIR's military capacity in Concepción. For example, the internal MIR report assessed GPM-1 as "one of the best organized" structures in the city, yet only five of its sixty-five members had "basic or special knowledge of military operations."[68] In at least one case, this prior knowledge consisted of a MIR militant's completion at age eighteen of the Chilean Armed Forces' obligatory military service the summer before he enrolled at the University of Concepción.[69] In Concepción province, where the MIR had proportionally the largest following in the country, only twenty-six MIR militants had at least some military training. The movement's total arsenal amounted to thirty-seven firearms—of which twenty were 9mm Walter 38 pistols—a standard issue World War II pistol used by the Chilean Armed Forces.[70]

The MIR's efforts to provide minimal military training for its militants began very late. In June 1973, poblador turned revolutionary Carlos Robles was on the verge of returning to Cuba to complete his second period of military training.[71] Following the Tanquetazo in Santiago on June 29, the trip was called off, and Robles and the other MIR militants selected for the trip "returned home to their workplaces and their mass fronts." Robles explained, "My front was pobladores in Penco."[72] As the only MIR militant in Penco with any military training, Robles began to give basic instruction on how to fire a gun to other miristas and pobladores in the area in July 1973.[73]

In preparation for a MIR conference to be held in Concepción in late July, the region's midlevel leaders met to discuss the military plan designed by the Fuerza Central. Mario Garcés from the GPM-1 leadership characterized this meeting with other MIR leaders in Concepción as "pretty disastrous."[74] For Garcés, the discussion "revealed the precariousness of the MIR in Concepción to confront a coup." From the outset, the MIR's contingency plan for a coup acknowledged that with "neither our own military force nor sufficient capacity to mobilize socially the city of Concepción cannot be defended, and so Concepción would not resist. The military, navy, and air forces already stationed in the region would take over, and our only viable strategy was to make a stand in the coal zone." Under this plan, the task assigned to the three MIR structures inside the city and university was "to create diversionary tactics to keep the enemy forces occupied" long enough to allow others to retreat to the coal zone and launch the resistance. A central part of this plan hinged on defending the only point of access to the coal zone: the two-kilometer-long bridge over the Bío Bío River. Faced with both the enormity and the improbability of this task, the conversation took a turn toward "the absurd, ending almost in a joking manner, with skepticism, and no small amount of impotence." Garcés recalled leaving the meeting "in a bad place emotionally." "It was one of the moments in the MIR when I was most depressed," he said. "I felt I was putting in a tremendous effort, and what we proposed to do paled in seriousness before the possibility of what could happen. No matter how much time and energy we invested, in the end, the national situation made the future uncertain."[75] It was not uncertainty alone that troubled him but the MIR's own inconsistency between its combative revolutionary discourse and its weak military preparation.

The failed coup attempt in late June gave urgency to the question of the Left's real military capabilities. These discussions within the MIR prompted in some militants a tacit recognition that "the MIR's military capability was nonexistent."[76] In Concepción province, several regional and midlevel MIR leaders perceived the growing gap between the rhetoric of revolutionary breakthrough and the real capacity of the MIR to respond to a military coup.[77] After the June Tanquetazo, when the MIR failed "to fuse with the workers' movement," FTR union leader Alejandro Alarcón concluded, "There was nothing more for me to do with the

MIR," and he quietly left the party.[78] Similarly, the Tanquetazo coupled with the growing number of military-led raids (*allanamientos*) against local factories shook Enzo La Mura's confidence in the MIR. "I did not see the situation as lost in Chile until almost the end," he admitted.

> Until June 1973, I shared the official [MIR] vision of the possibility to keep going forward [and] to find a favorable resolution for the popular sectors. But when the Tanquetazo happened, [and] was resolved with amnesty for the pro-coup military officials and the application of the arms control law, which delivered systematic blows against workers, pobladores, and peasants, I said to myself, "It's over."[79]

From that moment forward, La Mura, who had been an "officialist," stopped being a party man. His disillusionment with the MIR leadership would deepen in the weeks ahead. The experiences of Alejandro Alarcón and Enzo La Mura reveal how MIR militants navigated a turbulent revolutionary process that appeared unable to turn back the reactionary anti-Allende forces. The June 1973 failed coup attempt defeated La Mura months before the September 11, 1973, coup that brought Augusto Pinochet to power.

Meanwhile, midlevel militants in the provinces, who were largely isolated from internal power struggles, experienced this process of questioning in contradictory ways. For Mario Garcés in the GPM-1 leadership in Concepción's Barrio Norte, the distance between his own hesitancy about the military plan and its chances for success directly contradicted the optimistic vision advanced by national MIR leaders. He reflected that the "emphasis on proving your militancy made it difficult to disagree—not only with a specific orientation, but also with the larger project. To appear critical was equated with a lack of enthusiasm" for the revolutionary project.[80] After all, Miguel Enríquez, the MIR's general secretary, continually reminded miristas that "determination and courage" were the most "essential conditions" to ensure victory.[81] Garcés, unable to reconcile the difference between what he perceived as reality and what he was told was within reach, remained silent and disciplined: "I lived that final period very conflicted, with an intense inner dialogue, and I lived it alone."[82] While midlevel militants like Garcés immersed themselves in "the all-consuming daily existence as a militant," regional leaders like La Mura could also not openly acknowledge their skepticism about MIR preparations. La Mura admitted that he could only talk openly "with a few people in the coal zone because in reality the national MIR leadership imposed their interpretations."[83]

In the absence of open discussion within the party, the conflict between Santiago and Concepción leaders was manifested indirectly. After the Tanquetazo, the national MIR leadership sent two trusted MIR militants—Sergio Pérez and Ricardo Ruz—"to control and to reinforce" the presence of the Central Committee in Concepción.[84] This "intervention" of the Concepción MIR leadership was never acknowledged by national leaders or widely known in Concepción, even by members of the MIR Regional Committee. As former UdeC students from the earliest generation of MIR militants, their return to Concepción was not unusual, nor did Pérez and Ruz enter into open public conflict with the regional leaders. This indirect intervention was acknowledged only in whispers and rumors and never in "a process of ample and open discussion within the party" over the differences separating the regional and national leaderships.[85]

On the first anniversary of the Concepción People's Assembly, the MIR staged a public celebration of the official party line. Edgardo Enríquez arrived in Concepción to deliver a speech commemorating the Cuban Revolution's 26 of July Movement.[86] He echoed the Political Commission's optimistic interpretation of the national political situation and the balance of power as favoring workers and their allies. It was time, he concluded, for their final assault on power. In a private meeting, "to interpret the Tanquetazo" for regional leaders, Enríquez assured them that "we are close to a revolutionary breakthrough."[87] Longtime regional MIR leader Pedro Enríquez Barra recalled that "Edgardo Enríquez advanced a position that essentially advocated directly confronting the military."[88] To that end, he had convened the Concepción leadership to discuss the MIR's regional military plans, the same ones revealed just weeks earlier in the local press.

While Miguel Enríquez largely went unchallenged at the National Conference in February 1973, this was no longer the case by July 1973. No sooner had Miguel's brother Edgardo Enríquez concluded his presentation than a member of the regional leadership openly contradicted him. This time the voice of dissent came from the Argentine sociologist Néstor D'Alessio, who had recently been demoted from leadership of the GPM-2. Following a period of personal inner turmoil, Mario Garcés was relieved when D'Alessio spoke out: "This meeting was very important for me because it was the first time a party intellectual put a name on things."[89] The sociology professor took the floor and in front of the Political Commission representative laid out three alternatives for the MIR:

> The first was the official party line—the popular revolutionary counteroffensive—which in [his] judgment was unviable. Although it made some sense, with so little time the MIR would not be capable of confronting a coup d'etat, and so this position must be reevaluated. Civil war was the second alternative, which had a better chance for success if it produced a division within the armed forces. Even so, a reformist [Popular Unity] leadership was likely to continue, and the example of the Spanish Civil War was sufficiently graphic about the fate of a civil war with reformist leadership.[90]

D'Alessio's third alternative was prescient in warning that a coup was possible. He called on the MIR to start "a systematic preparation for the coup, which, among other things, required moving the party underground."[91] This intervention before a meeting of regional and midlevel MIR leaders marked the most public articulation of the Concepción leadership's dissenting perspective on Chile's political situation. His conclusion that the MIR should prepare immediately for a clandestine existence caught many of those present off guard. As Mario Garcés related, "This was a surprising proposal. We had been so caught up living in the moment, working against time in the logic of popular power—reinforcing social organizations, creating new connections, generating relationships between workers, students, and pobladores—that we had little room left to see the big picture."[92]

The MIR's work as an aboveground, mass party during the Popular Unity years meant that a clandestine existence could not easily be arranged for their several thousand militants, let alone for the workers, pobladores, peasants, and students who filled the ranks of the MIR's mass fronts.[93] Unlike the Communist Party, which had already survived a decade underground in the mid-twentieth century, the MIR, a political organization with less than seven years of existence, lacked precedent and prior preparation for a clandestine existence. The party's top leaders, Miguel Enríquez and the university reform generation of Concepción students turned national leaders, had not yet turned thirty. For a midlevel militant in his early twenties like Mario Garcés, who had silently begun to doubt whether "the MIR's official party line pushing revolution was sustainable," Néstor D'Alessio's sociological gaze at the "totality of factors" offered a critical perspective that had so often been suppressed by the internal party hierarchy. "I perceived then," reflected Garcés, "that as much as we fought against time, in the end, the situation was becoming more and more complex. The only response from the [MIR] leadership was to demand more effort, more commitment, more hours." The leaders' demands, however, were not "accompanied by an analysis, or by proposals that explained to us why this approach made sense, and whether or not we would actually be able to confront the coup by these means."[94]

This analytical discussion did not happen in July 1973. The conflict between the national and regional MIR leadership "became prolonged and was not resolved."[95] The Central Committee's only response was to send trusted confidants Sergio Pérez and Ricardo Ruz to Concepción after the Tanquetazo. Neither the regional MIR leaders nor the MIR bases in Concepción ever knew what their official role was within the party. Sometime in August 1973, the Central Committee suspended Mires and D'Alessio from the regional leadership—yet their suspension was unknown even to other local leaders.

Although sectors within the MIR leadership in Concepción recognized the need for a different strategy, they failed to advance an alternative in any meaningful way. For his part, Manuel Vergara manifested his dissenting opinions based on experiences in Concepción to the Central Committee, but he then misrepresented the Central Committee's policy prescriptions to regional MIR leaders. The criticism of the national leadership by Vergara, Mires, and D'Alessio never gained traction with the MIR. Nor did the regional leaders' attempt in Concepción to consolidate public support for a different strategy. The regional leadership's misgivings about the MIR's national strategy might have found wider support in the bases had they attempted to articulate it clearly. Vergara, Mires, and D'Alessio did not make allies with regional leaders like Enzo La Mura, who had become increasingly skeptical of the national party line. In the end, by August 1973, with no clear alternative, the MIR's regional leadership was deeply divided.

In early August 1973, building on the expanded organizing in the cordones industriales, the CUT in Concepción called for a massive march in support of Allende's government.[96] As in previous public demonstrations by the Left in Concepción province, the MIR's participation that day was never in doubt. Prior to the march, the regional MIR leaders had met, and Vergara designated La Mura, the MIR's regional coordinator for the Revolutionary Workers Front, to speak for the MIR at the rally. La Mura refused. Perceiving the situation as lost, he was simply at a loss for words. Instead of trying to take the now skeptical La Mura on as an ally, Vergara responded with scathing criticism. Yet Vergara did not volunteer to speak in La Mura's place.

'NO, WE HAVE TO WIN": THE WEIGHT OF THE VANGUARD PARTY, AUGUST 9, 1973

On the morning of August 9, 1973, twenty-one-year old Mario Garcés left his house early. The Concepción labor federation rally that day promised to be one of the province's largest.[97] As the second in command of the MIR's GPM-1, Garcés had the task of turning out MIR supporters in Concepción for the event. With two small Citroëns outfitted with loudspeakers, Garcés and another compañero traversed the city: "Starting at 7:00 in the morning, we passed through every neighborhood in Concepción, inviting people, passing out materials, and making contact with our [MIR] bases, with our [social] leaders."[98] Along the western edge of the city, the road to Talcahuano was already filled with workers from the steel mill and petroleum refineries marching with their hard hats—a sea of bobbing colors in the distance. Hugo Monsalves, MIR medical student and participant in the Coronel bakery takeover, arrived by bus, disembarking across the river in San Pedro.[99] As a demonstration of "the strength of the organized masses," the coal miners and their families marched from San Pedro across the two-kilometer-long bridge and into the city center.

By the afternoon, the 25,000 marchers converged on the central plaza outside the UdeC Theater, the site of the People's Assembly the year before. Pro–Popular Unity local newspaper *Diario Color* interviewed several participants to ask what the rally meant to them. A thirty-seven-year-old housewife and pobladora, Delfina Riquelme Riquelme, explained, "I am here in response to the call from the CUT to defend our President. I came today, because if I hadn't it would have been giving up and allowing the retreat of the revolution; I am here to condemn the fascists."[100]

Meanwhile, thirty-three-year-old worker Julio Mora Hidalgo answered simply, "I came to defend the rights obtained by the workers and to defeat the anti-patria that does not want to allow our government to advance."[101] FTR textile worker from Bellavista-Tomé, Nicanor Ibáñez, was moved by what he saw as he stood in the plaza: "For hours and hours people marched. They had come from all over— from Curanilahue, Lota, Coronel, Tomé, Chillán. It was an incredible sight to see that march with no beginning and no end."[102] Similarly, Mario Garcés remembered the sense of possibility in that moment. From the Citroën, megaphone in hand, Garcés led a series of MIR chants in the plaza: "It was amazing to be there before thousands of people, to have them respond to your calls, and to hear the workers and the masses shout "Power to the People! [¡Al poder!]."[103] Nicanor Ibáñez quoted one chant: "In the next march, we will have rifles!"[104]

The experience of witnessing thousands of people in the streets in August 1973 proved just as inspiring as it had the year before during the Concepción People's Assembly. Poblador and MIR militant Carlos Robles, who had come from Penco for the march, recalled his optimism in that moment: "I believed we were going to win. With the last march in Concepción, I had faith that we would win. It was a sea of people, and so I said to myself, 'No, we have to win.'"[105] Even Mario Garcés, filled with misgivings after the disastrous discussion of the MIR's regional military plan, regained some of his lost confidence that day.[106] He chastised himself for doubting: "Inwardly I felt almost like a little bourgeois, and I said to myself, 'Here is a lesson in front of you, before your own eyes, of a people so active, completely mobilized.'"[107] Garcés reasoned, even "if the party [the MIR] does not have the capabilities, the people are here, they are mobilized, and there is sufficient social force in this leftist city to generate some kind of resistance."[108] The revolutionary potential of the Chilean people manifested itself in sustained collective mobilization.

For these grassroots activists in the MIR, the 25,000-person march on August 9, 1973, offered affirmation of how far they had come in a few short years.[109] More people than ever turned out to affirm their support of Allende's government and Chile's revolution. By August 1973, MIR activists could point to unprecedented levels of participation and political mobilization as dividends of their grassroots organizing work centered on the direct empowerment of local people. The everyday revolutions had challenged local power relations and generated cross-class collective action. They had shaken the foundations of Chilean society. Yet these local processes of social transformation were not necessarily a revolution that could seize state power. The distance separating "taking state power" and "power to the people" soon became clear. The thousands of demonstrators converged on the central plaza only to find an empty stage.

In the midst of leading chants, Mario Garcés looked to "Manuel Vergara and other members of the regional leadership . . . to designate someone to give the MIR's main speech in the plaza." Yet the stage was empty. Garcés recalled his sense of confusion and uncertainty: "I felt orphaned, not understanding what was happening and why the MIR regional leadership did not take a more active role in the middle of this rally, with so many people mobilized." His responsibilities for the march had been to rally people: "I could not speak [on stage] and offer my perception of the facts."[110] The concentration of power within the MIR meant that midlevel leaders did not feel they had any authority to speak on behalf of the party.

Eventually his party superior, Carlos Rioseco, appeared and informed Garcés that the regional leadership was not going to speak and the march should proceed to the small plaza near the train station. While one portion of the rally turned toward the central market place to listen to speeches by Popular Unity figures, including FEC president Enrique Sepulveda (PS) and CUT president Juan Bautista Bravo (PC), Mario Garcés led MIR supporters to the train station, where FTR national leader and Bellavista-Tomé worker Alejandro Alarcón addressed the gathering.[111] Although Alarcón's speech "had at the very least given the MIR a visible voice at the rally," it was by and large a rehearsal of stock slogans rather than a political analysis. Garcés reflected, "We needed someone to get up there and give us instructions for the coup."[112] One of the largest popular rallies in Concepción ended without political leadership. Internal conflict between Santiago and Concepción leaders produced a rift that incapacitated local leaders. Going forward from this critical moment, the initiative for action came not from the leadership—the vanguard had disintegrated—but from the bases, who in circumstances not of their own making acted to carry forward their vision of justice in the present.

"IN TOMÉ, THE STORES DO NOT CLOSE": THE COUP AGAINST SOCIETY, AUGUST 21, 1973, 2:00 P.M.

Most scholarly treatments identify the August 22, 1973, ratification of the congressional vote declaring that Allende's government had violated the constitution as sealing the fate of Chile's socialist experiment.[113] The breakdown of the Chilean political system opened the door for military action against a democratically elected president whom Congress no longer recognized as legitimate. In Concepción province, however, the coup arrived the previous day. In response to two massive public demonstrations in Tomé and Concepción on August 21, the Chilean Navy and Army occupied the province and "never left."[114] The assault three weeks later on the Chilean presidential palace, La Moneda, thus was not the beginning but the culmination of the counterrevolution.

In late July, the Chilean Chamber of Commerce launched a new wave of strikes that promised to "shut down the economy as long as necessary to secure Allende's removal."[115] On August 21, the small business owners' federation called on its associates to adhere to a 48-hour strike.[116] The Tomé CUT warned that if shopkeepers closed, the workers would take to the streets and "open the stores by force."[117] When downtown shopkeepers shuttered their stores, the local labor federation kept its word.[118] No sooner had the textile factory whistles sounded than thousands of workers and townspeople filled Tomé's central streets. The widely shared attitude, as one MAPU member explained, was that "in Tomé, the stores do not close, the sirens will sound, and the people will go open them."[119] Local MIR leaders Miguel Ángel Catalán Febrero and Héctor Lepe Moraga were among those who had shown up ready for action, wire cutters in hand.[120] Their attitude emboldened others.

Much like the Coronel bakery takeover in January 1973, "the day we opened the shops" remains one of the most emblematic memories of the Popular Unity years for Tomé residents. "People still talk about it," remarked retired Bellavista worker Juan Reyes. "At first no one dared, but everyone wanted to."[121] Textile worker Eulogio Sanhueza, who years earlier had founded the MIR in Tomé, added, "It was the only time everyone got together with one single objective."[122] Not only were the textile unions and the entire spectrum of leftist political parties—the PC, PS, MAPU, and MIR—all present, but it appeared that "the entire town of Tomé" had turned out to show "what the people wanted."[123] As Sanhueza explained, "We opened the stores with all the people, everyone, the unions, [the parties], and left the owners inside to wait on people."[124]

As a demonstration of an organized people's power, the action in Tomé was effective. Only three businesses had their locks opened by force, and within two hours all three dozen shops had reopened. The demonstrators stationed guards to protect the stores; in many instances, the owners themselves opted to unlock their doors.[125] Even the opposition press conceded that there had been no looting in Tomé that day. The demonstrators did not ask for state intervention to expropriate the stores. Nor, as in the case of the Coronel bakery, did Tomé residents take over and run the shops themselves. In Eulogio Sanhueza's words, the textile workers and their families "opened the stores so that the owners would wait on them."[126] Guided by a sense of popular justice coupled with an abiding respect for private property, the textile workers "decided to make [obligar]" the stores open so that "in this way [the owners would] fulfill their obligation to provide services to the community."[127] Through collective action, Tomé's working-class residents sought recognition as equals.

Under Allende's government, the nationalization of the textile factories had brought higher employment and growing incomes for Tomé residents. The buying power of Chilean workers had never been greater. The shopkeepers in Tomé were not large businessmen. Jorge González, who had joined the MIR as a student in Tomé in 1968, reflected, "They disagreed with Allende's government, but they had guaranteed sales. The workers were earning good money and shopped at their stores, so the owners could hardly say they were not doing well."[128] Seen in this light, the action was not a declaration of class warfare against the owners but a petition that as workers they be allowed to enjoy the fruits of their labor. Yet, unlike in the past, Tomé residents did not wait for authorities to accede to their request. They took to the streets to ensure its compliance. They made a stand collectively, where individually they might not have done so, and found a boldness within themselves. The day's events seemed to be confirmation that willpower and collective action would be sufficient to resolve problems peacefully and justly.

In August 1973, Tomé residents transformed the cry for people's power into palpable collective action. They were not alone. All across Concepción province in August 1973 the extent to which everyday revolutions had been internalized was manifest in autonomous, day-to-day efforts to generate creative solutions to immediate problems. Faced with another Bosses' Lockout in the transportation sector, pobladores in Penco's Ho Chi Minh campamento requisitioned a bus to ensure residents' continued transportation to Concepción.[129] Students soon commandeered university-owned vehicles to "put them at the service of the people."[130] In a demonstration of "working-class solidarity to confront the aggression of the fascists," workers from three local industries collaborated through cordones industriales to protect drivers and vehicles transporting coal from the National Coal Company (ENACAR) in Lota and Coronel to the ceramics factory in Penco and the bottling plant in Costanera.[131] As workers held assemblies to debate production plans for 1974, many local unions took out newspaper ads proclaiming, "Participation Is Popular Power!"[132] In Concepción's Barrio Norte, pobladores and workers set up barricades around their neighborhood as a symbolic celebration of territorial autonomy.[133] A four-hundred-person price control board assembly in Talcahuano's Las Higueras neighborhood unanimously denounced "the daily acts of terrorism by ultra-right groups against workers," a reference to an escalating series of dynamite attacks on union leaders' homes and the local power grid.[134] The pobladores called on authorities to prosecute "the seditious leaders of the transportation strike" and the ultra-right groups "to the fullest extent of the law."[135]

During July and August 1973, under the pretext of looking for illegal weapons, the number of military-led raids on factories and working-class neighborhoods in Concepción province rose at an alarming rate. The MIR nationally and in Concepción province responded to these attacks with a propaganda campaign directed at Chile's conscript army. Slogans such as "Soldiers, do not fire on your brothers!" and "Soldiers, disobey the officers who incite a coup!" began to appear on buildings around the city.[136] After several MIR-affiliated students and a university drama instructor were arrested for distributing "seditious" flyers and charged with violating the Law for Internal State Security, grassroots organizations like the Las Higueras JAP and the Barrio Norte coordinating committee came to their defense, calling on authorities "to act more directly in favor of the people."[137]

The myriad popular mobilizations in Concepción province in August reflected how much Chilean society had changed during the intervening years. Even as the Chilean Left's major utopian projects—Allende's peaceful path to socialism and the MIR's proletarian revolution—appeared increasingly embattled, popular sectors continued to mobilize in ways that defended their vision of equality and justice in the present. While there were a few instances of acts against private property— stores had their locks broken, buses were commandeered, walls were covered in political slogans—these collective actions largely rejected violence. The revolution from below in Concepción province, as in the rest of Chile, was marked by the absence of violent revenge against individuals.[138]

As the Paños Oveja textile workers in Tomé declared in August, "In its long history of struggle, the working class has never used terrorist methods. On the contrary, the reactionary classes are the ones who have massacred workers and who now watch in desperation as the people advance with their government."[139] Socialist Party regional secretary Rafael Merino echoed these sentiments, noting it was not members of the Left but the Far Right who had assassinated two high-ranking military officials. Merino concluded that the "political action . . . of the entire Left is not conspiratorial" but instead seeks "to develop the strength of the people to create the conditions for this country to be governed by workers."[140] In the face of mounting counterrevolutionary violence—whether sabotage by the Far Right or violent raids by the military—the grassroots Left and their political leaders steadfastly sought strength in the will of a peaceful but organized people.

"TO DEFEND THE RIGHTS OF EVERY HUMAN": CONCEPCIÓN, AUGUST 21, 1973, 6:00 P.M.

By late afternoon on August 21, the crowds had dispersed from Tomé's downtown and the businesses had reopened. Meanwhile in Concepción, a third People's Assembly was getting under way inside the university theater on the central plaza. Although only the July 27, 1972, event was formally designated as the Asamblea del Pueblo de Concepción, in local memory Concepción had three People's Assemblies. The first, on May 12, 1972, demonstrated the strength of popular mobilization in the region. The improvised rally on campus and march on the city center exceeded political leaders' expectations. In response, regional political leaders organized the second People's Assembly on July 27 to project an alternative vision of power, one that proved unsustainable in the national political climate. Convened in late August 1973 to denounce human rights violations, this final People's Assembly presaged a darker future.

On August 10, 1973, Rear Admiral Jorge Paredes Wetzel announced that the Chilean Navy had arrested on charges of sedition several civilian workers at the Talcahuano Navy Yard (ASMAR) and sailors stationed at the Talcahuano Naval Base.[141] Soon the Socialist Party, the MAPU, and the MIR were implicated in an alleged plot to infiltrate the Chilean Armed Forces.[142] Secret meetings between civilian employees and national leftist leaders had indeed occurred, yet the initiative came not from above as a left-wing political conspiracy but from below. After low-ranking sailors and civilian workers overheard their superiors discussing a coup, they wanted to take action. They "decided to organize to defend Allende's government. They were not miristas or socialists, but leftist people who wanted to defend the constitutional government and, in particular, [President] Allende."[143] These everyday people placed in extraordinary circumstances sought guidance and support from leftitst political leaders. None of these behind-the-scenes efforts were known in August 1973.

Almost immediately, however, reports surfaced on August 10, 1973, that Talcahuano detainees had been tortured while in military custody.[144] Longtime MIR labor lawyer Pedro Enríquez Barra assumed the defense of the sailors and workers, but he along with their family members were continually denied access. The first substantiated reports of their condition came from the MIR regional secretary Manuel Vergara's teenage brothers, Pedro and René Vergara. They had been arrested during a navy-led raid on their apartment in Concepción and shared a cell with the sailors at the Talcahuano Naval Base.[145] Following their release on August 15, the brothers widely publicized the navy's use of torture against detained sailors.[146]

In response to this evolving situation, Concepción's key social organizations and regional leftist political leaders came together to form the Committee for the Defense of Human Rights in Chile.[147] The sponsors for the mass rally on August 21 included the University of Concepción's Consejo Superior, the student federation (FEC), the regional labor federation (CUT), the Concepción city cordon industrial, Christians for Socialism, the lawyers and attorneys union, and the pro-Allende Patriotic Front of Women and Professionals. The pillars of social justice in Concepción, the labor federation, the university, and the Catholic Church, all came together in the task of bearing witness and demonstrating solidarity "with the victims of arbitrary detentions and moral humiliations." The organizers called on the greater Concepción community to take a stand in defense "of the right of every human to have their legal personhood recognized" and to denounce all acts "that undermine the universal declaration of Human Rights."[148] Behind the scenes, regional party leaders from the PS, MAPU, and MIR, now joined by the Communist Party, mobilized their grassroots supporters for a massive turnout. The increasing frequency of military-led raids on local factories galvanized the wider Concepción community to express moral outrage over the abused sailors.

The August 1973 organizing of the human rights committee and the rally to defend the sailors was perhaps the regional MIR leadership's finest hour. In just eight years, the MIR had built a network of support among diverse constituents, which in turn had earned it a seat at the negotiation table with the regional Popular Unity. PS regional secretary Rafael Merino told reporters, "The MIR, without acknowledging it, has been in practice an ally of the Popular Unity, Allende's government, and its program."[149] This was certainly true of the MIR in Concepción province whose grassroots supporters collaborated in actions across the Left and whose leaders, on the basis of mutual respect, developed coordinated responses. Merino lamented that nationally the MIR had not "fully integrated with the Popular Unity coalition," noting that "sectarianism within the Left has inhibited the MIR from respecting the role that the Communists can play, and the Communists' sectarian attitude has not understood the role the MIR plays in the process."[150] The MIR's successful expansion in Concepción and its capacity for action derived from acting in alliance with a united Left. The human rights rally was no exception. In an open assembly, a range of speakers from grassroots organizations and political parties spoke, followed by the family members of the detained sailors and others who had recently been released from military detention. The rally concluded at 9:30 P.M. with the singing of the Chilean national anthem.[151]

"AFTERWARDS CAME THE REPRESSION":
CONCEPCIÓN PROVINCE, AUGUST 21, 1973, EVENING

In Concepción province, as in other regions in Chile, the military coup happened before September 11, 1973.[152] Opening the shops on August 21 marked a high point in Tomé for popular empowerment. Military repression followed. "From there everything started to go south [*quedar la escoba*]," explained Eulogio Sanhueza, "because we opened the shops and in the evening they sent the marines in. And they never left! It was as if they were getting ready for the coup here because Tomé was already occupied."[153] On the evening of August 21, Jorge González attended the human rights rally in Concepción. Upon exiting the theater, he said, "we were surrounded by police and military forces. The Third Army Division had cordoned off the entire plaza. Tear gas bombs exploded all around, shots rang out, and I tried desperately to escape from there, to disappear from the city center."[154] From the shops in Tomé to Concepción's central plaza in Concepción, Chileans in Concepción province feared—correctly—that they were under siege.

As a premonition of what followed, this last massive assembly occupies an outsized place in local memory. For many grassroots activists, the memory of the July 1972 People's Assembly has been transposed to this final rally in August 1973. Jorge González explained how the military repression made the entire experience of "the People's Assembly traumatic because we weren't expecting it. We didn't realize that the military was already trying to occupy the city."[155] One eyewitness reported fifty tear gas canisters being fired within five minutes, many of them directly into the theater.[156] For those trapped inside, the harrowing experience became etched in memory as "the first sign of what would follow."[157] The military dragged demonstrators from the theater "at bayonet point, forcing them to march with their hands on their head."[158] Then they made them stand with legs spread and hands against the walls of the regional government (Intendencia) for what seemed like an eternity, while soldiers patted them down in search of weapons they never found.[159] A total of 150 men and women were arrested that evening on charges of shouting insults at the military and failing to disperse immediately.[160] No one was spared. Nine students ended up in local hospitals, including the student federation vice president Jorge Ayala (MUI), who suffered a double fracture to his skull.[161]

In Concepción province, long known as a bastion of the Left, the local military commanders, General Washington Carrasco Fernández and Rear Admiral Jorge Paredes Wetzel, carried out their own "creeping coup," undercutting civilian rule weeks before September 11.[162] In response to the revived truckers' strikes and the escalating terrorist attacks by right-wing groups in early August, President Allende declared states of emergency in Concepción and other provinces and turned to the military to maintain order, as he had done during the 1972 Bosses' Lockout. On August 13, 1973, the Popular Unity government appointed Carrasco and Paredes jefes de plaza for Concepción and Tomé-Talcahuano, respectively, giving these local commanders centralized control over the national police and armed forces.[163] They used that authority to preemptively repress leftist supporters. When their coups on August 21 went unchecked by national authorities, military commanders acted with impunity in the weeks ahead to neutralize any possibility of regional resistance.[164]

"THEY CUT THE THREADS": CONCEPCIÓN PROVINCE, AUGUST 22 TO SEPTEMBER 11, 1973

In the prelude to a national coup, the military on August 21 in Concepción province consolidated its power through physical and symbolic violence. The following day, the marines raided the Paños Oveja textile union offices and the home of FTR Bellavista leader Raúl Moraga.[165] Police arrested local CUT president Jaime Sepúlveda (PC), the state-appointed general manager (*interventor*) of Paños Oveja Pedro Jorquera (MAPU), and a Paños Oveja socialist union leader.[166] Police used newspaper photographs from the August 21 demonstration to make additional arrests of suspected agitators. A few nights later, Juan Reyes was in the Bellavista-Tomé mill leading the workers' night watch. After the Bosses' Lockout in October 1972, Bellavista textile workers had formed a vigilance committee to protect their factory from acts of sabotage such as the arson that partially destroyed the Chiguayante-Caupolicán textile mill in November 1972. That night in late August 1973, recalled Reyes, two marines with bayonets fixed entered the factory. As they walked down the aisles past the looms, "they cut the threads" one by one. When Reyes came forward to confront them, demanding to know "what they were doing," they answered, "We want to know if the blades are sharp enough."[167] By destroying the textiles on the looms, the marines affirmed their power with didactic counterrevolutionary violence.

A concerted propaganda campaign that accompanied the military's actions contributed to the perception of a "climate of violence" under Allende's leadership.

On August 22, the day after the surprise attacks, local and national opposition media, including radio and television, devoted ample coverage to events in Tomé and Concepción, portraying the demonstrations as acts of violence and applauding the military repression that stopped them. *El Sur* gushed, "In a spectacular operation, military troops and police repressed the disturbances provoked by MIR, MAPU, and PS elements" inside the university theater.[168] The conservative Concepción daily, *La Crónica,* described how the array of speakers at the "human rights show" had "unloaded their artillery, concentrating their fire on the armed forces and the 'reactionary and pro-coup officer corps.'"[169] With the "mission to stop street demonstrations by miristas," the Third Army Regiment arrived to cordon off the plaza. Under the headline, "The MIR Got a Taste of Its Own Medicine," *La Crónica* reported, "[MIR militants] preached violence and called for civil war, for revolution, and for the conquest of power by force. Last night they found out . . . that the armed forces are a serious thing, with men [who] are made for war. To kill or be killed, not to fulfill police orders."[170] Already by late August 1973, the opposition press welcomed military repression.[171]

With thinly veiled class prejudice, the opposition media portrayed demonstrating Tomé workers as subhuman "hordes," "mobs," and "lumpen," manipulated by political leaders, singling out Communist labor federation president Jaime Sepúlveda.[172] The number of broken locks jumped from three confirmed cases to reports ranging from twenty-two to thirty-five affected businesses. Before an image of impending chaos, *La Crónica* offered a narrative of salvation: "These true hordes arrived with crowbars in hand, ready to destroy the metal curtains protecting the shops and thus prepare for an eventual night of pillage. Fortunately, this was impeded by the arrival of the marines sent in by Rear Admiral Jorge Paredes Wetzel."[173] Behind the shrill language is an open affirmation that only military intervention can restore an inverted social order. The everyday revolutions that promised to transform the foundations of Chilean society had shaken political and economic elites, whose decades of rule had been predicated on the subordination of Chile's popular classes. The media portrayals justified preemptive violence to reverse perceived transgressions against the social hierarchy.

The opposition media actively promoted visions of chaos and impending leftist violence—whether the MIR's radical rhetoric or the working class's presumed propensity for thievery—that could be used to persuade powerful institutions and leaders to put a stop to Chile's democratic experiment with socialism. Indeed, less than a week later, on August 25, 1973, Concepción again made national headlines. Only this time there was no precipitating popular mobilization, only fabricated headlines. During a raid in Talcahuano, *El Mercurio*'s correspondent in Concepción reported that the navy had uncovered an "enormous extremist arsenal."[174] At the time, the pro–Popular Unity newspaper, *Diario Color,* debunked the story by interviewing the home owner, who had surrendered two hunting rifles with expired permits and was dumbfounded by the alleged discovery of assault rifles and other light artillery.[175] By then, however, the story had been repeated dozens of times in other newspapers and on the radio. It marked the debut of "Plan Z," a propaganda campaign that swept the country in September and October 1973, warning of an impending "auto-coup" by Allende supporters to murder non-Marxist Chileans.[176] By 8:50 A.M. on September 11, 1973, the military had secured Concepción, Chile's third largest city; at 11:00 A.M., four Hawker Hunter jets took off from Concepción's El Carriel airport destined for La Moneda.

Epilogue

The Meaning and Memory of Radical Politics
in the Twenty-First Century

"I want you to understand this: we didn't change power relations, but we changed the Chilean people," retired textile worker Juan Reyes affirmed. Popular empowerment experienced in the moment as the transformation of subjectivities and the overturning of social hierarchies is a fundamental dimension of any revolutionary project. As Reyes explained, "people changed" during the Popular Unity years: "They were no longer content to be little people because they wanted to be more than that. Someone had opened their eyes, and now they could open [the eyes of] others."[1] Decades later, oral histories reveal that grassroots activism associated with the MIR empowered people to imagine a different role for themselves in society, and it is this story that lives on in local popular memory.

The enduring meaning of radical politics at the grassroots level invites us to consider the longer-term outcomes of activist mobilization beyond the immediate political defeats. Contained within a Cold War framework, most histories of Chile's revolution end with the September 11, 1973, military coup. The tragedy of that moment and subsequent years of violent repression made revisiting this era difficult. "I never had heard of Plan Z [before the coup]," Reyes said earnestly the first time we met. Initially, few Chileans believed the allegations that left-wing radicals had been plotting to kill several thousand non-Marxist Chileans. On September 10, 1973, few could imagine the violence that counterrevolutionary forces were prepared to unleash against Salvador Allende and his supporters. Yet with time, as the military junta consolidated its hold on power and a culture of fear took root, many Chileans started to give Plan Z greater credence: the sheer scale of brutality needed an explanation, a narrative to make sense of the unimaginable.[2]

Playing on fears of revolutionary violence and the rhetoric of the Marxist Left that endorsed armed struggle in the 1960s, Plan Z worked its way into the fabric of Chilean memory, justifying seventeen years of authoritarian rule as necessary to save the country from Marxist subversives, foremost among them the Movimiento de Izquierda Revolucionaria.

The vitriolic language of Plan Z press reports in August 1973 prefigured the campaign of extermination launched against the MIR by the military regime and its newly created secret police (DINA). Between 1973 and 1975, more than 400 MIR militants were detained and disappeared, or summarily executed. The secret police then set their sights on the Socialists and Communists. With genocidal precision, state agents assassinated more than 3,200 Chilean citizens in a campaign to eradicate leftist political culture from Chile.[3]

The August 1973 press coverage in Concepción province reflected the deep-seated anxiety and class prejudices that welcomed military intervention as necessary to right a social order overturned. The massive, systematic violation of human rights under General Augusto Pinochet's rule went beyond killing. More than 38,000 Chilean citizens passed through the regime's clandestine torture centers and survived; an additional 100,000 were tortured during raids (allanmientos) on their working-class neighborhoods.[4] Leftist militants or those sympathetic to leftist politics were often not high-level leaders but local people. The majority of political prisoners did not report formal political affiliations with the MIR or any other leftist party. As the urban and rural poor, their social class marked them as "other," just as the exercise of their historical agency in the 1960s and 1970s posed a threat to the status quo.

Scholars have widely debunked Plan Z as a regime fabrication, but its staying power for many Chileans meant that even four decades later, Juan Reyes felt the need to refute it. As Peter Winn has noted, revolutionary restraint characterized much of the Marxist and non-Marxist Chilean Left during the late sixties and early seventies.[5] Instead, it was those with a monopoly on power and force—the Chilean Armed Forces and their civilian supporters, encouraged by the U.S. government and military—who chose to use that force not just against political parties and a state-led transition to socialism, but Chilean society as a whole.

Decades of political and social repression in Chile succeeded in dismantling the physical sites that had bolstered leftist political culture—universities, shantytowns, factories, and unions—but it failed to dismantle the meaning of everyday revolutions for local activists. Forty years later, most of the young people and students who joined the revolutionary Left in Concepción are working in the fields of education, health care, and social work. Some completed advanced degrees in exile and returned to Concepción after 1990 as faculty members to reopen the sociology major that had been shut down by the dictatorship. Disrupted first by political activism and then by repression, others waited decades to complete their studies, with the assistance of government scholarships for former political prisoners. Many remain active in groups of former political prisoners, fighting to ensure access to adequate health care and to create local human rights memorials.

Though most are not members of political parties, they continue to identify as miristas. As a worker in Barrio Norte stated proudly, "I will die a mirista. It is something that I still carry inside of me."[6] The political education acquired within the MIR continues to inform how many engage with the world. "I never stopped being a militant. The experience I had as a MIR militant, and forming other militants, was beautiful," noted a health care worker from Tomé. He continued, "Some people might [be critical and] say that today I have nothing [to show for my activism][,] . . . but everything I have, who I am, I owe to the party."[7] People often refer to this ethical commitment as the "cultura mirista" to differentiate varying degrees of involvement with formal politics from ongoing social and cultural community engagement.[8] "What I learned in the MIR is still relevant today," reflected a social worker in her hometown of Coronel, "not just then, but now. I still believe in the need for equal opportunities, to work to improve people's lives, to have a government that truly allows people to thrive. I never stopped believing this."[9] The memories of these experiences continue to inform people's everyday commitments.

During the Popular Unity years, Concepción's radical politics focused not on taking state power but on changing local power relations through the creation of democratic, participatory spaces. The emergence of these spaces existed in tension with the Chilean Left's reliance on Marxist theory and the idea of the vanguard. In the 1960s, many people believed revolution was the way to create social change and that a revolution required a revolutionary party—a vanguard that would lead the way. The MIR's adherence to this model meant that despite innovations coming out of grassroots organizing, it remained a hierarchical, elite-led party. Since Allende's overthrow, "the big debate within the Chilean Left" has been, as Juan Reyes noted, "if we went too fast or if we went too slow"—a reflection of the binary positions of revolutionary versus reformist that have dominated scholarly and popular debates—the MIR versus Allende.[10] To the end, Allende steadfastly pursued his vision for a democratic transition to socialism, refusing at key junctures to arm the people and never veering from the institutionalism that guided his project. In June 1973, when pressed to mobilize his supporters, Allende responded, "How many 'masses' equal one tank?"[11] The MIR and the left wing of the Popular Unity coalition failed in their efforts to radicalize the revolutionary process and to stop the counterrevolution. In the end, neither was viable.

Ultimately, the transformative value of movement politics was evident in the shifts in political practice and culture that they initiated. Despite the tragedy of

1973, political culture in Chile *had* successfully started to move away from state- and party-centered models. Under the auspices of leftist political projects during the late sixties and early seventies, grassroots movements pursued transformations without the help of the state. In these, grassroots social struggle often defied the ideological narratives held by the Old Left and the New Left about enacting change. Unfolding contingencies generated unintended political opportunities. Rather than wait for external actors, local people mobilized to carry out their own visions and goals for revolution. Though their ideas were not implemented nationally, the Concepción People's Assembly, for instance, initiated a powerful conversation critiquing existing platforms for participatory democracy. Similarly, though the Coronel bakery takeover was not replicated as a model for grassroots control of basic consumption, involvement deeply informed participants' ongoing thinking about the necessary tools for democratic transformation. As one participant in the bakery takeover reflected, these "local democratic processes—marked by participation, strong organization, and creation of concrete proposals—these are historical experiences that we need today to help us think about the kind of democracy that we want."[12] The cultural and political traditions of everyday revolution endured in local communities and in the minds of participants long after the dictatorship silenced the most vocal of these "failed" leftist movements.

The same questions about democratic participation and a new social contract are once again on the horizon in Chile. Just like during the Popular Unity years, in 2011 young Chileans experienced personal and collective power in building a movement. In 2010, after twenty years in office, the center-left Concertación coalition lost the presidency. For the first time since the 1990 transition to democracy, the Right was in power. The election of businessman Sebastián Piñera sparked an opening for generalized social discontent to manifest. Inspired by massive marches for environmental protection, indigenous rights, and sexual liberation in early 2011, middle-class and working-class students saddled with stifling education debt launched a movement demanding free, quality education in June. Students challenged the dictatorship's legacy of political violence and neoliberal economic restructuring and the democratic transition's elite political class divorced from the realities of the majority of citizens. They drew from a historical repertoire of collective action—particularly the toma—as they occupied their schools and the streets with a fiesta atmosphere filled with puppets, street theater, and creative protest tactics. In July 2011, 2,500 students gathered in the central forum of the University of Concepción campus to spell with their bodies "No+Lucro"—No More Profits. Hired planes took aerial photographs that were widely disseminated on social media. Rather than memories of repression from the dictatorship, students mobilized deeper memories of joy and liberation to serve as powerful touchstones for imagining alternative futures.

Rejecting party hierarchies of the 1960s, young people in the 2010s view both the state and traditional political parties with skepticism. Horizontal power sharing and direct democracy drove much of the assembly-based movement. The distance between past and present political culture was perhaps best encapsulated in the chants that accompanied the massive rallies: the unofficial anthem of the Popular Unity years—"¡El Pueblo Unido Jamás Será Vencido!" (The People United Will Never Be Defeated!)—became "¡El Pueblo Unido Avanza sin Partido!" (The People United Go Forward without Parties!). Students embraced the idea that change must come from society and from a democratized political culture that validates grassroots participation. In 2013, four former student leaders were elected to Congress, which passed a 2015 law guaranteeing the right to free, public education. In the early twenty-first century, the Chilean student movement affirmed the power of social movements to change the political conversation.

Watching with exhilaration and trepidation as the protests unfolded, many of the 1960s grassroots activists I interviewed saw echoes of their past struggles. A Coronel social worker highlighted the "need to invent new forms of politics," pausing to ask, "How can the citizenry participate in making these decisions? Now more than ever it needs to be done!"[13] In the early 1970s, these young people believed that a profound restructuring of the social order was not just necessary, but possible, and that they could bring it about. Assessing the student movement, a schoolteacher from Coronel stated that when the time comes, "I'll be back in the streets but not telling the kids what to do, because young people today are well educated, they know what they want, they know where they are going, [they have ideas] that they learned from their grandparents."[14] His comments reflect the importance of the intergenerational transfer of memories but also an abdication of his vanguard status with confidence that a new generation will find its own way.

The resurgence of social movements in 2011 opened up a new interpretation of the MIR from below. At its finest, most generous moment, Chile's revolutionary Left found a way to articulate a project for radical political transformation with grassroots social struggle. Across Latin America, the relative success of Revolutionary New Left groups hinged on opening up spaces of cross-class sociability. The MIR in Concepción excelled in this regard. Chileans participated in effective grassroots movements centered on expanding platforms for people to be heard, developing critical thinking skills through political education, and fighting to expand access to social rights, including education, health care, housing, and basic consumption. Collective action inspired people in ways both emotional and political. Participants bridged different life experiences and emphasized the value of each person's contribution. The enduring legacy of grassroots revolution in Concepción was a set of tools for changing everyday lives.

It will likely take decades to assess the full impact of the 2011 Chilean student movement. But past experiences indicate that immediate political gains may not be the best measure of long-term outcomes. As thousands of young people came to politics for the first time, the experience of being part of a movement changed them. Even as a movement subsides or goes in different directions, those experiences continue to shape lives. Participants carry with them the skills learned in taking a stand, in formulating political positions, in carrying out direct actions, and in becoming agents of their own destinies.

Appendix

Sponsoring Organizations for the
Concepción People's Assembly, July 27, 1972

UNIONS

1. Sindicato Único CAP
2. Sindicato Industrial Paños Oveja
3. Sindicato Industrial Bellavista
4. Sindicato Industrial FIAP
5. Sindicato Metalúrgico de Lota
6. Sindicato Metalúrgico de Schwager
7. Sindicato Industrial Minero de Schwager
8. Sindicato de Empleados de Schwager
9. Sindicato Industrial Caupolicán Chiguayante
10. Sindicato Industrial INCHALAM
11. Sindicato Petroquímica Chilena
12. Sindicato Industrial FANALOZA
13. Sindicato Industrial COSAF
14. Sindicato Industrial VIPLA
15. Sindicato Profesional Cantera Lonco
16. Sindicato Profesional MASISA
17. Sindicato Lota-Green
18. Sindicato Celadores de Lota
19. Sindicato Industrial CCU
20. Sindicato Industrial MADESAL
21. Sindicato Industrial Maestranza Universal
22. Sindicato Industrial Muebles Roma
23. Sindicato Provincial de Periodistas
24. FENATS Concepción

25. Comando permanente de Defensa de los Trabajadores de Sindicatos Sigdo Koppers S.A.; Tecsa, Delegación Cerrillos y Atevo Belfi
26. Sindicato Constructora Bío Bío
27. Sindicato Claro y Vicuña
28. Sindicato Obra Rene Schneider (CORMU)
29. Sindicato Obra LAN A-4 (CORMU)
30. Sindicato Carlos Valck
31. Sindicato Claudio Arancibia
32. Sindicato Hermanos Peredo (Pedro González Asuar)
33. Sindicato Obra Simmons (Maqri Hepner)
34. Sindicato Edwards y Ceruti
35. Sindicato Obra Torre Carlos Cortés (CORMU)
36. Sindicato Constructora Cerrillos (Hualpencillo)
37. Sindicato Único Barhkan Talcahuano
38. Sindicato Cerrillo (Lenin)
39. Sindicato Constructora Dolmén
40. Sindicato Constructora APTECAR
41. Sindicato Constructora Ramón Zoñé
42. Sindicato Profesional de Bencineros
43. Sindicato Profesional de Choferes de Camiones
44. Sindicato Constructora Jorge Morales Geldres
45. Sindicato Departamental Construcción de Lota
46. Sindicato Constructora Osvaldo Band
47. Sindicato Constructora Augusto Bellolio
48. Sindicato Departamental de la Construcción de Tomé
49. Sindicato Departamental de la Construcción de Talcahuano
50. Sindicato Constructora Xilo Técnica
51. Sindicato Molino Santa Rosa
52. FENATS Coronel
53. Asociación del Personal de Astilleros y Maestranzas de la Armada (ASMAR)
54. Trabajadores de Obras Portuarias
55. Sindicato Industrial Gacel
56. Sindicato Profesional del Diario EL SUR
57. Sindicato Industrial BALCO
58. Sindicato Industrial El Tibet
59. Sindicato Profesional Mauricio Gleissner
60. Frente Único Pesquero
61. Frente de Trabajadores Revolucionarios

PEASANTS

1. Federación Campesina Los Valientes de la Concepción
2. Consejo Comunal Campesino de Cabrero
3. Consejo Comunal Campesino de Yumbel

4. Movimiento de Campesinos Revolucionarios
5. Comité Unidad Campesina: Pequeños Propietarios, Medieros e Inquilinos de Hualqui
6. Trabajadores del Fundo Leonera de Hualqui

CAMPAMENTOS

1. Campamento Lenin
2. Campamento Luciano Cruz
3. Campamento Camilo Torres
4. Campamento Sierra Maestra No. 1
5. Campamento Sierra Maestra No. 2
6. Campamento Hilario Contreras
7. Campamento Bellavista Sur
8. Campamento Che Guevara
9. Campamento Luis Emilio Recabarrren
10. Campamento Arnoldo Ríos
11. Campamento Tencha de Allende
12. Campamento Ránquil
13. Campamento Manuel Rodríguez
14. Campamento José Tohá
15. Campamento Lucha Obrera
16. Campamento Las Vertientes
17. Campamento René Schneider
18. Campamento El Pantano
19. Campamento El Edén
20. Campamento Carlos Cortés
21. Campamento 30 de Noviembre
22. Campamento Fidel Castro
23. Campamento Jorge Fernandez
24. Campamento Cuba
25. Comité Sin Casa Tencha de Allende
26. Comité Sin Casa Arnoldo Ríos
27. Comité Sin Casa Ránquil
28. Comité Sin Casa FERBIO
29. Comité Sin Casa Pedro de Valdivia
30. Comité Sin Casa Pedro del Río
31. Comité Sin Casa Playa Negra
32. Movimiento de Pobladores Revolucionarios

STUDENTS

1. Federación de Estudiantes Secundarios de Concepción
2. Federación de Estudiantes de Concepción

3. Federación de Estudiantes de la UTE
4. Centro de Estudiantes de Medicina
5. Centro de Ingeniería de Ejecución
6. Centro de Sociología
7. Centro de Estudiantes de Periodismo
8. Centro de Estudiantes de Economía
9. Centro de Estudiantes de Filosofía
10. Centro de Estudiantes de Servicio Social
11. Consejo Superior de la Universidad de Concepción
12. Docentes y Trabajadores de la UTE
13. Movimiento Universitario de Izquierda
14. Centro Estudiantil Secundario y Universitario de Santa Juana
15. Centro de Alumnos Escuela Agrícola de Santa Juana
16. Liceo de Chiguayante
17. Centro Juvenil Rene Schneider, Lota

MOTHERS' CENTERS

1. Centro de Madres La Piedad
2. Centro de Madres Manuel Rodríguez
3. Centro de Madres Pedro Aguirre Cerda
4. Centro de Madres Campamento Teniente Merino
5. Centro de Madres Nueva Aurora
6. Centro de Madres Tania
7. Centro de Madres La Pólvora
8. Centro de Madres Santa Cecilia
9. Centro de Madres Corporación de Obras Urbanas
10. Centro de Madres Cooperativa Lo Galindo
11. Centro de Madres Lala Carmona
12. Centro de Madres Santa Maria
13. Centro de Madres Julieta
14. Centro de Madres La Unidad
15. Centro de Madres María Maluje
16. Centro de Madres Las Golondrinas
17. Centro de Madres Pabla Jaraquemada
18. Centro de Madres Nuestra Señora de Fátima
19. Centro de Madres Villa CAP
20. Centro de Madres Flor de Durazno
21. Centro de Madres Las Violetas
22. Centro de Madres Isabel Riquelme
23. Centro de Madres Estrellita del Sur
24. Centro de Madres Las Laboriosas
25. Centro de Madres Juanita de Cerda

26. Centro de Madres Unión Ferroviaria
27. Centro de Madres La Mujer Campesina de Hualqui

POLITICAL PARTIES

1. Partido Socialista
2. Movimiento de Izquierda Revolucionaria
3. Movimiento de Acción Popular Unitaria
4. Partido Radical
5. Izquierda Cristiana

Source: "Asamblea del Pueblo: Nómina de organizaciones adherentes," *El Sur,* July 27, 1972, 11.

NOTES

INTRODUCTION

1. Juan Reyes, interview by author, Tomé, Chile, October 11, 2011.
2. Peter Winn, "The Furies of the Andes: Violence and Terror in the Chilean Revolution and Counterrevolution," in *A Century of Revolution: Insurgent and Counterinsurgent Violence during Latin America's Long Cold War,* ed. Greg Grandin and Gilbert M. Joseph (Durham, NC: Duke University Press, 2010), 241.
3. Steve J. Stern, *Remembering Pinochet's Chile: On the Eve of London 1998* (Durham, NC: Duke University Press, 2004); Steve J. Stern, *Battling for Hearts and Minds: Memory Struggles in Pinochet's Chile, 1973–1988* (Durham, NC: Duke University Press, 2006); Steve J. Stern, *Reckoning with Pinochet: The Memory Question in Democratic Chile, 1989–2006* (Durham, NC: Duke University Press, 2010); Alexander Wilde, "Irruptions of Memory: Expressive Politics in Chile's Transition to Democracy," *Journal of Latin American Studies* 31:2 (May 1999): 473–500.
4. Important exceptions include Peter Winn, *Weavers of Revolution: The Yarur Workers and Chile's Road to Socialism* (New York: Oxford University Press, 1986) and *La revolución chilena* (Santiago: LOM, 2013); Florencia Mallon, *Courage Tastes of Blood: The Mapuche Community of Nicolas Ailío and the Chilean State, 1906–2001* (Durham, NC: Duke University Press, 2005); Heidi Tinsman, *Partners in Conflict: The Politics of Gender, Sexuality, and Labor in the Chilean Agrarian Reform, 1950–1973* (Durham, NC: Duke University Press, 2002); Frank Gaudichaud, *Poder popular y cordones industriales: Testimonios sobre el movimiento popular urbano, 1970–73* (Santiago: LOM, 2004). For innovative approaches that incorporate cultural history, see Camilo Trumper, *Ephemeral Histories: Public Art, Politics, and the Struggle for the Streets in Chile* (Oakland: University of California Press, 2016); César Albórnoz and Claudio Rolle, *1973: La vida cotidiana de un año crucial* (Santiago: Planeta Historia y Sociedad, 2003); Patrick Barr-Melej, *Psychedelic Chile: Youth, Counterculture, and Politics on the Road to Socialism and Dictatorship* (Chapel Hill: University of North Carolina Press, 2017).

5. Henry A. Landsberger and Tim McDaniel, "Hypermobilization in Chile, 1970–1973," *World Politics* 28.4 (July 1976): 502–41.

6. *Informe de la Comisión Nacional de Verdad y Reconciliación sobre la violación a los derechos humanos en Chile, 1973–1990* (Santiago: Ministerio Secretaría General de Gobierno, 1991).

7. Between 1973 and 1975, the military regime executed or disappeared 424 MIR militants. Magdalena Garcés Fuentes, "Terrorismo de Estado en Chile: La campaña de exterminio de la DINA en contra del MIR" (PhD diss., Universidad de Salamanca, 2016); José Leonel Calderón López, "La política del Movimiento de Izquierda Revolucionaria (MIR) durante los dos primeros años de la dictadura militar (1973–1975): Entre la lucha por convertirse en actor político y la lucha por sobrevivir" (Undergraduate thesis, Universidad de Santiago de Chile, 2009).

8. Mario Garcés Durán, "Prólogo," in *Miguel Enríquez y el proyecto revolucionario en Chile: Discursos y documentos del Movimiento de Izquierda Revolucionaria,* ed. Pedro Naranjo et al. (Santiago: LOM; Centro de Estudios Miguel Enríquez, 2004), 6. On Argentina, see Pilar Calveiro, *Política y/o violencia: Una aproximación a la guerrilla de los años 70* (Buenos Aires: Siglo Veintiuno, 2013).

9. For the classic interpretation of the theory of the two demons, see Jorge G. Castañeda, *Utopia Unarmed: The Latin American Left after the Cold War* (New York: Vintage Books, 1993). For revisionist historiography on the Southern Cone, see Valeria Manzano, *The Age of Youth in Argentina: Culture, Politics, and Sexuality from Perón to Videla* (Chapel Hill: University of North Carolina Press, 2014); Aldo Marchesi, *Latin America's Radical Left: Rebellion and Cold War in the Global 1960s* (Cambridge: Cambridge University Press, 2017); Vania Markarian, *El '68 uruguayo: El movimiento estudiantil entre molotovs y música beat* (Buenos Aires: Universidad Nacional de Quilmes, 2012); Lindsey Churchill, *Becoming the Tupamaros: Solidarity and Transnational Revolutionaries in Uruguay and the United States* (Nashville, TN: Vanderbilt University Press, 2014); Victoria Langland, *Speaking of Flowers: Student Movements and the Making and Remembering of 1968 in Military Brazil* (Durham, NC: Duke University Press, 2013).

10. Mario Garcés Durán, *El despertar de la sociedad: Los movimientos sociales en América Latina y Chile* (Santiago: LOM, 2012).

11. This study is on leftist grassroots movements and therefore does not explore the lives and experiences of conservative movements or the Chilean military. See Margaret Power, *Right-Wing Women in Chile: Feminine Power and the Struggle against Allende, 1964–1973* (University Park: Pennsylvania State University Press, 2002); Verónica Valdivia, *Nacionales y gremialistas: El parto de la neuva derecha política chilena, 1964–1973* (Santiago: LOM, 2008).

12. The research for this book draws on three years of fieldwork in Chile (in 2006, 2008, and 2009, from 2010 through 2011, and in 2013, 2014, and 2015). The sixty formal oral history interviews that I conducted took place between 2010 and 2011. The historians Sebastián Leiva, Eugenia Palieraki, Gina Inostroza, and Mariel Ruiz Muñoz graciously enabled me to consult oral history transcripts from interviews they conducted between 2004 and 2016. The majority of participants were MIR militants, members of the MIR's mass fronts, or MIR sympathizers. A handful of other participants were from the MAPU, the Socialist Party, the Communist Party, and Catholic Action, as well as Cristian Democrats and leftist sympathizers. The interviews were semistructured to cover key themes, including when individuals arrived in Concepción, engagement with politics, decision to join the MIR, activism

during the Popular Unity period, and events of regional and national significance such as the 1972 People's Assembly and the Bosses' Lockout. Group interviews proved to be particularly dynamic experiences of recovering historical memory. As I listened, other stories emerged. In addition, in 2014, I interviewed University of Concepción activists about the Chilean Winter student movement.

13. John Beverley, "Rethinking the Armed Struggle in Latin America," *Boundary 2* 36.1 (2009): 47–59.

14. For an exemplary memoir in this vein, see Max Marambio, *Las armas de ayer* (Madrid: Debate, 2008). For a pioneering study on memory narratives by the 1960s generation, see Katherine Hite, *When the Romance Ended: Leaders of the Chilean Left, 1968–1998* (New York: Columbia University Press, 2000).

15. I use "Concepción" to refer to both the city and the surrounding province.

16. Jody Pavilack, *Mining for the Nation: The Politics of Chile's Coal Communities from the Popular Front to the Cold War* (University Park: Pennsylvania State University Press, 2011).

17. Ibid., 1–2.

18. Juan José Salinas Valdés, "Poder popular provincial: Los casos de Concepción-Talcahuano y Constitución, 1970–1973" (Undergraduate thesis, Universidad de Concepción, 2008).

19. Igor Goicovic, *Movimiento de Izquierda Revolucionaria* (Concepción: Ediciones Escaparate, 2012).

20. For a similar grassroots approach in Argentina, see Javier Salcedo, *Los Montoneros del barrio* (Buenos Aires: EDUTREF, 2013).

21. Hasan Kwame Jeffries, *Bloody Lowndes: Civil Rights and Black Power in Alabama's Black Belt* (New York: New York University Press, 2009), 5.

22. Jeffrey Gould and Aldo A. Lauria-Santiago, *To Rise in Darkness: Revolution, Repression, and Memory in El Salvador, 1920–1932* (Durham, NC: Duke University Press, 2008); Thomas Miller Klubock, "Ránquil: Violence and Peasant Politics on Chile's Southern Frontier," in Grandin and Joseph, *A Century of Revolution*, 121–59. For a U.S. comparison, see Kathryn Olmsted, *Right out of California: The 1930s and the Big Business Roots of Modern Conservatism* (New York: New Press, 2015).

23. Arturo Valenzuela, *The Breakdown of Democratic Regimes: Chile* (Baltimore, MD: Johns Hopkins University Press, 1978); Winn, *Weavers of Revolution*, 6.

24. Julio Pinto Vallejos, ed., *Cuando hicimos historia: La experiencia de la Unidad Popular* (Santiago: LOM, 2005); and *Fiesta y drama: Nuevas historias de la Unidad Popular* (Santiago: LOM, 2014).

25. Kristin Ross, *May '68 and Its Afterlives* (Chicago: University of Chicago Press, 2002), 73–74.

1. "WE LIVED THOSE YEARS WITH A LOT OF PASSION"

1. "Margarita González," interview by author, Santiago, Chile, March 24, 2011. At the request of the interviewee a pseudonym has been used. All other names have been used with permission of interviewees.

2. Jeffrey Gould, "Solidarity under Siege: The Latin American Left, 1968," *American Historical Review* 114.2 (April 2009): 348–75.

3. University reform movements were formative experiences for the Chilean New Left, represented primarily by the MIR and the Movimiento de Acción Popular Unitaria (MAPU). In 1969, the left wing of the Christian Democratic Youth formed the MAPU. The founders included many protagonists in the Santiago university reform movements, particularly the toma of the Universidad Católica in 1967 and the hanging of a banner proclaiming "*El Mercurio miente* [lies]" across the Universidad de Chile's Casa Central. See Carlos M. Huneeus, *Movimientos universitarios y generación de elites dirigentes: Estudio de casos* (Santiago: Corporación de Promoción Universitaria, 1973).

4. In his memoirs, Juan Saavedra, law student at the University of Concepción and early MIR member, identifies the slogan of their movement as "Universidad para todos" (University for Everyone). Juan Saavedra Gorriateguy, *Te cuento otra vez esa historia tan bonita* (Santiago: Editorial Forja, 2010), 59.

5. Ibid., 59.

6. Between 1961 and 1973, total enrollment went from 25,612 students to 145,663. Saaveda, *Te cuento otra vez*, 58–59.

7. Following the implementation of the university reforms, the Universidad de Concepción enrolled 19,437 students in 1973. Saaveda, *Te cuento otra vez*, 58–59; *Memoria de la Universidad de Concepción correspondiente al año 1968* (Concepción: Imprenta Univeristaria), 26; *Memoria de la Universidad de Concepción correspondiente al año 1972–1973* (Concepción: Editorial Universitaria, 1977), 343.

8. González interview, March 24, 2011.

9. Miguel Enríquez, Bautista Van Schouwen, and Luciano Cruz enrolled in the UdeC medical school in 1961. All three were members of the MIR's national leadership from 1967 until their deaths. Cruz died in a domestic accident in August 1971; Van Schouwen was arrested and killed by military officials in December 1973; Enríquez died in a gunfight with secret police agents in October 1974.

10. Eugenia Palieraki, *¡La revolución ya viene! El MIR chileno en los años sesenta* (Santiago: LOM, 2014), chap. 3.

11. On the 1964 election, see Marcelo Casals Araya, *El alba de una revolución: La izquierda y el proceso de construcción estratégica de la "vía chilena al socialismo,"* 1956–1970 (Santiago: LOM, 2010), 121–55; Marcelo Casals Araya, *La creación de la amenaza roja: Del surgimiento del anticomunismo en Chile a la "campaña del terror" de 1964* (Santiago: LOM, 2016); and José Tomás Labarca, "'Por los que quieren un gobierno de avanzada popular': Nuevas prácticas políticas en la campaña presidencial de la Democracia Cristiana, Chile, 1962–1964," *Latin American Research Review* 52.1 (2017): 50–63. On the founding of the MIR, see Palierka, *La revolución ya viene;* and Carlos Sandoval Ambiado, *MIR (una historia)* (Santiago: Sociedad Editorial Trabajadores, 1990).

12. MIR, "Declaración de Principios," in Naranjo et al., *Miguel Enríquez y el proyecto revolucionario en Chile.*

13. In *Guerrilla Warfare,* Ernesto "Che" Guevara elaborated his foco theory—the idea that a small band of dedicated revolutionaries could inspire a mass uprising. For a critique of how Guevara's theory actually misrepresented the historical conditions in prerevolutionary Cuba, see Julia E Sweig, *Inside the Cuban Revolution: Fidel Castro and the Urban Underground* (Cambridge, MA: Harvard University Press, 2002).

14. Luis Vitale, *Contribución a la historia del MIR (1965–1970)* (Santiago: Instituto de Investigación de Movimientos Sociales "Pedro Vuskovic," 1999), 8. For more on the limited scope of the MIR's military abilities, see Marco Álvarez Vergara, *La constituyente revolucionaria: Historia de la fundación del MIR chileno* (Santiago: LOM, 2015), which includes the never before published 1965 Political-Military Thesis. For a comparative look at Southern Cone revolutionary Left groups, see Aldo Marchesi, *Latin America's Radical Left: Rebellion and Cold War in the Global 1960s* (Cambridge: Cambridge University Press, 2017).

15. Palieraki, *¡La revolución ya viene!*, chap. 1.

16. The Vanguardia Revolucionaria Marxista-Rebelde (VRM) was led by an older generation of Trotskyists, including Enrique Sepúlveda and Pedro Enríquez Barra, who became the first MIR general secretary and regional secretary, respectively, in Concepción. The VRM also contained a younger generation of dissident Socialist Youth members, including Miguel and Edgardo Enríquez, Bautista Van Schouwen, and Sergio Pérez Molina from Concepción. Dissident socialists associated with the Trotskyist-oriented Partido Socialista Popular (PSP) formed the second largest delegation. The PSP had briefly been in the Ibáñez government (1953–53) and had deep roots in the labor movement with well-known public figures like Humberto Valenzuela and Luis Vitale. As with the MUI in Concepción, many nonaffiliated communists and socialists filled the MIR's initial ranks.

17. MIR, "Declaración de Principios."

18. The principal leaders in the MUI quickly rose to leadership positions in the MIR.

19. Juan José, "El MUI de Concepción," *Punto Final* 2.14 (October 1966): 9.

20. In 1964, during the MUI's first year, a PS-PC backed candidate, Claudio Sepúlveda, a socialist medical student, won the MUI nomination for 1964 FEC president by assembly. The following year, also by assembly, the MUI nominated a more left-wing candidate, Miguel Enríquez, formerly of the VRM and now a member of the newly formed MIR.

21. Students marginalized from the Juventudes Comunistas (JJCC) in 1962 over the Sino-Soviet split initiated conversations with students from the VRM, including Miguel Enríquez, Bautista Van Schouwen, and Martín Hernández, who had been expelled from the Socialist Youth Party at the PS National Congress in February 1964, as well as Luciano Cruz, one of the few former JJCC members who joined the VRM.

22. Enzo La Mura, interviews by author, Concepción, Chile, April 1 and 29, 2011.

23. According to La Mura, the MUI founders drew inspiration from Allende's assessment. La Mura interview, April 1, 2011.

24. La Mura interview, April 1, 2011.

25. Nelson Gutiérrez Yáñez, interview by Eugenia Palieraki, Concepción, Chile, January 13, 2005.

26. Guitérrez interview, January 13, 2005; Saavedra, *Te cuento otra vez*, 53. The PC and PS only participated in the MUI from November 1964 to October 1965.

27. Saavedra, *Te cuento otra vez*, 53–54.

28. Martín Hernández, interview by Sebastián Leiva, Concepción, Chile, March 25, 2005.

29. La Mura interview, April 1, 2011.

30. "Malestar general por alza en tarifas de locomoción," *La Patria*, April 16, 1965, 1; "De 55 y no de 50 por ciento es alza en la locomoción," *La Patria*, April 17, 1965, 1.

31. "Aumenta efervescencia por el alza en la locomoción," *La Patria*, April 20, 1965, 1, 6.

32. For more on the April 1957 protests, see Gabriel Salazar Vergara, *La violencia política popular en las "grandes alamedas": La violencia en Chile 1947–1987* (Santiago: LOM, 2006), 209–20; Pedro Milos, *Historia y memoria: 2 de abril de 1957* (Santiago: LOM, 2007).

33. Vitale, *Contribución a la historia del MIR*, 4–5.

34. The older generation of MIR founders, including Clotario Blest, were also deeply influenced by 1957, which revealed for the first time the "masa popular" and its insurrectionary capacity, particularly pobladores. With its emphasis on labor organizing, the Old Left was initially slow to organize pobladores and conceive of them as revolutionary subjects equal to workers.

35. Students threw coins and ridiculed *El Sur*'s false announcement of fare decreases. Earlier in the march, medical student Miguel Enríquez and law student Juan Saavedra insulted press photographer Hernán Bernales Hinojosa by shouting "Death to the Reactionary Press!" as they attempted to grab his camera. The local press widely covered the incident, publishing photographs of the two accused students. "Acción universitaria: Quisieron agredir a reporteros gráficos," *La Patria*, April 21, 1965, 1.

36. "Protesta estudiantil por alzas de la locomoción," *La Patria*, April 21, 1965, 1, 6.

37. Headlines like "Violence in Concepción," "Bloody Night on the Diagonal," "Sticks, Rocks, Water, and Gunshots," "Police Used Gas Bombs and Police Clubs," "Debut of the 'Guanaco' in Violent Incidents," and "Students Won the 'Battle' in the Barrio Universitario," as well as many pages of coverage and photo spreads, capture both sensationalism and shock. *La Patria*, April 22, 1965, 1, 3, 7.

38. A joint MUI-Radical proposal not to attend classes on April 22 passed by general assembly vote, 883 to 249. "Violencia alcanzaron los graves disturbios callejeros: Treinta y tres detenidos en Choque de policía y estudiantes," *El Sur*, April 22, 1965, 1, 16.

39. "Gremios se unen a protesta de estudiantes penquistas," *La Patria*, April 23, 1965, 2.

40. "Protesta por alzas e intervención policía," *La Patria*, April 25, 1965, 3.

41. "Represión policial en el Recinto de la U origina seria protesta," *El Sur*, April 24, 1965, 1, 14.

42. Ibid.

43. "Piden sesión especial de la cámara por atentado a 'U,'" *El Sur*, April 27, 1965, 7; "Dos mil estudiantes salen en defensa de la Universidad," *El Sur*, April 27, 1965, 7.

44. MUI students from Concepción composed one-third (7 of 21) of the MIR's first Central Committee. The first general secretary, however, was a member of the older generation, as were the five members of the Secretariado Nacional. Pedro Naranjo, "La vida de Miguel Enríquez y el MIR," in Naranjo et al., *Miguel Enríquez y el proyecto revolucionario en Chile*, 45.

45. Saavedra, *Te cuento otra vez*, 56.

46. "Declaraciones a Granel por incidentes en universidad," *La Patria*, November 16, 1965, 7.

47. Saavedra, *Te cuento otra vez*, 56.

48. "Acción anti-imperialista: Estudiantes del MIR expulsaron a Senador Kennedy de recinto universitario," *El Rebelde* 4.34 (January 1966): 2.

49. Saavedra, *Te cuento otra vez*, 57.

50. "Declaraciones a Granel por incidentes en universidad," *La Patria*, November 16, 1965, 7.

51. "Las juventudes políticas frente a frente," *El Sur,* June 28, 1967, 17.

52. "Renuevan directiva: Universitarios harán foro de candidatos en emisoras locales," *El Sur,* October 28, 1965, 10.

53. Ibid.

54. Saavedra, *Te cuento otra vez,* 59.

55. Modernization reform was based on the formation of central institutes. Rector Stitchkin oversaw the creation of the basic science institutes (math, biology, physics, and chemistry) in 1959. The second phase, designed to create the social science institutes and the first-year core curriculum known as the propedéutico, was implemented under Rector Ignacio González Ginouvés in 1965. The latter phase coincided with the university reform movement and became a central focus of student demands, particularly in the propedéutico and sociology institute opened in 1965 and 1966, respectively. See *Objectives of the Academic Reorganization and Integrated Urbanization Plan of the University of Concepción* (Santiago: Editorial Universitaria, 1958); Jaime García Molina, *El campus de la Universidad de Concepción: Su desarrollo urbanístico y arquitectónico* (Concepción: Universidad de Concepción, 1994); "Dos pasos significativos en el plan de reestructuración de la Universidad penquista: Los ojos del continente puestos en Concepción," *La Patria,* June 5, 1958.

56. "Más de cuatro mil alumnos fuera de la Universidad; Canceladas las matrículas," *El Sur,* October 22, 1966, 1.

57. "Continúa la huelga: Alumnos piden participar en el directorio de la U," *El Sur,* September 27, 1966, 7.

58. "Comenzó congreso Interno extraordinario de la FEC," *El Sur,* October 8, 1966, 10; "Piden cogobierno de la Universidad; Reformas fundamentales planteó el Congreso Interno de la FEC," *El Sur,* October 15, 1966, 9.

59. Miguel Enríquez summarized these goals in "Balance de la lucha en la Universidad de Concepción," *Punto Final* 2.40 (October 1967): 36–37.

60. "Alumnos exigen salida de los cuerpos de paz," *La Patria,* October 15, 1966, 12.

61. Nadia Torres Hidalgo, "La francmasonería y su influencia en la educación en Concepción" (Undergraduate thesis, Universidad de Concepción, 2002).

62. Carlos Huneeus, *La reforma universitaria: Veinte años después* (Santiago: Corporación de Promoción Universitaria, 1988), 73.

63. *Acta de Sesión Extraordinaria de Directorio* (No. 21), October 19, 1966, 305, Archivos Generales Universidad de Concepción (AGUdeC).

64. Ibid., 301.

65. Huneeus, *La reforma universitaria,* 73.

66. Eduardo Aquevedo served as FEC vice president in 1967. In May 1969, Aquevedo participated in the formation of the MAPU.

67. "Comienza análisis del problema universitario," *El Sur,* November 11, 1966, 8.

68. "En defensa de su universidad: La ciudad penquista paraliza hoy sus actividades," *La Patria,* November 15, 1966, 1.

69. Saavedra, *Te cuento otra vez,* 61.

70. Enríquez, "Balance de la lucha en la Universidad de Concepción."

71. Under the current system, a specially convened 135-member Claustro Pleno, composed of the Assembly of Associates and full-time academic faculty selected the new rector. Saavedra, *Te cuento otra vez,* 63.

72. "Candidato a rector llegaría el jueves," *El Sur,* February 27, 1968, 8.

73. "Rector electo: impulsaré reformas en la 'U,'" *El Sur,* March 16, 1968, 9.

74. The 1968 *Memoria* for the Universidad de Concepción locates the origins of the university reform process in "the desire of the university community—faculty and students—to replace the university structures, democratizing the election of authorities and granting participation at all levels to students." As quoted in Edgardo Enríquez Frödden, "La reforma en la Universidad de Concepción," in *La reforma universitaria en Chile (1967–1973),* ed. Luis Cifuentes and Raúl Allard (Santiago: Editorial Universidad de Santiago, 1997), 127.

75. The Consejo Superior replaced the academic functions of the Consejo Universitario and the administrative and economic powers of the Directorio. The Consejo Superior was composed of 40 members, 10 of them students, including the FEC president, and three additional nonvoting representatives of nonacademic personnel. The Claustro Pleno had 1,500 members, an increase from 135. Hunneus, *La reforma universitaria,* 75.

76. Enríquez, "La reforma en la Universidad de Concepción," 128.

77. Ibid., 129–30. The 1973 enrollments include the UdeC branch campuses in Chillán, Los Ángeles, and the Universidad de Carbón, founded under Enríquez's leadership. At the beginning of Rector Enríquez's term in March 1969, the University of Concepción had 4,600 students. When he stepped down in January 1973, it enrolled 17,200. For the 1973 school year, UdeC enrolled 19,437 students. *Memoria de la Universidad de Concepción correspondiente al año 1972–1973,* 94–95.

78. Gutiérrez interview, January 13, 2005.

79. Letter to UdeC Rector Edgardo Enríquez Frödden from Institute Director Francisco Brevis, Professor Alejandro Saavedra, Sociology Student President Tulio Ríos, and FEC President Nelson Gutiérrez, March 4, 1969, AGUdeC.

80. For more on the experiences of foreign professors at UdeC during the Popular Unity years, see Klaus Meschkat, "Las ciencias sociales en un mundo globalizado," *Sociedad Hoy* 18 (2010): 131–42.

81. "Concepción: Guerra de los botones," *Ercilla* 1684 (September 13, 1967): 7.

82. Luciano Cruz traveled to Cuba at the invitation of Fidel Castro to attend the July 26 anniversary in 1968. He remained there until early December 1968. "Luciano Cruz regresó de Cuba," *El Sur,* December 24, 1968, 8. According to Vitale, in mid-1968 the MIR Central Committee voted to send Cruz to Cuba to develop a closer relationship with the Cuban leadership and "to train himself at a higher level than our embryonic 'military units.'" The national tour with Clotario Blest and Luciano Cruz never materialized, according to Vitale, due to lack of financial resources. Vitale, *Contribución a la historia del MIR,* 12, 21.

83. González interview, March 24, 2011.

84. Between 1965 and 1968, the MUI continued to be more than merely a MIR mass front. The majority of MUI participants were independent leftists. The MUI remained an alliance between the MIR and other political groups, including the Maoist-oriented Partido Comunista Revolucionaria (PCR), the Grupo de Avanzada Marxista (GRAMA) in the engineering school, former members of the Communist Youth and the Socialist Youth, and, in growing numbers, Christians and former Christian Democrats. Over time many of the smaller Marxist groups would either dissolve and join the MIR, as GRAMA did in 1967, or leave the MUI coalition, as the PCR did in 1969.

85. In Concepción province, the MIR made overtures to recruit progressive Christians into the party. As early as 1966, Vitale and medical student president Edgardo Condeza initiated an effort to create a Christian front within the MIR. The MUI's leadership within the reform movement explains why some Christian students came to see the MIR as the best vehicle for creating lasting social change. Other left-wing Christian Democrats joined the MAPU (1969) and Christian Left (1971). One notable example of a DC-to-MIR convert was the medical student Arturo Hillerns. In December 1967, Hillerns headed the DC ticket in FEC elections, eventually losing to MUI nominee Luciano Cruz. Two years later, Hillerns was a MIR militant and led a medical mission to Puerto Saavedra that was instrumental in establishing contacts with nearby Mapuche communities. For more on the Parroquia Universitaria and its early connection to the MIR in Concepción, see the memoirs of Julián Bastías Rebolledo, *Memorias de la lucha campesina: Cristiano, mestizo y tomador de fundos* (Santiago: LOM, 2009). For more on the grassroots health advocacy promoted by Hillerns in collaboration with Mapuche communities, see Mallon, *Courage Tastes of Blood*, 150, 161.

86. In mid-1967, the MIR sent Miguel Enríquez to Cuba; he returned in time for the MIR Congress, at which he was elected general secretary, according to Vitale, as a gesture to the younger generation following the death of Che Guevara.

87. At the 1967 MIR Congress, 10 of 15 Central Committee members and the five-person Secretariado Nacional were from "nontraditional" sectors of Concepción and Santiago. In Miguel Enríquez's own typology, the "nontraditional" MIR sectors were those that had broken with the Old Left after 1959, principally the Juventudes Comunistas, marginalized in 1962 over the Sino-Soviet split, and the dissident Juventudes Socialistas, which left in 1963 and 1964. Naranjo, "La vida de Miguel Enríquez y el MIR," 52–53.

88. Only Zorrilla studied at the Universidad de Chile in Santiago; the other four Secretariado Nacional members were University of Concepción students. Bautista Van Schouwen took over as MIR regional secretary in Concepción in 1968, replacing labor lawyer Pedro Enríquez Barra, who remained in the regional MIR leadership. In 1968 Miguel Enríquez and Van Schouwen both graduated with medical degrees; Luciano Cruz had abandoned his studies.

89. In 1966, the MIR published the first Chilean edition of "El hombre nuevo y el socialismo," in *Estrategia*.

90. Vitale, *Contribución a la historia del MIR*, 22–23. Vitale celebrated Van Schouwen's "audacious political plan to support the labor struggles in the region, particularly in the coal zone, the Tomé textile mills, the Huachipato steel mill, and among pobladores and campesinos from Talca to Puerto Montt."

91. Ibid., 23.

92. Miguel Enríquez, "Algunos antecedents del Movimiento de Izquierda Revolucionaria" (March 1971), in Naranjo et al., *Miguel Enríquez y el proyecto revolucionario en Chile*, 91.

93. Lily Rivas, interview by author, Concepción, Chile, October 11, 2011.

94. Enríquez, "Algunos antecedentes," 91.

95. Marcelo Ferrada Noli, "Nelson Gutiérrez In Memoriam," accessed June 15, 2012, http://ferrada-noli.blogspot.com/2008/10/nelson-gutierrez-in-memoriam.html.

96. Miguel Enríquez, "Sin lastre avanzaremos más rápido" (July 1969), cited in MIR, "Anexos a los Documentos Internos 2-a correspondientes a 1973," in *La izquierda chilena*

(1969–1973): Documentos para el estudio de su línea estratégica, ed. Víctor Farías, vol. 6 (Santiago: Centro de Estudios Públicos, 2000), 3894.

97. The party later passed resolutions forbidding actions against individuals, such as kidnapping. The Osses incident produced a rift between General Secretary Miguel Enríquez and his former classmates from the University of Concepción, who retained the MIR's regional leadership after Enríquez left for Santiago. Characterized derisively as "hotheads," the regional MIR was sanctioned, and in the internal debates that followed, the national MIR concurred that any kind of terrorist acts directed against individuals would not be tolerated or promoted within the organization.

98. MIR did not hold another party congress until 1988, on the eve of the democratic transition in Chile.

99. Naranjo, "La vida de Miguel Enríquez y el MIR," 58–59.

100. Vitale, *Contribución a la historia del MIR,* 27.

101. Enríquez, "Algunos antecedentes," 90.

102. Naranjo, "La vida de Miguel Enríquez y el MIR," 61.

103. Ricardo Frödden, interview by Eugenia Palieraki, February 2, 2005, Santiago, Chile.

104. "Sin lastre avanzaremos más rápido," in Farías, *La izquierda chilena,* 3894.

105. Ibid.

106. Ibid.

107. Enríquez, "Algunos antecedentes," 92.

108. Eugenia Palieraki, "La opción por las armas: Nueva izquierda revolucionaria y violencia política en Chile (1965–1970)," *Revista Polis* 19 (March 2008): 7; Naranjo, "La vida de Miguel Enríquez y el MIR," 62.

109. Naranjo, "La vida de Miguel Enríquez y el MIR," 58. GPMs appeared first in Concepción and Santiago and then throughout Chile by the end of 1969.

110. Ibid., 61.

111. Ibid., 62.

112. La Mura interview, April 1, 2011.

113. Palieraki, "La opción por las armas."

114. Bastías Rebolledo, *Memorias de la lucha campesina,* 18–19.

115. "Socializar la medicina," *Revolución* 2.6 (July 1971): 3; "Estudiantes de medicina a la opinión pública," *Mensaje* 20.201 (August 1971): 363–64.

116. González interview, March 24, 2011.

117. González interview, March 24, 2011. On the figure of the "repentant guerrilla," see John Beverley, "Rethinking the Armed Struggle in Latin America," *Boundary 2* 36.1 (2009): 47–59. For more on the 1968 generation in Chile, see Hite, *When the Romance Ended.*

2. "TO CREATE A MORE JUST SOCIETY"

1. Founding members included three textile workers—Tránsito del Carmen Cabrera Ortiz ("Tatín") and Jacinto Segundo Flores ("Titín") from the FIAP mill and Eulogio Sanhueza Bustos ("Sergio") from the Bellavista mill—and a student who attended technical school in Concepción, Héctor Lepe Moraga ("Rojas"). The names enclosed in parentheses and in quotation marks are the men's political names within the MIR.

2. Eulogio Sanhueza, interview by author, Tomé, Chile, October 14, 2011.

3. For a parallel example from the Panguipulli region in southern Chile, see memoirs by the forestry worker José Bravo Aguilera, *De Carranco a Carrán: La tomas que cambiaron la historia* (Santiago: LOM, 2012).

4. MIR, "Programa del Movimiento de Izquierda Revolucionaria," in Naranjo et al, *Miguel Enríquez y el proyecto revolucionario en Chile*, 105.

5. Ibid.

6. Juan Reyes, interview by author, Tomé, Chile, June 2, 2011.

7. Reyes interview, June 2, 2011.

8. Reyes interview, June 2, 2011.

9. For more on the MIR's construction of revolutionary masculinity and its working-class appeal, see Florencia Mallon, "*Barbudos,* Warriors, and *Rotos:* The MIR, Masculinity, and Power in the Chilean Agrarian Reform, 1965–1974," in *Changing Men and Masculinities in Latin America,* ed. Matthew C. Gutmann (Durham, NC: Duke University Press, 2003).

10. Reyes interview, June 2, 2011.

11. FTR-Bellavista member, interview by author, Tomé, Chile, November 2, 2011. The interviewee requested to remain anonymous; quotes are from field notes from the unrecorded interview.

12. Ibid.

13. Many of the historic generation of MIR leaders in Concepción had been members of the Socialist Party Youth until their expulsion from the party in 1964. Casals, *El alba de una revolución,* 111–13.

14. Nicanor Ibáñez, FTR-Bellavista group interview by author, Tomé, Chile, July 20, 2011. The practice of short-changing workers was substantiated by Alejandro Alarcón during April 2011 oral history interviews.

15. Nicanor Ibáñez, FTR-Bellavista group interview by author, Tomé, Chile, June 10, 2011. Handwritten notes; interview was not recorded.

16. Juan Reyes, FTR-Bellavista group interview, July 20, 2011. Elías Lafertte and Luis Emilio Recabarren were founding members of the Chilean Communist Party.

17. FTR-Bellavista group interview, July 20, 2011.

18. Reyes, FTR-Bellavista group interview, July 20, 2011.

19. Reyes interview, June 2, 2011.

20. Palieraki, *¡La revolución ya viene!,* 30.

21. Ibid., 40.

22. Espejo, FTR-Bellavista group interview, July 20, 2011.

23. Sanhueza interview, October 14, 2011.

24. Reyes, FTR-Bellavista group interview, July 20, 2011.

25. Reyes interview, June 2, 2011; Reyes, FTR-Bellavista group interview, July 20, 2011.

26. Ibáñez, FTR-Bellavista group interview, July 20, 2011.

27. See interview with Bellavista mill foreman and FTR leader Juan Avila in the French documentary, *A seis meses de la Unidad Popular* (May 1971). http://www.theclinic.cl/2012/05/26/de-culto-a-seis-meses-de-la-unidad-popular/

28. "Bellavista-Tomé: FTR—Una sola línea y ahora a la CUT," *El Rebelde* 6.31 (May 23, 1972), 2.

29. Reyes interview, June 2, 2011; Reyes, FTR-Bellavista group interview, July 20, 2011.

30. FTR-Bellavista member interview, November 2, 2011.

31. Reyes interview, June 2, 2011.

32. Reyes and Espejo, FTR-Bellavista group interview, July 20, 2011.

33. Jorge González, Coronel MIR group interview by author, Coronel, Chile, April 30, 2011.

34. Álvarez Vergara, *La constituyente revolucionaria.*

35. For discussion on violent discourse as effective propaganda as opposed to real military capacity, see Palieraki, "La opción por las armas."

36. The model of five members with one designated leader (*jefe*) that the MIR instituted appears to have been taken from the PS, likely due to Concepción MIR leaders' former involvement with the Socialist Party Youth. Casals, *El alba de una revolución,* 111–13. See also Teresa Veloso, interview by author, Concepción, Chile, August 4, 2011; Sanhueza interview, October 14, 2011; Jorge González, interview by author, Coronel, Chile, June 16, 2011.

37. Espejo, FTR-Bellavista group interview, July 20, 2011.

38. Bautista Van Schouwen, "Solo una revolución entre nosotros puede llevarnos a una revolución en Chile," May 1969 document prepared for IV MIR Congress.

39. González interview, June 16, 2011.

40. Steven F. Lawson and Charles Payne, "'This Transformation of the People': An Interview with Bob Moses," in *Debating the Civil Rights Movement, 1945–1968,* 2nd ed. (Lanham, MD: Rowman and Littlefield, 2006), 170–88.

41. Naranjo, "La vida de Miguel Enríquez," 47. Although Naranjo refers to the coal zone as Lota and Coronel, all of the MIR's contacts in this period were in the town of Coronel and its Schwager coal mines, not in Lota, where the Communist presence was considerably greater. See also Hernán Reyes, interview by Eugenia Palieraki, Coronel, Chile, March 7, 2005.

42. The four initial recruits were Edmundo "Ademir" Galindo, Guillermo "Chalao" Cánovas, Eulogio "Duro Pablo" Fritz, and Juan "Peneco" Sanhueza. Naranjo, "La vida de Miguel Enríquez," 47; Aníbal Cáceres [pseudonym], interview by author, Coronel, Chile, June 19, 2011.

43. Naranjo, "La vida de Miguel Enríquez," 47–48.

44. The general secretary of the Concepción VRM, lawyer Pedro Enríquez Barra, was named the first regional secretary of the newly formed MIR in Concepción. Pedro Enríquez Barra, interview by author, Concepción, Chile, August 25, 2011.

45. Lautaro López, interview by author, Talcahuano, Chile, June 15, 2011. Daniel López himself had been elected to Congress as a Socialist *diputado* for the southern city Puerto Montt, before the family moved north to Concepción province in 1960.

46. Nationally, the Frente de Estudiantes Revolucionarios existed for university and high school students. In Concepción, however, the prior tradition of the MUI remained the MIR's mass front in the University of Concepción, while local high school students organized in the FER.

47. "Aníbal Cáceres," Coronel MIR group interview by author, Coronel, Chile, April 30, 2011.

48. Cáceres interview, June 19, 2011.

49. Enzo La Mura, interview by author, Concepción, Chile, April 29, 2011; Grecia Quiero, Coronel MIR group interview by author, Coronel, Chile, April 30, 2011. The sports clubs La Alianza in the Colonia neighborhood and the Independiente in Villa Mora were both

spaces in which the MIR garnered support. For more on the role of sports clubs and politics, see Brenda Elsey, *Citizens and Sportsmen: Fútbol and Politics in Twentieth-Century Chile* (Austin: University of Texas Press, 2011).

50. Cáceres interview, June 19, 2011.

51. Pedro Enríquez Barra, interviews by author, Concepción, Chile August 29 and October 11, 2011.

52. For more information about Cautín province, see Bravo Aguilera, *De Carranco a Carrán*; Bastías Rebolledo, *Memorias de la lucha campesina*.

53. "Gume Figueroa," interview by author, July 23, 2011, Tomé, Chile. At the request of the interviewee, I am using his political name.

54. "Últimos contingentes para los trabajos de verano," *El Sur*, February 2, 1971, 7.

55. Enzo La Mura, interview by author, Concepción, Chile, April 1, 2011.

56. La Mura interview, April 1, 2011.

57. Cáceres interview, June 19, 2011; Quiero, Coronel MIR group interview, April 30, 2011.

58. La Mura interview, April 1, 2011. MUI founder and FEC leader Juan Saavedra decided to finally complete his law degree. Afterwards, he returned to his native Temuco and organized the MIR there. See Saavedra, *Te cuento otra vez*, 59.

59. In Tomé no rift emerged between the local miristas and the regional leadership in Concepción, in part because of the continuity of the MIR-Tomé's leadership: two of the four founding textile workers, Eulogio Sanhueza and Tránsito del Carmen Cabrera, remained in leadership positions there.

60. Enríquez, "Algunos antecedentes," 92; La Mura interview, April 29, 2011.

61. La Mura interview, April 29, 2011. The other names for the Brigade included Brigada Sindical del MIR en Coronel and Brigada Sindical del Carbón.

62. "El Mono" Escalona, interview by author, Coronel, Chile, May 7, 2011; at interviewee's request his last name has been used with his nickname. See also Quiero interview, May 11, 2011; Cáceres interview, June 19, 2011; La Mura interview, April 1, 2011.

63. La Mura interview, April 1, 2011; La Mura interview, April 29, 2011; Cáceres interview, June 19, 2011.

64. For more on the CIA's collaboration with right-wing forces in Chile, see Peter Kornbluh, *The Pinochet File: A Declassified Dossier on Atrocity and Accountability* (New York: New Press, 2004).

65. Reyes interview, June 2, 2011; Ibáñez, FTR-Bellavista group interview, June 20, 2011.

66. Miguel Enríquez lamented in 1974 the decision not to prioritize mass fronts after the coup because it meant the MIR "lost half the prerevolutionary period" to organize. Naranjo, "Prólogo," in Naranjo et al., *Miguel Enríquez y el proyecto revolucionario en Chile*, 21, 67. The *foquista*-oriented sectors within the MIR, who believed that guerrilla struggle was still the priority, had already largely abandoned the MIR and formed other parties, including the Movimiento Revolucionario and the Vanguardia Organizada del Pueblo (VOP). The older generation of MIR founders, who left the MIR in 1967 to start the MIR–Frente Revolucionario, actively campaigned for Allende.

67. FTR-Bellavista group interview by author, Tomé, Chile, July 20, 2011.

68. "Gume Figueroa" interview, July 23, 2011; Darwin Rodríguez, interview by author, Tomé, Chile, October 31, 2011.

69. These experiences held true for MIR recruitment in Coronel and for the work of the MAPU in Tomé.

70. During the first months of the Pinochet dictatorship in 1973, navy officials executed Miguel Ángel Catalán Febrero along with two other leaders of the Tomé GPM, Carmen Cabrera Ortiz and Héctor Lepe Moraga.

71. "Ola de huelgas en Concepción," *La Crónica*, July 23, 1970, 3.

72. Winn, *Weavers of Revolution*, 151.

73. "Obreros ocuparon fábrica de Paños Bellavista-Tomé," *El Sur*, April 2, 1970, 1.

74. FTR Bellavista-Tomé member interview, November 2, 2011.

75. "El FTR en Concepción en la Industria textil: Más fábricas para el pueblo," *El Rebelde* 5.3 (June 16, 1971): 6–7.

76. Alarcón, interview by author and Aníbal Navarette, Santiago, Chile, April 13, 2011.

77. Sanhueza interview, October 14, 2011.

78. FTR Bellavista-Tomé member interview, November 2, 2011.

79. FTR Bellavista-Tomé member interview, November 2, 2011.

80. "Actividades gremiales: Marcha sobre Concepción realizan obreros textiles," *El Sur*, September 26, 1970, 9; FTR-Bellavista group interview by author, handwritten notes, June 10, 2011.

81. "Hoy llega a estatizar Lota-Schwager," *El Sur*, December 31, 1970, 1, 12.

82. Salvador Allende, "Discurso en el mineral de Carbón de Lota, el 31 de diciembre de 1970," in *Salvador Allende: La revolución chilena* (Buenos Aires: EUDE; reprint Archivos Salvador Allende).

83. "El FTR en Concepción en la industria textil: Más fábricas para el pueblo," *El Rebelde* 5.3 (June 16, 1971), 6–7.

84. Ibid. For more on the CUT-UP agreement that formalized worker participation in theory in the nationalized sector, see Peter Winn, "Workers into Managers: Worker Participation in the Chilean Textile Industry," in *Popular Participation in Social Change: Cooperatives, Collectives, and Nationalized Industry*, ed. June Nash et al. (The Hague: Mouton, 1976), 577–601.

85. Reyes, FTR-Bellavista group interview, July 20, 2011.

86. Reyes, FTR-Bellavista group interview, July 20, 2011.

87. "El MIR lleva un candidato al sindicato," *La Crónica*, November 26, 1970, 16.

88. "Coronel: Empate en elección sindical," *El Sur*, December 18, 1970, 10.

89. Enzo La Mura, interview by author, Concepción, Chile, May 12, 2011.

90. La Mura interview, May 12, 2011.

91. Bravo interview, quoted in Rosa Ogalde, Marta García, and Mario Gutiérrez, *Coronel y ayer y hoy: Cómo vivirá el tercer milenio* (Coronel, Chile: Marta García, 2003): 361–67.

92. Carillo, Coronel MIR group interview, March 5, 2011.

93. Lautaro López, Coronel MIR group interview by author, San Pedro de la Paz, Chile, March 5, 2011.

94. On the question of worker participation in Chile's nationalized sector, Espinosa and Zimbalist found that industries with a Communist *interventor* (state-appointed manager) had minimal worker participation in practice. Juan G. Espinosa and Andrew S. Zimbalist, *Economic Democracy: Workers' Participation in Chilean Industry, 1970–1973* (New York: Academic Press, 1981).

95. La Mura interview, April 1, 2011.

96. "El Programa de Lucha del FTR del Carbón," *El Rebelde* 6.12 (January 7, 1972): 7. See also "Por esto pelearemos en la CUT" (Plataforma del FTR a la CUT), *El Rebelde* 6.30 (May 16, 1972): 5. First public mention of FTR is "El FTR en Concepción en la Industria textil: Más fábricas para el pueblo," *El Rebelde* 5.3 (June 16, 1971): 6–7. Previously workers who identified with the MIR ran on MIR platforms, but not all of these workers would go on to become militants of the MIR. Many remained active in the FTR, the MIR's mass front for workers.

97. "El Programa de Lucha del FTR del Carbón," *El Rebelde* 6.12 (January 7, 1972): 7.

98. La Mura interview, April 1, 2011.

99. "Declaración del FTR," *El Sur,* January 4, 1972, 8.

100. "FTR del Carbón: Renovación sindical y movilización revolucionaria," *El Rebelde* 6.12 (January 7, 1972): 7; "FTR del Carbón: Importante victoria," *El Rebelde* 6.13 (January 19, 1972): 7.

101. "Nueva victoria del FTR en el Carbón," *El Rebelde* 6.26 (April 18, 1972): 8.

102. "FTR del Carbón: Renovación sindical y movilización revolucionaria," *El Rebelde* 6.12 (January 7, 1972): 7.

103. Carillo, Coronel MIR group interview, March 5, 2011.

104. La Mura interview, May 12, 2011.

105. Cáceres interview, June 19, 2011.

3. "BY OUR OWN MEANS"

1. "De una 'pichanga' nació el 'Lenin,'" *El Sur,* May 24, 1970, 14.

2. "400 familias participaron en toma ilegal de terrenos," *El Sur,* May 9, 1970, 1, 16.

3. Newspaper reports identified by name the marginal neighborhoods of Hualpencillo, Manuel Rodríguez, Esmeralda, Prieto Cruz, as well as the outlying towns of Chiguayante and Coronel.

4. "De una 'pichanga' nació el 'Lenin,'" *El Sur,* May 24, 1970, 14.

5. Salinas Valdés, "Poder popular provincial," 82, 84, 149. In 1960, the combined population was 231,687; by 1970, it had grown by nearly another 100,000. The total population of Concepción province in 1970 was 642,163, with just over 40,000 recent migrants from other Chilean regions. The population of Concepción province doubled from 1940 to 1970, from 310,663 to 642,163, while the 1960 earthquake destroyed many of the older tenements in the city center.

6. Mario Garcés, *Tomando su sitio: El movimiento de pobladores de Santiago, 1957–1970* (Santiago: LOM, 2002); Edward Murphy, *For a Proper Home: Housing Rights in the Margins of Urban Chile, 1960–2010* (Pittsburgh: University of Pittsburgh Press, 2015); Alison J. Bruey, *Bread, Justice, and Liberty: Grassroots Activism and Human Rights in Pinochet's Chile* (Madison: University of Wisconsin Press, 2018).

7. Boris Cofré, *Campamento Nueva La Havana: El MIR y el movimiento de pobladores, 1970–1973* (Concepción: Ediciones Escaparate, 2007), 67.

8. Centro para el Desarrollo Económico y Social de América Latina (DESAL), *América Latina y desarrollo social,* 2 vols. (Santiago: DESAL, 1965).

9. Cofré, *Campamento Nueva La Havana,* 24.

10. Murphy, *For a Proper Home,* 89–90.

11. Angela Vergara, "Revisiting Pampa Irigoin: Social Movements, Repression, and Political Culture in 1960s Chile," *Radical History Review* 124 (January 2016): 43–54.

12. In an industrial province like Concepción, peasants were less present and thus have not been included in this study. On MIR activism in Cautín province, see Mallon, *Courage Tastes of Blood.*

13. Manuel Castells, "Movimiento de pobladores y lucha de clases en Chile," *EURE: Revista de Estudios Urbano Regionales* 3.7 (1973): 25.

14. Cofré, *Campamento Nueva La Havana,* 63–64.

15. Garcés, *Tomando su sitio,* 410. See also Cofré, *Campamento Nueva La Havana,* 72–84.

16. Nelson González, interview by author, Concepción, Chile, July 19, 2011, August 28, 2011.

17. The May 1970 toma of Campamento Lenin in Talcahuano prefigured the toma and consolidation of the MIR's emblematic Campamento Nueva La Havana in Santiago six months later. For more on the MIR's activism in Santiago poblaciones, see Garcés, *Tomando su sitio;* Palieraki, *¡La revolución ya viene!*

18. Humberto Fernández, interview by Mariel Ruiz Muñoz, Talcahuano, Chile, February 2012.

19. "La Población 'Lenin' vive horas de tensión," *La Crónica,* May 9, 1970, 3. See also "Aislado el Campamento Lenin," *El Sur,* May 10, 1970, 17.

20. Palieraki, *¡La revolucion ya viene!,* chap. 1.

21. Víctor Rebolledo, interview by author, Población Diego Portales (formerly Población Lenin), Talcahuano, Chile, November 1, 2011. At the time, Sigdo Kopper held the contract to build the Dow Chemical subsidiary, Petrodow.

22. In November 1970, a study carried out by the UP government identified 32,245 families with urgent housing needs in Concepción province. Calculating an average family size of five, the total number of individuals affected was 161,225. "10 mil casas es el Plan inicial para la provincial," *El Sur,* November 15, 1970, 4; "El sombrío presente de la vivienda," *El Sur,* November 15, 1970, 5.

23. J. C. M., "Campamento Lenin: Experiencia de lucha obrera," *Punto Final* 105 (May 26, 1970): 8–9.

24. Fundo San Miguel, also sometimes referred to as Fundo Macera. Héctor Jego, interview by author, Concepción, Chile, April 19, 2011.

25. Pedro Enríquez Barra, interview by author, Concepción, Chile, October 11, 2011. At the time government authorities accused the press of fomenting the toma by announcing the MINVU's plan to expropriate Fundo San Miguel.

26. "De una 'pichanga' nació el 'Lenin,'" *El Sur,* May 24, 1970, 14.

27. Jego interview, April 19, 2011; "La Población 'Lenin' vive horas de tensión," *La Crónica,* May 9, 1970, 3; "Aislado el Campamento Lenin," *El Sur,* May 10, 1970, 17.

28. "Policía impidió nueva ocupación," *El Sur,* May 11, 1970, 22.

29. "La Federación de Estudiantes, por intermedio de la presente, se permite solicitarle un préstamo de E 45.000 . . . ," Sergio Riffo letter to Secretary General, "Carpeta FEC," Archivos Generales Universidad de Concepción (AGUdeC).

30. Ana Sandoval, interview by Mariel Ruiz Muñoz, Concepción, Chile, February 2012.

31. "Salieron con la suya en Campamento Lenin; siguen en pie 'milicias' y 'olla común,'" *La Crónica*, May 14, 1970, 5; "Levantado el cordón policial; Campamento 'Lenin' se queda donde está," *El Sur*, May 14, 1970, 1, 14.

32. "Campamento 'Lenin' rechazó solución dada por gobierno," *El Sur*, May 12, 1970, 1.

33. "Salieron con la suya en Campamento 'Lenin,'" *La Cronica*, May 14, 1970, 5.

34. Garcés, *Tomando su sitio*, 411.

35. "Aislado el Campamento Lenin," *El Sur*, May 10, 1970, 17.

36. "El Intendente: Es un abierto desafío; el gobierno no tratará con sediciosos," *El Sur*, May 10, 1970, 9; "Urrejola: 'No hay solución por vía de violencia,'" *El Sur*, May 11, 1970, 9.

37. "De una 'pichanga' nació el 'Lenin,'" *El Sur*, May 24, 1970, 14.

38. Juan José Salinas Valdés, "Campamento Lenin: Expresión de poder popular en Talcahuano/Concepción, 1970–1973" (MA thesis, Universidad de Concepción, 2012), 178–80.

39. Humberto Fernández interview, February 2012.

40. Jego interview, April 19, 2011.

41. Sandoval interview, February 2012; Rosa Jara, interview by Gina Inostroza Retamal, Talcahuano, Chile, March 19, 2016.

42. Rebolledo interview, November 1, 2011.

43. Murphy, *For a Proper Home*, 35–37.

44. "400 familias participaron en toma ilegal de terrenos," *El Sur*, May 9, 1970, 1, 16.

45. Guevara's March 1965 essay, originally titled "From Algiers," is credited with developing the idea of "the new man." In 1966, the MIR circulated the first Chilean edition of Guevara's essay in their magazine *Estrategia*.

46. "Aislado el Campamento Lenin," *El Sur*, May 10, 1970, 17.

47. "La Población 'Lenin' vive horas de tensión," *La Crónica*, May 9, 1970, 3.

48. Banned activities included "1. Pelea entre pobladores; 2. Comportamiento irresponsable con la familia; 3. Desaseo general en la vivienda; 4. No concurrencia injustificada a las asambleas generales; 5. Falta de cooperación en la recolección de ayuda; 6. Llegar curado e introducir trago al campamento; 7. Prohibida toda clase de juegos de azar; 8. Negarse injustificadamente a hacer guardia; 9. Abandonar la guardia; 10. Robo; 11. Permanencia en el campamento." "11 son los mandamientos de los ocupantes," *La Crónica*, May 11, 1970, 2. Among the documents seized at the failed toma of Fundo Bellavista in August 1970 was a similar version of the "Reglamento interno de los pobladores." Those detained claimed no knowledge of the document or its origins.

49. Humberto Fernández interview, February 2012.

50. Humberto Fernández interview, February 2012.

51. "La Población Lenin vive horas de tensión," *La Cronica*, May 9, 1970, 3.

52. Humberto Fernández interview, February 2012.

53. Amanda Galindo Mardones, quoted in "Aislado el Campamento Lenin," *El Sur*, May 10, 1970, 17.

54. Ibid.

55. "La Población 'Lenin' vive horas de tensión," *La Crónica*, May 9, 1970, 3; "2.680 personas habitan la población denominada 'Campamento Lenin,'" *El Sur*, May 25, 1970, 9.

56. "Salieron con la suya en Campamento Lenin: Siguen en pie 'milicias' y 'olla común,'" *La Crónica*, May 14, 1970, 5.

57. "Dirigentes de la 'Lenin' partieron a Santiago," *El Sur*, May 27, 1970, 70.

58. Ernesto Herrera, quoted in "Aislado el Campamento Lenin," *El Sur,* May 10, 1970, 17.

59. "Aislado el Campamento Lenin," *El Sur,* May 10, 1970, 17;"400 familias participaron en toma ilegal de terrenos," *El Sur,* May 9, 1970, 16.

60. Eduardo Cruz, "Acerca de Rudy," Memoria Viva, accessed April 15, 2012, www .memoriaviva.cl. See also various testimonies cited in Salinas, "Campamento Lenin," 167–74.

61. "La Población 'Lenin' vive horas de tensión," *La Crónica,* May 9, 1973, 3.

62. "Inhumanas condiciones de vida en Población 'Lenin,'" *El Sur,* May 30, 1970, 1, 16.

63. Patrick Barr-Melej, "Siloísmo and the Self in Allende's Chile: Youth 'Total Revolution,' and the Roots of the Humanist Movement," *Hispanic American Historical Review* 86.4 (November 2006): 747–84; Barr-Melej, *Psychedelic Chile.*

64. "Inhumanas condiciones de vida en Población 'Lenin,'" *El Sur,* May 30, 1970, 1, 16.

65. "Polémica en torno al Campamento 'Lenin': Otarola vs. dirigentes," *La Crónica,* June 1, 1970, 4.

66. "Inhumanas condiciones de vida en Población 'Lenin,'" *El Sur,* May 30, 1970, 16.

67. "Pobladores responden a delegado de CORHABIT," *El Sur,* May 31, 1970, 21.

68. "Polémica en torno al Campamento 'Lenin': Otarola vs. dirigentes," *La Crónica,* June 1, 1970, 4.

69. *El Sur,* March 2, 1971, 7; March 4, 1971, 9.

70. "Se vislumbra solución en toma de 'San Miguel,'" *La Crónica,* May 11, 1970, 3.

71. "Polémica en torno al Campamento 'Lenin': Otarola vs. dirigentes," *La Crónica,* June 1, 1970, 4.

72. Salinas, "Poder popular provincial," 179.

73. Mario Garcés, "El movimiento de pobladores durante la Unidad Popular, 1970–1973," *Atenea* 512 (July–December 2015): 43.

74. Jego interview, April 19, 2011.

75. Sandoval interview, February 2012.

76. Jara interview, 2016. Women also participated in Santiago's Nueva La Havana. See also Colin Henfrey and Bernardo Sorj, *Chilean Voices: Activists Describe Their Experiences of the Popular Unity Period* (Atlantic Highlands, NJ: Humanities Press, 1977), 137.

77. Lusvenia Fernández, interview by Gina Inostroza, Talcahuano, Chile, March 19, 2016.

78. Elisabeth Jean Wood, *Insurgent Collective Action and Civil War in El Salvador* (Cambridge: Cambridge University Press, 2003).

79. "Entrevista con pobladora y su marido del Campamento Lenin (Diego Portales)," unpublished interview by the nonprofit organization Servicios de Estudios Regionales (SER), 1990.

80. "2.680 personas habitan la población denominada 'Campamento Lenin,'" *El Sur,* May 25, 1970, 9. For more on the olla común, see "Salieron con la suya en Campamento Lenin: Siguen en pie 'milicias' y 'olla común,'" *La Crónica,* May 14. On May 14, 1970, approximately 300 people received food from the communal pot.

81. Jara interview, March 19, 2016.

82. Ida Subiabre, interview by author, Población Diego Portales (formerly Población Lenin), Talcahuano, Chile, November 1, 2011.

83. Celinda Opazao, quoted in "Pobladores muestra la otra cara de la toma," *El Sur,* June 6, 1970, 8.

84. Subiabre interview, 2011.

85. Tinsman, *Partners in Conflict.*

86. Lusvenia Fernández, Ida Subiabre, and Víctor Robolledo interviews.

87. In a 1974–75 interview in exile, "Laura," a MIR housing activist, describes a similar process in Santiago's Nueva La Havana shantytown, observing that even if adults did not immediately change gender relations, their efforts provided important examples to young people who did seem to reflect these new attitudes. Henfrey and Sorj, *Chilean Voices,* 139.

88. Lusvenia Fernández interview, March 19, 2016; Jara interview, March 19, 2016.

89. "Partidos políticos en pugna por la Población 'Lenin,'" *El Sur,* June 3, 1970, 1.

90. Ibid. 1,16.

91. "Comenzaron expulsiones, 'Lista negra' en el Campamento 'Lenin,'" *El Sur,* June 5, 1970, 1, 16.

92. "Alcohol y delincuencia en el Campamento Lenin," *El Sur,* March 2, 1971, 7.

93. "En Campamento 'Lenin': No aceptan comandos de los 'presidenciables,'" *La Crónica,* June 3, 1970; Murphy, *For a Proper Home,* 91–92.

94. "Celedonio," quoted in Jose del Pozo, *Rebeldes, reformistas y revolucionarios: Una historia oral de la izquierda chilena en la época de la Unidad Popular* (Santiago: Ediciones Documentas, 1992), 30.

95. Jego interview, April 19, 2011. Although the MIR mass front for pobladores (MPR) was formally founded in October 1970, throughout 1970 and much of 1971 the Concepción MIR—not the MPR—appeared as the primary public actor in revolutionary shantytown activities.

96. "400 familias participaron en toma ilegal de terrenos," *El Sur,* May 9, 1970, 1, 16.

97. Helmut Frenz, *Mi vida chilena: Solidaridad con los oprimidos,* trans. Sonia Plaut (Santiago: LOM, 2006), 57.

98. Ibid., 59, 61.

99. *El Sur,* July 13, 1970, 19.

100. Frenz, *Mi vida chilena,* 65. The landowner Carlos Macera initially pressed a lawsuit against those responsible for building the shelter. Thanks to connections and the influence of their members, the German Lutheran community managed to avoid a legal conflict with him.

101. Jego interview, April 19, 2011.

102. Jorge Fuentes, Sesión de Claustro Pleno, July 23,1970, foja 23, AGUdeC.

103. Between May and August 1970, the sixteen tomas in Concepción province were in Talcahuano, 9; Penco, 3; Barrio Norte Concepción, 2; San Pedro de la Paz, 1; and Hualqui, 1. Two tomas can be linked to Popular Unity parties; six tomas can be linked directly to the Campamento Lenin leadership and University of Concepción students associated with the MIR and the FEC. For additional information, see the Concepción data compiled by Mario Garcés and Susana Costamagna, "El movimiento de pobladores durante la UP: De las 'tomas de sitios' a la formación de poblaciones." The author wishes to thank Garcés and Costamagna for sharing their unpublished data. July 1970 witnessed a new wave of MIR-backed land takeovers in Santiago that paralleled those in Concepción.

104. Jego interview, April 19, 2011.

105. "185 detenidos en otra toma: La 'Lenin' amplió sus dominios," *El Sur,* August 31, 1970, 30.

106. Murphy, *For a Proper Home,* 119.

107. Pedro Cifuentes Jara, "Ursupación de terrenos en Fundo Bellavista," AJC.

108. Julio Cuevas Gática, "Ursupación de terrenos en Fundo Bellavista," AJC. After paying a fine, the 134 men and 16 students were released within a few days. When the police failed to build a case against the MIR students for lack of witnesses, the case was closed.

109. "El MIR lleva un candidato al sindicato," *La Crónica,* November 26, 1970, 16.

110. "Distribuyen la tierra en la Lenin," *La Crónica,* August 31, 1970, 3.

111. *El Sur,* August 25, 1970, 1; August 27, 1970, 12; *La Crónica,* August 25, 1970, 1; "Playa Negra: 'Somos del pabellón de la vergüenza,'" *La Crónica,* August 26, 1970, 20.

112. Garcés, "El movimiento de pobladores durante la Unidad Popular," 37–40.

113. Jorge Fuentes, *Actas del Consejo Superior* (No. 64:4), October 7, 1970, AGUdeC.

114. Alejandro Saavedra, *Actas del Consejo Superior* (No. 64:4), October 7, 1970, AGUdeC.

115. *Actas del Consejo Superior* (No. 64:4), October 7, 1970, AGUdeC.

116. *El Sur,* December 17, 1970, 11.

117. *Actas del Consejo Superior* (No. 18:8), May 26, 1971, AGUdeC.

118. "Tranquilo congreso en Campamento Lenin," *Diario Color,* May 8, 1971, 1, 6.

119. Víctor Toro, interview by author, Bronx, NY, July 27, 2012.

120. Toro, quoted in "Congreso de Pobladores: Sin casa renuncian a tomas," *El Sur,* May 10, 1971, 15.

121. Toro, quoted in "Congreso de Pobladores."

122. In an oral history interview, Víctor Toro recalled that among the delegates were Talcahuano dockworkers, Tomé textile workers, and Coronel coal miners. He noted his own surprise at so many unionized workers without homes, which differentiated Concepción province from his experiences organizing pobladores in Santiago. Toro interview, July 27, 2012.

123. Toro interview, July 27, 2012.

124. Toro interview, July 27, 2012.

125. Robles interview, August 2, 2011.

126. Robles interview, August 2, 2011.

127. Robles interview, August 2, 2011.

128. Robles interview, August 2, 2011.

129. Murphy, *For a Proper Home,* 117.

130. Toro interview, July 27, 2012.

131. Toro interview, July 27, 2012.

132. "Dirigente del MIR vino a organizar ocupantes ilegales," *El Sur,* December 5, 1971, 12.

133. Toro interview, July 27, 2012.

134. Jara interview, March 19, 2016.

4. "LET THE PEOPLE SPEAK!"

1. Estimates of total attendance range from 3,000 to 6,000, likely depending on how the crowd outside was counted. Newspaper reports agree that Teatro Concepción's 1,122-person seating capacity was completely full and that crowds overflowed, filling the Plaza de Independencia and nearby streets. MAPU leader Eduardo Aquevedo emphasized the representativeness of the gathering but estimated the attendance to be between 500 and 600

people. People had started arriving at 6:00 P.M., the first round of formal speeches started at 7:35 and ended at 9:30 P.M. The meeting itself stretched past midnight. "30 oradores en la Asamblea," *Diario Color,* July 28, 1972, 5; Silva, *Los cordones industriales,* 175; Cancino, *Chile: La problemática del poder popular,* 263; Ramón Riquelme, "Las tareas que dejó planteada la primera asamblea del pueblo," *Punto Final* 6.164 (August 15, 1972): 12; Eduardo Aquevedo, interview by author, Santiago, Chile, October 20, 2011.

2. Mario Garcés, interview by author, Santiago, Chile, December 9, 2011.

3. "Fernando Manque," interview by Gina Inostroza and Marco Contreras, Concepción, Chile, July 16, 2014.

4. Manuel Antonio Garretón, *The Chilean Political Process,* trans. Sharon Kellum (Boston: Unwin Hyman, 1989)0.

5. "30 oradores en la Asamblea," *Diario Color,* Concepción, Chile, July 28, 1972, 5.

6. Oral histories provide evidence of collaboration in the bases across leftist party lines going back to the late 1960s. See Aquevedo interview, October 20, 2011; Saéz interview, August 31, 2011; González interview, June 16, 2011; Rodríguez interview, October 31, 2011.

7. "Asamblea del Pueblo: nómina de las organizaciones adherentes," *El Sur,* July 27, 1972, 11.

8. Joint press statement issued by PS, MAPU, IC, and MIR, "Documento de Concepción," *Diario Color,* May 24, 1972, 13.

9. Trumper, *Ephemeral Histories,* 6–7. See also Gabriel Salazar V. and Julio Pinto V., *Historia contemporánea de Chile V: Niñez y juventud* (Santiago: LOM, 2002), 217; Salazar, *La violencia política popular en las "grandes alamedas."*

10. Organizers had hired a chain of regional radio stations to cover it but cancelled their contract at the last minute, citing an "orden superior." No recording of the event survives. "Asamblea sin voz," *El Sur,* July 28, 1972, 1.

11. "Asamblea del Pueblo aprueban sectores UP de Concepción,"*El Mercurio,* July 29, 1972, 1, 16. See also descriptions in *Chile Hoy* of conservative reactions in *La Prensa.*

12. "Una 'Lesera' dura calificativo del Senador Montes para 'Asamblea del Pueblo,'" *El Sur,* July 28, 1972, 1.

13. "Enérgico rechazo de Allende a la 'Asamblea del Pueblo,'" *El Mercurio,* August 1, 1972, 8.

14. Hugo Cancino Troncoso, *Chile: La problemática del poder popular en el proceso de la vía chilena al socialismo, 1970–1973* (Aarhus, Denmark: Aarhus University Press, 1988), 247.

15. Miguel Silva, *Los cordones industriales y el socialismo desde abajo* (Santiago: Imprenta Lizor, n.d); Danny Gonzalo Monsálvez Araneda, "La Asamblea del Pueblo en Concepción: La expresión del poder popular," *Revista de Historia* 16 (2006): 37–58; Salinas Valdés, "Poder popular provincial"; Sebastián Leiva, *Revolución socialista y poder popular: Los casos del MIR y PRT-ERP, 1970–1976* (Concepción: Ediciones Escaparate, 2010).

16. Greg Grandin, "Living in Revolutionary Time: Coming to Terms with the Violence of Latin America's Long Cold War," in *A Century of Revolution: Insurgent and Counterinsurgent Violence during Latin America's Long Cold War,* ed. Greg Grandin and Gilbert M. Joseph (Durham, NC: Duke University Press, 2010), 4.

17. Grandin, "Living in Revolutionary Time," 20.

18. Brian Loveman, *Chile: The Legacy of Hispanic Capitalism,* 3rd ed. (New York: Oxford University Press, 2010).

19. The Frei administration extended the right to vote to illiterate adults. The 1970 presidential election was the first with the newly expanded electorate. In *Mining for the Nation,* Jody Pavilack makes a similar argument about the Popular Front in the coal zone in the 1940s in which a period of popular mobilization and unique local leftist coalitions ended in state repression.

20. Peter Winn documented a similar encounter over who leads and who follows in the meeting between striking Yarur textile workers and President Allende; see Winn, *Weavers of Revolution,* 185–86, 192–93.

21. Garcés interview, December 9, 2011. Garcés refers to the Argentinian sociologist José Nun as developing this concept in relation to social movements elsewhere in Latin America.

22. Winn, "The Furies of the Andes," 240–42.

23. Power, *Right-Wing Women around the World.* See also Trumper, *Emphemeral Histories.*

24. Pobladores in Concepción carried out 117 land takeovers in 1971; by comparison, in the same period Santiago saw just 3 new land takeovers and Valparaíso 22. By January 1972, just under 15,000 residents of Concepción lived in campamentos that resulted from land takeovers. Garcés, "El movimiento de pobladores durante la Unidad Popular."

25. Víctor Toro, interview by author, Bronx, NY, July 27, 2012.

26. At the time Andrés Pascal Allende was a member of the MIR Political Commission and nephew of the president. Andrés Pascal Allende, interview by author, Santiago, Chile, December 12, 2011.

27. The Popular Unity agreed to back the MUI candidates in Concepción student federation elections, which allowed Nelson Gutiérrez (MIR) to win 59% of the vote for his second term as FEC president in 1971. As the first three chapters revealed, MIR control of the student federation proved critical for expanding support in the region.

28. The Popular Unity broke off this round of talks (December 1970–June 1971) at the behest of the PC. Fidel Castro initiated the second round between December 1971 and January 1972; the Popular Unity also ended these talks. Negotiations opened again between April and May 1972 and were broken off following the May 12 march in Concepción and the Concepción Manifesto. As a condition of the talks, the MIR insisted that their results be made public. Pedro Naranjo, "La vida de Miguel Enríquez el MIR," in Naranjo et al., *Miguel Enríquez y el proyecto revolucionario en Chile,* 70–71; and Miguel Enríquez, "Informe de la CP al CC sobre las conversaciones MIR-UP" (May 20, 1972), in Naranjo et al., *Miguel Enríquez y el proyecto revolucionario en Chile,* 153–59.

29. "Penquistas también realizarán marcha," *El Sur,* April 9, 1972, 12.

30. Gwynn Thomas, "The Legacies of Patrimonial Patriarchalism," *Annals of the American Academy of Political and Social Science* 636.1 (July 2011): 69–87; Gwynn Thomas, *Contesting Legitimacy in Chile: Familial Ideals, Citizenship, and Political Struggle, 1970–1990* (University Park: Pennsylvania State University Press, 2012).

31. "Declaración del FTR," *El Sur,* January 4, 1972, 8.

32. "Lider del MIR proclamó a candidatos del FTR," *El Sur,* April 24, 1972, 16. See also "Lo que dijo el MIR en el Carbón," *El Rebelde* 6.27 (April 25, 1972): 8–10.

33. "Todos desean marcha el 12," *El Sur,* May 6, 1972, 14.

34. "FTR quiere discutir el mismo día que lo haga la oposición ¿Qué hará la autoridad?," *El Sur,* May 5, 1972, 8. The Sindicato Único de la Construcción in Concepción province was

formed in September 1972. See "Se constituye Sindicato Único de la construcción," *El Sur*, September 23, 1972, 7.

35. "Acuerdo MIR-UP: 'Impedir marcha de la democracia,'" *El Sur*, May 10, 1972, 1.

36. "Mañana marcha sólo la oposición: Determinación del gobierno (Santiago)," *El Sur*, May 11, 1972, 16.

37. "Gobierno postergó marchas de la unidad popular y del MIR; militantes se tomarán las calles," *Diario Color*, May 11, 1972, 7.

38. PS, MAPU, PR, IC, and MIR, "Declaración Conjunta (Concepción)," May 10, 1972, printed in "Mañana marcha sólo la oposición: Determinación del gobierno (Santiago)," *El Sur*, May 11, 1972, 16.

39. La Mura interview, April 29, 2011.

40. "La CUT," *Diario Color*, May 12, 1972, 5.

41. "A las 17 horas se reúne la oposición: plenas garantías asegura el gobierno," *El Sur*, May 12, 1972, 16.

42. "Hoy marcha la patria," *El Sur*, May 12, 1972, 7.

43. Convocatoria para el 12 de mayo, "Llamamos al pueblo a ocupar las calles de Concepción e impedir los desmanes y provocaciones de los grupos fascistas de Patria y Libertad, del PDC y del PN," *El Sur*, May 12, 1972, 10. This group closely maps onto the signatories of the July 27 People's Assembly in Concepción. Organizations denoted with an asterisk (*) appeared on both *convocatorias* printed in the local press: CUT; Comando Provincial de Pobladores; *FEC; *FEPRESCO; Consejo Provincial Campesino; *Partido Socialista; *Partido Radical; *MAPU; *IC; *MIR; *Sindicato Industrial, Metalúrgico y de Empleados de Schwager; FENATS Provincial; *Sindicato Industrial CAP; *Sindicato Sigdo Koppers; *Sindicato ASMAR; *Sindicato INCHALAM; Sindicato del Cuero y el Calzado; *Sindicato Industrial FANALOZA, Penco; *Sindicatos Fábricas Bellavista, FIAP y Oveja; Sindicato Ralco; *Sindicato Industrial CCU; Frente Provincial de Pobladores y Campamentos; *Sindicato Provincial de Periodistas; *Sindicato General de Empleados y Obrero del Diario el SUR.

44. "Concepción: Unidad revolucionaria contra el fascismo y la conciliación," *El Rebelde* 6.30 (May 16, 1972): 3.

45. "Suspendida marcha de oposición: orden expresa del Presidente de la República," *El Sur*, May 13, 1972, 1.

46. Ibid.

47. "Izquierdistas marcharon desde el foro de la 'U,'" *Diario Color*, May 13, 1972, 5.

48. "Heridos y detenidos," *El Sur*, May 13, 1972, 1.

49. Ibid.

50. Reports of the number of speakers range from 21 to 53. See "Izquierdistas marcharon desde el foro de la 'U,'" *Diario Color*, May 13, 1972, 5; "Documento de Concepción,"*Diario Color*, May 24, 1972, 13; Marcial Muñoz, interview by author, Santiago, Chile, January 7, 2011.

51. "Nelson Gutiérrez (Secretario Nacional del MIR): Debate con Salvador Allende en la Universidad de Concepción," *Punto Final* 132 (June 8, 1971).

52. "Izquierdistas marcharon desde el foro de la 'U,'" *Diario Color*, May 13, 1972, 5.

53. "Heridos y detenidos," *El Sur*, May 13, 1972, 1.

54. The subsequent speeches alternated between unionists and students, including representatives from the municipal workers, the journalist union, the high school student federation FEPRESCO, and many more. The MIR's mass fronts appear overrepresented among

the speakers identified by the local press, perhaps a decision by *El Sur* to hype the event as MIR dominated. Yet the MIR's May 12 rally was originally planned as a campaign launch for FTR candidates running in CUT elections; thus it makes sense that many social leaders associated with the MIR had planned to speak that day.

55. Marcial Muñoz, interview by author, Santiago, Chile, January 7, 2011. His version is consistent with the fact that newspaper accounts only identified by name the more recognizable leaders, referring to others as, for example, "a MAPU shantytown leader."

56. Muñoz interview, January 7, 2011.

57. Estimates for attendance at the two marches vary. The MIR newspaper *El Rebelde* listed 25,000 for the Left and 2,000 for the Right; the FEC president, Manuel Rodríguez (PS), also reported 25,000 on the campus. The local conservative newspaper *El Sur* estimated attendance at the opposition march to be 6,000. Years later in an interview, MIR leader Pedro Enríquez Barra noted that it was the largest march he had ever seen in Concepción and estimated the turnout to be between 15,000 and 20,000. "Concepción: Unidad revolucionaria contra el fascismo y la conciliación," *El Rebelde* 6.30 (May 16, 1972): 3; "Suspendida marcha de oposición: Orden expresa del Presidente de la República," *El Sur,* May 13, 1972, 1; "La FEC a la comundiad universitaria, a los trabajadores de Concepción, y opinión pública en general," *Diario Color,* May 15, 1972, 15. Pedro Enríquez Barra, interview by author, Concepción, Chile, August 25, 2011.

58. "Heridos y detenidos," *El Sur,* May 13, 1972, 1.

59. Muñoz interview, January 7, 2011.

60. González interview, August 28, 2011.

61. "Izquierdistas marcharon desde el foro de la 'U,'" *Diario Color,* May 13, 1972, 5.

62. Muñoz interview, January 7, 2011.

63. Enríquez Barra interview, August 25, 2011; "La izquierda no sale a la calle esta tarde," *La Crónica,* May 24, 1972, 3.

64. Álvaro Riffo, interview by Eugenia Palieraki, Concepción, Chile, January 10, 2005.

65. Muñoz interview, January 7, 2011.

66. Alberto Vidal, interview with author, Concepción, Chile, April 5, 2011. On the astonishment at the massive turnout, which surpassed all expectations, see also Enríquez interviews, August 25 and October 11, 2011; Monsalves interview, August 15, 2011; Veloso interview, August 4, 2011; Riffo interview, January 10, 2005.

67. PS, MAPU, PR, IC, and MIR, "Al pueblo de Concepción," *Diario Color,* May 14, 1972, 15.

68. Manuel Rodríguez, "La FEC a la comunidad universitaria, a los trabajadores de Concepción, y opinión pública en general," *Diario Color,* May 15, 1972, 15. Members of the Communist Ramona Parra Brigade shot MIR students Arnoldo Ríos and Oscar Lynch on the UdeC campus; Ríos later died of his wounds. Cruz died in a domestic accident. Eladio Caamaño died of his injuries on May 13. He belonged to the Maoist-oriented Revolutionary Communist Party (PCR) but received a MIR-FER funeral.

69. Ibid. The Group of Five also demanded the dismissal of Communist governor Wladimir Chávez and the immediate dissolution of the reviled riot police, the Grupo Móvil, as originally outlined in the 40-point program of the Popular Unity government.

70. "Declaración de la Comisión política del Partido Comunista," insert, *Noticias de Última Hora,* May 17, 1972, 4.

71. Manuel Castells, "La lucha política de clases y la democracia burguesa en Chile," *Documento del Trabajo No. 60* (Santiago: Universidad Católica de Chile, Centro Interdisciplinario de Desarrollo Urbano, December 1972), 82.

72. Silva, *Los cordones industriales,* 172; "La UP no está dividida," *El Sur,* May 17, 1972, 1.

73. Aquevedo interview, October 20, 2011; Enríquez Barra interview, October 11, 2011.

74. For example, MIR leader Pedro Enríquez Barra and Socialist leader Rafael Merino were second cousins. Enríquez Barra interview, August 25, 2011.

75. Enríquez Barra interview, October 11, 2011.

76. Enríquez Barra interview, August 25, 2011.

77. Joaquín Undarraga, "La lucha por la calle (2)," *Diario Color,* May 23, 1972, 2.

78. Joint press statement issued by PS, MAPU, IC, and MIR, "Documento de Concepción," *Diario Color,* May 24, 1972, 13. Reprinted in its entirety as "El 'Manifiesto de Concepción,'" *Punto Final* 6.159 (June 6, 1972), 4–7. The drafting of the document appears to have been a collaborative effort among regional leaders.

79. Joaquín Undarraga, "La lucha por la calle (2)," *Diario Color,* May 23, 1972, 2.

80. Joint press statement issued by PS, MAPU, IC, and MIR, "Documento de Concepción," *Diario Color,* May 24, 1972, 13.

81. Ibid.

82. Ibid. *Comunal* denotes *comuna*-wide. A *comuna* is roughly equivalent to a county or municipality—the smallest administrative subdivision in Chile, followed by departments and then provinces. While "commune" carries connotations in English not applicable in Chile, "municipality" in Chile carries connotations linked to top-down 1974 territorial and administrative reorganization imposed during the Pinochet dictatorship. For these reasons, *comuna* is used throughout this study in the original Spanish.

83. Miguel Enríquez, quoted in "Documentos," *Punto Final* 6.159 (June 6, 1972); Cancino, *La problemática del poder popular,* 251–53.

84. Joint press statement issued by PS, MAPU, IC, and MIR, "Documento de Concepción," *Diario Color,* May 24, 1972, 13.

85. Winn, *Weavers of Revolution,* 233–34. For more on the Lo Curro meeting, see Sergio Bitar, *Chile: 1970–1973* (Mexico City: Siglo Veintiuno, 1979), 156–57.

86. Communist leaders demanded that the Allende government break off talks with the MIR initiated during Fidel Castro's visit in December 1971 and renewed in April 1972. Cuban intelligence officer Ulises Estrada recalled an eventual compromise "reached with Allende whereby Cuba would continue offering armed training to the MIR . . . but would provide it with no new arms until or unless there was a coup, at which point the Cubans would hand over a stockpile of weapons that they would now begin assembling in Santiago." Tanya Harmer, *Allende's Chile and the Inter-American Cold War* (Chapel Hill: University of North Carolina Press, 2011), 155; Cancino, *La problemática del poder popular,* 277–78.

87. Castells, "La lucha política de clases," 84.

88. Winn observed that "the failure of compromise in July 1972 and the advent of confrontation politics one month later were indications that the Opposition was not going to give the Lo Curro strategy the opportunity to succeed." *Weavers of Revolution,* 234.

89. The more radical wings of the MAPU and the PS dominated the Concepción regional leaderships and memberships. See Manuel Rodríguez, interview by author, San Pedro de la Paz, Chile, October 7, 2011; Aquevedo interview, October 20, 2011.

90. Aquevedo interview, October 20, 2011; Enríquez Barra interview, October 11, 2011.

91. *Programa básico de gobierno de la Unidad Popular* (Santiago, 1969).

92. Ibid.

93. Cancino, *La problemática del poder popular,* 251–52.

94. FTR-MIR, "Documento sobre el VI Congreso de la Central Única de Trabajadores," in Farías, *La izquierda chilena (1969–1973),* 1669. In the FTR's platform, the Asamblea Popular sounded remarkably similar in composition and function to the Consejos de Trabajadores. The Asamblea Popular would have the participation of workers, peasants, employees, artisans, professionals, soldiers, pobladores, and students and would be organized locally, communally, provincially, and nationally. "Documentos," *Punto Final* 6.159 (June 6, 1972).

95. Aquevedo interview, October 20, 2011; Silva, *Los cordones industriales,* 173.

96. Enríquez Barra interview, October 11, 2011.

97. In CUT elections held on May 30–31, 1972, the Communist Party garnered 30.69% of the votes, ahead of the PS and DC. "Resultados oficiales de elección de la CUT," *El Sur,* July 25, 1972, 7.

98. Aquevedo interview, October 20, 2011.

99. Silva, *Los cordones industriales,* 173.

100. Aquevedo interview, October 20, 2011.

101. "Declaración pública de Sindicato del EL SUR," *El Sur,* July 20, 1972, 7.

102. See "En la UTE piden formar la 'Asamblea del Pueblo,'" *El Sur,* July 20, 1972, 7; "'Implementar una movilización de masas' propone MAPU," *El Sur,* July 20, 1972, 7; "El MUI en busca de 'una alternativa revolucionaria,'" *El Sur,* July 22, 1972, 7.

103. "Apoyo a las Asambleas del Pueblo," *Diario Color,* July 23, 1972, 6.

104. Rodríguez interview, October 7, 2011.

105. Between May and July, the balance of power within the provincial CUT shifted. In May 1972 CUT elections, the Communist Party obtained 31%, the Socialist Party 27%, the Christian Democrats 20%, the MAPU 6%, PR 5%, and the FTR less than 4%. Yet according to a pact between the PS, MAPU, and MIR, the two *consejeros*-elect from the MAPU and the one from the FTR would back "the Socialist compañero for general secretary," giving him a one vote margin over the Communists. However, MIR leader Pedro Enríquez Barra recalled that "word came down from Santiago that the CUT in Concepción was reserved for the Communists and we had to step aside"; in late July, socialist labor leader Oscar González accepted the second-in-command position. Enríquez Barra interview, October 11, 2011.

106. "Apoyo a las Asambleas del Pueblo," *Diario Color,* July 23, 1972, 6.

107. "¡Todos a la Asamblea del Pueblo para denunciar el caracter contrarrevolucionario del parlamento y para rendir homenaje a la gloriosa Revolución cubana!," *El Sur,* July 23, 1972, 19. Also in *Diario Color.*

108. In 1972, Fernando Manque's small MCR group had recently won a stunning victory in gaining leadership positions within the provincewide Peasant Federation Los Valientes de la Concepción. As a worker on the Fundo Leonora in Hualqui, a member of the Campesino Unity Committee in Hualqui, a leader in the Peasant Federation Los Valientes de la

Concepción, and finally a militant of the MCR, Manque alone was associated with four of the six peasant groups that signed on as official sponsors of the July People's Assembly.

109. On the formation of Campamento Arnoldo Ríos, named for the slain UdeC MIR student, see "Ocupación de terrenos en Hualqui," *El Sur,* January 18, 1971, 14. Manque also participated in the creation of Campamento Che Guevara of Fundo Vaquería. See "MCR ocupó fundo en Hualqui," *El Sur,* May 22, 1971, 1, 14.

110. Manque interview, July 16, 2014.

111. Manque interview, July 16, 2014.

112. Manque interview, July 16, 2014.

113. Silva, *Los cordones industriales,* 174.

114. "Asamblea del Pueblo' plantea quiebre UP," *El Sur,* July 26, 1972, 1, 6; "Partidos ante Asamblea del Pueblo," *Diario Color,* July 26, 1972, 8.

115. Ibid.

116. *Diario Color,* July 26, 1972.

117. *Diario Color,* July 26, 1972,11.

118. "PS: Nada con los ultras," *El Sur,* July 27, 1972, 12.

119. A list of sponsoring organizations for the Concepción People's Assembly, July 27, 1972, can be found in the appendix.

120. Asamblea," *El Sur,* July 27, 1972, 1. According to the version reported in *Chile Hoy* by Marta Harnecker, the Group of Five had agreed "to eliminate the formal participation of the political parties to give the stage to representatives from social organizations." Yet the MIR and UP parties failed to reach an agreement about the format; the terms of this disagreement are unknown. Silva, *Los cordones industriales,* 175.

121. Lily Rivas Labbé, interview with author, Concepción, Chile, October 11, 2011.

122. Rivas interview, October 11, 2011.

123. "Debutó Asamblea del Pueblo," *El Sur,* July 28, 1972, 7; Silva, *Los cordones industriales,* 175.

124. The speaking order for predesignated representatives was Enrique Torres (MAPU union leader from coal zone), Ramón Riquelme (MIR/MCR, president of Chilean-Cuban Cultural Institute), Ricardo Bozzo (IC leader), Humberto Bravo (PR regional secretary), Manuel Vergara (MIR regional secretary), and Manuel Rodríguez (Socialist city councilman and president of the Student Federation of Concepción). At the time, Bozzo, Vergara, and Rodríguez were all UdeC students. The event was presided over by the same six social leaders who had called for its celebration in the July 23 newspaper announcement, with the exception of Marcial Muñoz, who was not in Concepción that day. "Debutó Asamblea del Pueblo," *El Sur,* July 28, 1972, 7.

125. "30 oradores en la Asamblea," *Diario Color,* July 28, 1972, 5.

126. Garcés interview, December 9, 2011.

127. Silva, *Los cordones industriales,* 175.

128. Oral histories confirm that MIR militants who attended the People's Assembly did not have prior knowledge of the "Let the people speak" chant or that there would be open microphones; rather, they too joined the spontaneous demand to transform the event into an open assembly. See Garcés interview, December 9, 2011.

129. Garcés interview, December 9, 2011.

130. Rodríguez interview, October 7, 2011.

131. Manque interview, July 16, 2014.

132. Rivas interview, October 11, 2011.

133. Rodríguez interview, October 7, 2011. See also Aquevedo interview, October 20, 2011.

134. "30 oradores en la Asamblea," *Diario Color*, July 28, 1972, 5.

135. Silva, *Los cordones industriales*, 175.

136. Rodríguez interview, October 7, 2011. MAPU leader Eduardo Aquevedo noted that the People's Assembly had been "prepared in advance to not get away from us and become a show of the ultra-Left." Aquevedo interview, October 20, 2011.

137. Manuel Castells summarized the motions presented by the UP and MIR as "coinciding in the need to take on political tasks beyond the government initiatives[,] . . . in particular the organization of Community Councils of Workers to coordinate and promote the leadership and popular control in different mass fronts (factories, schools, fundos, poblaciones, health, etc.)." Castells, "La lucha política de clases," 83.

138. Manque interview, July 16, 2014.

139. Jeff Goodwin, James M. Jasper, and Francesca Poletta, *Passionate Politics: Emotions and Social Movements* (Chicago: University of Chicago Press, 2001); Nicole Fabricant and Nancy Postero, "Contested Bodies, Contested States: Performance, Emotions, and New Forms of Regional Governance in Santa Cruz, Bolivia," *JLACA* 18.2 (2013): 187–211.

140. Garcés interview, December 9, 2011.

5. "BUILDING THEIR OWN POWER"

1. "Coronel sin pan," *El Sur*, October 5, 1972, 1.

2. "Miembros del FTR ocuparon panadería," *El Sur*, January 14, 1973, 14. All interviewed Coronel residents agreed the bread was of terrible quality. Hugo Monsalves, Lautaro López, Tito Carrillo, and Rodemil Galindo, group interview by author, San Pedro de la Paz, March 5, 2011; Aníbal Cáceres, Juan González, Grecia Quiero, and "El Mono" Escalona, interview by author, Coronel, Chile, April 30, 2011.

3. Hugo Monsalves, interview by author, San Pedro de la Paz, Chile, August 15, 2011.

4. Monsalves interview, August 15, 2011.

5. Cáceres interview, June 19, 2011.

6. La Mura interview, October 12, 2011.

7. Cáceres interview, June 19, 2011.

8. For more on the role of women in the JAP, see Esperanza Díaz Cabrera, "La participación de las mujeres en las Juntas de Abastecimiento y Precios (JAP) en el Gran Concepción, 1971–1973" (Undergraduate thesis, Universidad de Concepción, 2011).

9. "Miembros del FTR ocuparon panadería," *El Sur*, January 14, 1973, 14.

10. "Querella por panadería tomada," *El Sur*, January 16, 1973, 9.

11. "Miembros del FTR ocuparon panadería," *El Sur*, January 14, 1973, 14. This version is corroborated in Lautaro López Stefoni and Tito Carrillo Mora, "Una historia por contar: La toma de la panadería en Coronel," *Puña y Letra* 3.3 (December 2001): 14–15.

12. Kornbluh, *The Pinochet File*, 36.

13. "No darán fuerza pública: Acto público de trabajadores textiles," *El Sur*, August 1, 1972, 7; "Detenido dirigente del MUI," *El Sur*, August 1, 1972, 7; "Universitarios defienden a

trabajadores de Caupolicán," *El Sur,* August 3, 1972, 8; "Apoyo a los Trabajadores Industria Textil Caupolicán Chiguayante [desde la] Asociación Zonal de los Trabajadores del Banco del Estado de Chile, Concepción," Insert, *El Sur,* August 5, 1972, 7; "Apoyo universitario a textil Caupolicán [declaración del Sindicato de Empleados y Obreros de la Universidad de Concepción]," *El Sur,* August 6, 1972, 12; "Declaración de Gacel: Unidad en defensa de un trabajador," *El Sur,* August 6, 1972, 12.

14. "Trabajadores no devuelven la Caupolicán," *Diario Color,* July 29, 1972.

15. Ibid.

16. Ibid.

17. "Textil Caupolicán: Expira el plazo para apelar," *Diario Color,* July 31, 1972.

18. "No darán fuerza pública: Acto público de trabajadores textiles," *El Sur,* August 1, 1972, 7.

19. "Trabajadores no devuelven la Caupolicán," *Diario Color,* July 29, 1972.

20. "No darán fuerza pública: Acto público de trabajadores textiles," *El Sur,* August 1, 1972, 7.

21. "Frente a fallo judicial: 'Requisión de Caupolicán es irreversible,'" *El Sur,* July 30, 1972, 5.

22. Manuel Rodríguez, interview by author, San Pedro de la Paz, Chile, October 7, 2011.

23. Eduardo Aquevedo, interview by author, Santiago, Chile, October 20, 2011.

24. "Asamblea del Pueblo aprueban sectores UP de Concepción,"*El Mercurio,* July 29, 1972, 1, 16. See also descriptions in *Chile Hoy* of conservative reactions in *La Prensa.* The choice of "People's Assembly"—a reference to the Popular Unity program—was the central point of contention. Many leftists, following Marxist-Leninist theory, understood popular power as a means to an end: replacing parliament and eventually the state.

25. "Enérgico rechazo de Allende a la 'Asamblea del Pueblo,'" *El Mercurio,* August 1, 1972, 8.

26. Silva, *Los cordones industriales,* 176.

27. Aquevedo interview, October 20, 2011.

28. Aquevedo interview, October 20, 2011.

29. Aquevedo interview, October 20, 2011.

30. Rodríguez interview, October 7, 2011.

31. "Debutó Asamblea del Pueblo," *El Sur,* July 28, 1972, 7.

32. "Esta es la política del MIR," *El Rebelde* 6.41 (August 1, 1972): 3. The 1971 FTR Program also outlines the creation of an Asamblea Popular at local, regional, and national levels.

33. "Asamblea en Concepción: Sólo el pueblo es victoria," *El Rebelde* 6.41 (August 1, 1972): 3.

34. The MIR's national leadership came out in support of the People's Assembly and never publicly questioned the Concepción MIR leadership. The MIR's national newspaper, *El Rebelde,* reprinted the regional MIR's proposal from the People's Assembly and subsequent issues celebrated "what the people decided in Concepción." *El Rebelde* 6.40 (July 25, 1972) and 6.41 (August 1, 1972).

35. Enríquez interview, October 11, 2011.

36. "El pueblo comenzó a ser poder," *El Sur,* July 30, 1972, 19. The editorial in *El Rebelde* formed the basis of weekly discussions in MIR bases. "Asamblea en Concepción: Sólo el pueblo es victoria," *El Rebelde* 6.41 (August 1, 1972): 3; "La asamblea mostró el camino:

Construir con las masas el poder popular! [Editorial]," *El Rebelde* 6.42 (August 8, 1972): 3. *El Rebelde* also printed examples of endorsements to the People's Assembly. "Solidaridad combativa," *El Rebelde* 6.42 (August 8, 1972): 5.The speech's subsequent dissemination in *El Rebelde* meant that it would be read and discussed by both national MIR militants and grassroots sympathizers.

37. Manuel Vergara, "El pueblo comenzó a ser poder," *El Sur*, July 30, 1972, 19.

38. Miguel Enríquez, *Lo Hermida: La cara más fea del reformismo*, 48. The regional Socialist Party leaders also prioritized the immediate formation of Consejos Comunales de Trabajadores. "PS: 'Tenemos el respaldo del comité central,'" *El Sur*, August 3, 1972, 7.

39. Garcés interview, December 9, 2011; Toro interview, July 27, 2012.

40. Riffo interview, January 10, 2005.

41. Riffo interview, January 10, 2005.

42. Fernando Mires, "Notas sobre un capítulo de mi vida," *POLIS: Política y Cultura* (August 10, 2016), https://polisfmires.blogspot.com/2016/08/fernando-mires-notas-sobre-un-capitulo_7.html. Accessed September 13, 2017.

43. Garcés interview, December 9, 2011.

44. Garcés interview, December 9, 2011.

45. Chilean historian Boris Cofré uses the term "historical popular power" to describe grassroots experiences and the term "theoretical popular power" to distinguish the theoretical debates over the term's meaning drawn from Marxist-Leninist thought. Cofré, *Campamento Nueva la Havana*.

46. "Levanta polvareda la marcha del 30," *El Sur*, August 28, 1972, 15; "Gobierno no autorizó la marcha: 'En resguardo de la seguridad y el orden,'" *El Sur*, August 28, 1972, 1, 13. The API also joined the PC and the initiative of the Group of Five parties.

47. Winn, *Weavers of Revolution*, 235.

48. Thomas C. Wright, *Latin America in the Era of the Cuban Revolution* (Westport, CT: Praeger, 2001), 142.

49. Winn, *Weavers of Revolution*, 237.

50. La Mura interview, October 12, 2011.

51. Enzo La Mura, interviews with author, Concepción, Chile, April 1, April 29, May 11, October 12, 2011. La Mura asserted that in their instructions to MIR militants, the leaders were clear that miristas should not act alone but rather as "catalysts [*movilizadores*] for local people to confront the strike."

52. "El comercio abre sus puertas," *Diario Color*, October 16, 1972, 5; "A la opinión pública—Panos Oveja Tomé," *Diario Color*, October 30, 1972, 8; "Actas del Sindicato Industrial de Bellavista Tomé," October 19, 1972, 227–28.

53. "El poder es esto que estamos construyendo, en las comunas, esta libertad, esta unión, esta fuerza," *El Rebelde* 5.54 (October 30–November 5, 1972): 5.

54. "A la opinión pública—Paños Oveja Tomé," *Diario Color*, October 30, 1972, 8. In October 1972, Paños FIAP and Paños Bellavista had been fully nationalized and were state owned, while Paños Oveja Tomé and Textil Caupolicán Chiguayante were only requisitioned.

55. Ibid.

56. "Lo nuevo en textil: De la mano del trabajador a la mano del pueblo," *Diario Color*, November 5, 1972, 20. The insert was signed by the Comité Textil CORFO and *las empresas textiles del Área Social*.

57. "Atentado de depósito de paños," *Diario Color,* November 5, 1972, 1.

58. "Gobernador subrogante Tomé," *Diario Color,* November 5, 1972, 8.

59. " Declaración del Departamento de Medicina preventiva y social de la UdeC," *Diario Color,* October 20, 1972, 5.

60. Gabriel Sanhueza interview, in Rody Oñate Z., "El Surazo en tres dimensiones: Análisis de una experiencia," *Comunicación y Cultura* 1 (July 1973): 226–36; and "Surazo," *El Rebelde* 6.54 (October 30, 1972): 7.

61. Pedro Enríquez Barra, interview by author, Concepción, Chile, October 11, 2011.

62. Enríquez Barra interview , October 11, 2011.

63. Winn, *Weavers of Revolution,* 237.

64. "Normal atención en los barrios," *Diario Color,* October 14, 1972, 5; "Se constituyó Comité Provincial de Abastecimientos," *Diario Color,* October 14, 1972, 5; "Orden del día de la UP provincial," *Diario Color,* October 18, 1972, 8.

65. "El comercio abre sus puertas," *Diario Color,* October 16, 1972, 5.

66. On October 17, 1972, the Partido Nacional and Patria y Libertad mobilized their militants to protest in Concepción streets in the morning. Leftist militants occupied the streets in the afternoon. Both incidents were controlled by military and police presence. *Diario Color,* October 18, 1972, 1.

67. "El poder es esto que estamos construyendo, en las comunas, esta libertad, esta unión, esta fuerza," *El Rebelde* 5.54 (October–November 1972): 5.

68. "Gigantesco incedio en la Textil Chiguayante," *Diario Color,* October 23, 1972, 1; "Incendio en 'Caupolican' deja mas de un 50% en pérdidas," *Diario Color,* October 24, 1972, 1.

69. "Concepción: Con el comité somos más fuertes," *Diario Color,* October 30, 1972, 4–5.

70. "El PS instruye a sus bases," *Diario Color,* October 21, 1972, 5.

71. "Concepción: Los coordinadores son poder," *El Rebelde* 6.53 (October 23, 1972): 5.

72. Ibid.

73. "Comité coordinador en Chiguayante," *Diario Color,* October 26, 1972, 8.

74. Ibid. *Diario Color*'s description of the Chiguayante Comité Coordinador matched the vision offered in *El Rebelde* of the Five Comités Coordinadores Comunales in Chiguayante, Penco, Concepción, Tomé, and Talcahuano. "Concepción: Los coordinadores son poder," *El Rebelde* 6.53 (October 23, 1972): 5.

75. For the MIR these priorities crystallized a new platform known as the "Pliego del Pueblo," which was widely disseminated by the FTR and other mass fronts during the Bosses' Lockout through *El Rebelde* and in open discussions in assemblies. "Pliego del Pueblo" (October 1972), in Naranjo et al., *Miguel Enríquez y el proyecto revolucionario en Chile,* 171–88. Enzo La Mura recalled that the "spontaneous tendency" in the bases was "to go and open the businesses that closed," and so as regional MIR leaders "we focused on creating an organization of this type" that could mobilize people and have "an ability to defend ourselves" in street conflicts. Enzo La Mura interview, October 12, 2011. For more on the MAPU's proposals, see "MAPU y PR ante el Paro," *Diario Color,* October 23, 1972, 8; "El MAPU llama a parar el fascismo con las masas y pasar a la ofensiva," *Diario Color,* October 25, 1972, 12.

76. "Concepción: Con el comité somos más fuertes," *Diario Color,* October 30, 1972, 4–5.

77. Carlos Robles was not a JAP leader, yet he met Señora Neña, his local JAP leader, when he organized an assembly for a toma. In Lirquén and Penco, Robles noted that many JAP leaders, like Señora Neña, were also the owners of the local corner stores. Robles reflected on his role assisting Señora Neña to create better distribution and organization, explaining "pero tiene que distribuirlo así, justamente." He also noted that Señora Neña and her husband were much more sympathetic to the MIR than other political groups. González and Robles interview, August 2, 2011.

78. Díaz Cabrera, "La participación de las mujeres en las Juntas de Abastecimiento y Precio (JAP)," 75–76.

79. By 1973, the JAP Comunales in Concepción and Coronel were led by MIR members.

80. "El poder es esto que estamos construyendo, en las comunas, esta libertad, esta unión, esta fuerza," El Rebelde 5.54 (October 30–November 5, 1972): 5. García went on to project the future creation of a Comité Coordinador de Coronel, linking workers, pobladores, and students. Yet it was the JAP Comunal, not the coal unions, that would convene the first meeting of the Coordinating Committee in March 1973.

81. Iván Quintana, interview by author, Concepción, Chile, August 26, 2011. See also my interview with Communist diputado-obrero representing Lota, Luis Fuentealba Medina, Lota Alto, Chile, December 21, 2006.

82. Aníbal Cáceres, interview by author, Camilo Olavarría sector, Coronel, Chile, June 19, 2011.

83. Cáceres interview, June 19, 2011.

84. López interview, June 15, 2011.

85. Cáceres interview, June 19, 2011. According to Tito Carrillo, the majority of the JAP leaders in the Coronel neighborhoods of Schwager, Camilo Olavarría, Villa Mora, la Colonia, and La Central were MIR members. Tito Carrillo, Coronel MIR group interview by author, San Pedro de la Paz, Chile, March 5, 2011.

86. Lautaro López characterized this sense of a mirista ethic as a legacy of the historic generation of MIR leaders in the Universidad de Concepción and their work creating MIR bases in the region. López interview, June 15, 2011.

87. Hugo Monsalves, interview by author, San Pedro de la Paz, Chile, August 15, 2011.

88. Monsalves interview, August 15, 2011.

89. López interview, June 15, 2011.

90. Carrillo interview, March 5, 2011. The half liter of milk for every school age child was one of the most popular and most remembered programs implemented by the Popular Unity government. It figured among the 40 measures proposed in the UP platform.

91. Carrillo interview, March 5, 2011.

92. Cáceres interview, June 19, 2011.

93. Cáceres interview, June 19, 2011.

94. López interview, June 15, 2011.

95. Hugo Monsalves, Coronel MIR group interview by author, San Pedro de la Paz, Chile, March 5, 2011.

96. Comunal denotes comuna-wide. Comuna is defined in note 82, page 199.

97. López interview, June 15, 2011.

98. La Mura interview, October 12, 2011.

99. Cáceres interview, June 19, 2011. "Querella por panadería tomada," *El Sur,* January 16, 1973, 9.

100. Juan Alarcón and Mario Gutiérrez, interview by author, Communist Party headquarters, Coronel, Chile, May 2, 2011.

101. Following the bakery occupation, the FTR attained greater support in coal mine union elections in February 1973. Enzo La Mura interviews, April 1 and October 12, 2011.

102. Cáceres interview, June 19, 2011; "El Mono" Escalona, interview by author, Coronel, Chile, May 7, 2011.

103. Cáceres interview, June 19, 2011.

104. López interview, June 15, 2011.

105. Carrillo, Coronel MIR Group interview, March 5, 2011.

106. "Miembros del FTR ocuparon panadería," *El Sur,* January 14, 1973, 14.

107. López interview, June 15, 2011.

108. López interview, June 15, 2011.

6. "LIVING WITHIN A SPECIAL WORLD"

1. Alejandro Alarcón, interview by author, Santiago, Chile, April 27, 2011.

2. Formed in 1971, the Comisión Política served as the political leadership in the Central Committee. The 48-member Central Committee was the largest and most representative body in the MIR. It was composed of the Political Commission, regional secretaries and delegations, and national leaders from mass fronts and special tasks. In practice, however, it did not function as a deliberative body for collective leadership (Enzo La Mura, interview by author, Coronel, Chile, October 11, 2011). For more on the limitations of the CP, see Pedro Naranjo, "La vida de Miguel Enríquez el MIR," in Naranjo et al., *Miguel Enríquez y el proyecto revolucionario en Chile,* 73.

3. In late August 1973, arrest warrants were issued for Carlos Altamirano, Oscar Garretón, and Miguel Enríquez, general secretaries of the PS, MAPU, and MIR respectively, for alleged subversion of the armed forces.

4. Lily Rivas Labbé, interview by author, Concepción, Chile, October 11, 2011; Nelson González, interview by author, Concepción, Chile, July 19, 2011.

5. Jorge González, grassroots MIR activist in Tomé, put it succinctly: "When the coup happened, the Political Commission was exposed. Not just the top leadership, the coup caught all of us with our pants down because the military training we were given was insufficient." Jorge González, interview by author, June 16, 2011, Coronel, Chile.

6. Alejandro Alarcón, interview by author and Aníbal Navarette, Santiago, Chile, April 13, 2011.

7. Alarcón interview, April 27, 2011.

8. Alarcón interview, April 27, 2001.

9. Enzo La Mura, interview by author, Concepción, Chile, April 1, 2011. After being tapped to join the Central Committee, La Mura continued to live in Concepción and remained one of the region's most public MIR leaders.

10. The Fourth Party Congress was suspended after the Osses incident in 1969. As a result, all subsequent members added to the Central Committee were "co-opted by the historic leadership," which tended to reproduce a sense of loyalty and unquestioning confidence in the established leaders. La Mura interview, April 1, 2011.

11. MIR, "Informe de la Comisión Política al Comité Central restringido sobre la crisis de octubre y nuestra política electoral" [Confidential Internal Document], November 3, 1972, in Farías, *La izquierda chilena (1969–1973),* 2:3416–46.

12. Andrés Pascal Allende, interview by author, Santiago, Chile, December 12, 2011. See also La Mura interview, October 11, 2011.

13. Garcés interview, December 6, 2011.

14. Martín Hernández, interview by Eugenia Palieraki, October 30, 2004.

15. Other leftist students echoed this characterization of UdeC student politics. MAPU leader Eduardo Aquevedo, for example, distinguished himself in debates by the amount of citations he could marshal to support his position. Juan Carlos Feres, interview by author, Santiago, Chile, January 5, 2011.

16. La Mura interview, April 1, 2011.

17. For more on Fernando Mires's perspective from within the regional MIR leadership see his blog, "Notas sobre un capítulo de mi vida," *POLIS: Política y Cultura* (August 10, 2016), https://polisfmires.blogspot.com/2016/08/fernando-mires-notas-sobre-un-capitulo_ 7.html (August 10, 2016), accessed September 13, 2017.

18. Paradoxically, the loyalty that worked to ensure the CP's hold on power also prevented it from removing Vergara from the regional leadership. Vergara had been one of the earliest MIR members in Concepción, and "Miguel Enríquez was always very fond of him," explained CC member and MPR national leader Víctor Toro. Víctor Toro, interview by author, Bronx, NY, July 27, 2012.

19. La Mura interview, April 29, 2011; Pascal Allende interview, December 12, 2011.

20. La Mura interview, October 11, 2011.

21. La Mura interview, April 1, 2011.

22. Enzo la Mura, correspondence with author, February 26, 2013; La Mura interview, April 1, 2011.

23. Álvaro Riffo, interview by Eugenia Palieraki, Concepción, Chile, January 10, 2005.

24. Hernández interview, October 30, 2004.

25. The Movimiento Gremial emerged in the Universidad Católica in the 1960s. Contrary to the portrayal of the Chilean Right's resurgence as a scared reaction to Frei's centrist reforms and Allende's proposed socialism, Verónica Valdivia argues the New Right emerged as a consciously political project, jettisoning the traditional Right's reliance on co-optation. Valdivia, *Nacionales y gremialistas.*

26. Wright, *Latin America in the Era of the Cuban Revolution,* 144.

27. Naranjo, "La vida de Miguel Enríquez el MIR," 79. The Central Committee's deliberations were not made public until January 1973, when the MIR sent a letter to the Socialist Party outlining their position on elections. The letter was widely disseminated as "Carta del MIR al PS," *El Rebelde* 7.67 (January 30, 1973): 11–13.

28. Martín Hernández, interview by Sebastián Leiva, Concepción, Chile, March 25, 2005.

29. "Carta del MIR al PS," *El Rebelde* 7:67 (January 30, 1973): 11–13.

30. MIR, "Informe de la Comisión Política al Comité Central restringido sobre la crisis de octubre y nuestra política electoral" [Confidential Internal Document], 3479–82.

31. Ibid.

32. Garcés interview, December 11, 2011. For more on the life of Carlos Rioseco, see the memoir written by his widow, Hilda E. Espinoza Figueroa, *Las buganvillas de Carlos: Una historia inconclusa* (Concepción: Ediciones Escaparate, 2005).

33. Garcés interview, December 11, 2011. Garcés joined the leadership of GPM-1 in December 1972 after completing MIR work organizing a Christian Front in Concepción and after refusing to take over the Tomé GPM leadership.

34. Winn, *Weavers of Revolution*, 239.

35. Popular Unity candidates elected included CUT labor leader Oscar González (PS), former FEC president Manuel Rodríguez (PS), Oscar Guillermo Garretón (MAPU) representing the radical wing of his party, and Communists Iván Quintana from Tomé and Fernando Agurto from Concepción. *El Mercurio*, March 6, 1973.

36. Miguel Enríquez, "Análisis del resultado electoral, perspectivas y tareas," March 10, 1973, in Naranjo et al., *Miguel Enríquez y el proyecto revolucionario en Chile*, 224.

37. Hernández interview, October 30, 2004.

38. Despite the UdeC students figuring prominently in the MIR, most student militants had been assigned to off-campus tasks, including open political organizing work in Concepción, Coronel, and Tomé, as well as more clandestine "special tasks, military tasks, and intelligence tasks." However, as evidenced by the 1971 FEC elections, the MIR's mass front—the MUI—had broad support, despite the relatively small number of MIR militants assigned to political work in the university. Hernández interview, October 20, 2004.

39. "Operación Comando," *El Sur*, July 8, 1973, 1. Of the 89, full-fledged militants numbered 65, with the other 24 aspiring members.

40. Ibid.

41. Garcés interview, December 11, 2011.

42. Garcés interview, December 11, 2011.

43. Torres remembered his frustration at Bravo's "relaxed attitude," adding that in the MIR "we never trusted the loyalty of the [armed forces] to the government." Manuel Torres, interview by author, Concepción, Chile, September 6, 2011.

44. Garcés interview, December 11, 2011.

45. Stern, *Battling for Hearts and Minds*, 17–18.

46. Garcés interview, December 11, 2011.

47. Torres interview, September 6, 2011.

48. Garcés interview, December 11, 2011.

49. "CUT Provincial: Ocupar industria es una orden cuerda," *El Sur*, July 7, 1973, 7.

50. The largest cordón connected the interrelated petroleum industries in Talcahuano's "Four Corners" sector with dockworkers at the San Vicente port. Its leadership board consisted of three Socialists, two miristas, and one MAPU member. In addition to a cordón in Coronel, by July 12, 1973, six other cordones were operating in Concepción and Talcahuano: Cordón Costanera, Cordón Centro de Servicios y Equipamentos, Cordón Estación Andalién, Cordón Penco and Lirquén, Cordón San Pedro, and Cordón San Vicente-Talcahuano, or Cordón Cuatro Esquinas. Three of the six, Cordón Costanera, Cordón Centro de Servicios, and Cordón Estación Andalién, were located in GPM-1 territory. See "CUT Provincial:

Ocupar industria es una orden cuerda," *El Sur,* July 7, 1973, 7; "Quinto cordón industrial CUT: Cercado el Barrio Pedro de Valdivia," *El Sur,* July 7, 1973, 1, 6; "CUT creó otro cordón," *El Sur,* July 10, 1973, 7; "Inquietud en Pedro de Valdivia: CUT: 8 'cordones' para Concepción," *El Sur,* July 12, 1973, 1, 10; "Formado córdon centro y de servicios," *Diario Color,* July 28, 1973, 16.

51. *Diario Color,* July 13, 1973.

52. "CUT creó otro cordón," *El Sur,* July 10, 1973, 7.

53. Garcés interview, December 11, 2011.

54. Miguel Enríquez, "La clase obrera y el pueblo no retrocederán," radio address, July 7, 1973, in Naranjo et al., *Miguel Enríquez y el proyecto revolucionario en Chile,* 256.

55. Enríquez, "La clase obrera y el pueblo no retrocederán," 256. "Today more than ever the working classes and the pueblo have demonstrated that there is enough strength to continue the counteroffensive. . . . Today it is clearer than in October the class character of the social and political confrontations: the workers versus the bosses" (257).

56. Ibid., 259.

57. Peter Winn, "Salvador Allende: His Political Life . . . and Afterlife," *Socialism and Democracy* 19.3 (2005): 155.

58. "CUT reclama por los allanamientos," *El Sur,* July 25, 1973, 8.

59. Miguel Enríquez, "Abrir la contraofensiva revolucionaria y popular," June 14, 1973, in *La izquierda chilena,* 4703.

60. Miguel Enríquez, "Vivimos un momento histórico fundamental," in Naranjo et al., *Miguel Enríquez y el proyecto revolucionario en Chile,* 269.

61. Héctor Jego, interview by author, Concepción, Chile, April 19, 2011.

62. Jego explained that although the Fuerza Central had one representative on the regional MIR committee, the Fuerza Central-Concepción responded directly to the national political-military plans. Jego interview, April 19, 2011.

63. Jego interview, April 19, 2011.

64. The Navy and FACH both used the Carriel Sur airport in Concepción. Sometime in mid-August 1973, General Gustavo Leigh ordered the transfer of the Chilean Air Force's four Hawker Hunter airplanes from Santiago to Concepción. Speculation about this decision points to Leigh's fears that planes were too close to Cordón Cerrillos in Santiago or that by then Concepción was already occupied by the military.

65. The Encargado de los Operativos for the Fuerza Central–Concepción took the secret plans to his home to store them, where they were discovered by his sibling, who then turned them over to *El Sur.* Fuerza Central–Concepción member Héctor Jego did not dispute the veracity of the information printed in *El Sur.* On March 13, 1973, the Christian Democratic Party purchased Concepción's papers *El Sur* and *La Crónica.* The editorial line of *El Sur* moved sharply to the Right after the owners recovered the paper from the workers who occupied it during the October Bosses' Lockout.

66. "Operación Comando,"*El Sur,* July 8, 1973, 1. The story referred to the MIR's Grupos Políticos-Militares as paramilitary groups.

67. Jego interview, April 19, 2011.

68. "Operación Comando,"*El Sur,* July 8, 1973, 1. In the case of GPM-2 in the UdeC, only 4 of the 138 members had military training. GPM-4 had 5 members with military training, GPM-5 had 4 members "with complete instructions on military operations," GPM-6 in Talcahuano had 3 members, and GPM-7 had 5 members.

69. Garcés interview, December 11, 2011.

70. *El Sur* reported, "The array recorded in secret extremist documentation reaches .38 20 Walter, 3 Mauser, 3 M-1, 3 M-2, 2 Springfield rifles, 2 12 semiautomatic shotguns, three .22 caliber rifles, a shotgun 16." "Operación Comando,"*El Sur,* July 8, 1973, 1.

71. In a 2004 interview, Ulises Estrada, head of Chilean operations at the Cuban DGLN (1970–73), recalled that Cubans provided military training in Chile and Cuba to "hundreds" of miristas and nearly two thousand Chileans. The historian Tanya Harmer concludes, "The junta's fears that the Cubans could lead mass resistance, nurtured over the course of three years of psychological campaigns to play up Cuban involvement in Chile, was exaggerated. Even with prior knowledge and unity, it is far from certain whether a few hundred (or even a few thousand) partially trained Chilean militants could have resisted Chile's armed forces. The Chilean Left was hopelessly divided and was unprepared to face the military onslaught that followed, having been severely weakened by the arms raids in the weeks leading up to the coup." Tanya Harmer, *Allende's Chile and the Inter-American Cold War* (Chapel Hill: University of North Carolina Press, 2011), 233, 246. In his unsubstantiated narrative of pre-coup subversion in Chile, Manuel Contreras, former head of the Chilean DINA, included annexes of Chilean immigration records used by DINA agents to identify Chileans who had traveled to Cuba. According to these documents, 59 MIR militants completed a military *curso* in Cuba, 15 completed a "curso de guerrillas," and 16 received training in the use of explosives. Manuel Contreras Sepúlveda, *La verdad histórica: El ejército guerrillero abril de 1967 al 10 de septiembre de 1973*, vol. 1 (Santiago: Ediciones Encina, 2000), 240–49.

72. Carlos Robles, interview by author, Penco, Chile, August 2, 2011.

73. Carlos Robles noted that he later received help from a Concepción MIR student who had also trained in Cuba, but the training they gave to "*los cabros* here in Bellavista sur" never went beyond basic use of firearms. Robles interview, August 2, 2011.

74. Garcés interview, December 11, 2011. The leaderships from GPM-1 in Barrio Norte, GPM-2 in the UdeC, and a new GPM being formed in Puchacay attended this meeting.

75. Garcés interview, December 11, 2011.

76. Osvaldo Torres G., "La izquierda revolucionaria latinoamericana: Derrotas y readecuaciones: Los casos del Movimiento de Liberación Nacional-Tupamaros, MLN-T, de Uruguay y el Movimiento de Izquierda Revolucionaria, de Chile" (PhD diss., Universidad de Chile, 2011). Torres was a MIR militant in Santiago during the Popular Unity.

77. Garcés interview, December 11, 2011.

78. Alarcón interview, April 27, 2011.

79. La Mura interview, April 1, 2011.

80. Garcés interview, December 11, 2011.

81. Enríquez, "La clase obrera y el pueblo no retrocederán," 259.

82. Garcés interview, December 11, 2011.

83. La Mura interview, April 1, 2011.

84. "¡A fortalecer nuestro partido! Los golpes recientes, algunas lecciones y la reorganización de las direcciones" [Documento de Comisión Política a Comité Central y a las bases del partido], June 1974, in Miriam Ortega and Cecilia Radrigan, *Miguel Enríquez: Con vista a la esperanza* (Santiago: Escaparate, 1998), 358. In early August 1973, Ricardo Ruz participated in meetings with marines in Talcahuano who sought guidance on how to resist a coup

from within. Jorge Magasich Airola, *Los que dijeron "No": Historia del movimiento de los marinos antigolpistas de 1973*, vol. 2 (Santiago: LOM, 2008), 110.

85. Martín Hérnandez interview, October 30, 2004. Political Commission member Andrés Pascal Allende similarly recalled that the intervention in Concepción was never explicit.

86. Edgardo Enríquez, "Discourse in Homage to Cuban Revolution," *El Rebelde*, July 26, 1973, 5–8.

87. La Mura interview, October 11, 2011.

88. Pedro Enríquez Barra, interview by author, Concepción, Chile, August 29, 2011.

89. Garcés interview, December 11, 2011.

90. Garcés interview, December 11, 2011.

91. Garcés interview, December 11, 2011.

92. Garcés interview, December 11, 2011.

93. As a member of the Political Commission and the Central Committee, Andrés Pascal Allende acknowledged decades later that this was a fundamental weakness in the MIR's national strategy. Pascal Allende interview, December 12, 2011.

94. Garcés interview, December 11, 2011.

95. For a description of the party's expulsions of Regional Committee and Central Committee members Manuel Vergara, Enzo La Mura, and Víctor Bomballet following their decision to seek asylum, see "¡A fortalecer nuestro partido! Los golpes recientes, algunas lecciones y la reorganización de las direcciones," 356–59.

96. "Orden de la CUT: Para a las 15 horas," *Diario Color*, August 9, 1973, 6.

97. "Combativo acto de la CUT," *Diario Color*, August 10, 1973, 1; "En paro de la CUT: Le dieron duro a las FF. AA.," *La Crónica*, August 10, 1973, 2; "Una concentración más," *El Sur*, August 10, 1973, 6.

98. Garcés interview, December 11, 2011.

99. Hugo Monsalves, interview by author, San Pedro de la Paz, Chile, August 15, 2011.

100. "Combativo acto de la CUT," *Diario Color*, August 10, 1973, 1.

101. Ibid.

102. Nicanor Ibáñez, FTR-Bellavista group interview by author, Tomé, Chile, July 20, 2011.

103. Garcés interview, December 11, 2011.

104. Ibáñez interview, July 20, 2011.

105. Robles interview, August 2, 2011.

106. Robles interview, August 2, 2011.

107. Garcés interview, December 11, 2011.

108. Garcés interview, December 11, 2011.

109. "Movilización laboral arrojó saldo positivo," *Diario Color*, August 15, 1973, 7.

110. Garcés interview, December 11, 2011.

111. "Combativo acto de la CUT," *Diario Color*, August 10, 1973 1.

112. Garcés interview, December 11, 2011.

113. Stern, *Battling for Hearts and Minds*, 17.

114. Eulogio Sanhueza, interview by author, Tomé, Chile, October 14, 2011.

115. Wright, *Latin America in the Era of the Cuban Revolution*, 145.

116. "Adhesión de comercio de Tomé," *El Sur*, August 22, 1973, 10.

117. "Tomé: Descerrajan 22 negocios," *El Sur,* August 22, 1973, 1. According to Darwin Rodríguez, the CUT's decision had been made prior to the rally and was supported by the local UP Committee in Tomé and the Tomé MIR leadership. Darwin Rodríguez, interview by author, Tomé, Chile, October 31, 2011.

118. "Adhesión de comercio de Tomé," *El Sur,* August 23, 1973, 10. The owners of neighborhood corner stores in the hills surrounding Tomé did not participate in the strike.

119. This determined attitude was reinforced by the example of the drivers who transported Tomé textiles to Santiago. Faced with a parallel truckers' strike, they joined forces with other pro-government truckers to ensure their products reached their destination. The nationwide organization of leftist drivers was called Movimiento Patriótico de Recuperación (MOPARE). Rodríguez interview, October 31, 2011.

120. Sanhueza interview, October 14, 2011; Juan Reyes, interview by author, Tomé, Chile, October 14, 2011.

121. Reyes interview, October 14, 2011.

122. Sanhueza interview, October 14, 2011.

123. Rodríguez interview, October 31, 2011; Sanhueza interview, October 14, 2011. As a relatively new party, the Izquierda Cristiana did not have a significant presence in Tomé.

124. Sanhueza interview, October 14, 2011.

125. "Incidentes en Tomé por cierre del comercio,"*Diario Color,* August 21, 1973, 7. Both oral sources and newspaper accounts from the pro-UP *Diario Color* contend that only three shops had their locks broken.

126. Sanhueza interview, October 14, 2011.

127. "Incidentes en Tomé por cierre del comercio,"*Diario Color,* August 21, 1973, 7.

128. Jorge González, interview by author, Coronel, Chile, June 16, 2011.

129. "Pobladores solucionan su problema de movilización," *Diario Color,* August 9, 1973, 4.

130. "La respuesta de los estudiantes al paro de los empresarios," *Diario Color,* August 9, 1973, 4.

131. "El salario del valor: Trabajadores de ENACAR y FANALOZA impiden paralización de industria," *Diario Color,* August 19, 1973, 9. See also "Trabajadores impidieron paralización del la CCU," *Diario Color,* August 21, 1973, 4.

132. Primer Encuentro de Trabajadores Refractarios Lota-Green Empresa del Área Social, "Participación es poder; los trabajadores ahora participamos," *Diario Color,* August 19, 1973; Primer Encuentro de Trabajadores de FANALOZA, "Participación es poder popular," *Diario Color,* August 22, 1973.

133. "Poder popular en Barrio Norte," *Diario Color,* August 16, 1973, 7.

134. At the time, many people attributed the attacks to Patria y Libertad's fascist squads. In fact, new evidence suggests that the Chilean Navy was directly responsible for carrying out attacks across the country. See "Dinamitaron post de alumbrado público," *Diario Color,* August 11, 1973, 7; "Ultraderecha enloquecida: Dos criminales atentados en Concepción y Talcahuano," *Diario Color,* August 12, 1973, 1; "Terrorismo en pleno centro de Concepción," *Diario Color,* August 14, 1973, 1; "Sigue adelante ola de terror en Concepción," *Diario Color,* August 17, 1973, 6. For more on the navy's role, see Winn, "Furies of the Andes," 261.

135. "Exigen aplicación de medidas drásticas contra Huelguistas," *Diario Color,* August 18, 1973, 4.

136. "Llamado a desobedencia militar: Interceptado camión del MIR," *El Sur,* July 15, 1973, 1.

137. "A la justicia militar por portar panfletos subversivos," *Diario Color,* August 14, 1973, 7; "Poder popular en Barrio Norte," *Diario Color,* August 16, 1973, 7.

138. Winn, "Furies of the Andes," 250.

139. "Declaración de trabajadores de Paños Oveja," *Diario Color,* August 9, 1973, 5.

140. "Rafael Merino: 'Son otros los sectores que han tratado de infiltrar las FF.AA.,'" *Diario Color,* August 13, 1973, 8.

141. "Armada desbarató golpe: Brote subversivo en base de Talcahuano," *El Sur,* August 10, 1973, 1; "En base naval: 30 detenidos. Sedición extremista debía estallar en los próximos 60 días," *El Sur,* August 11, 1973, 1.

142. The arrests took place on August 9, 1973. By early September, the military's internal investigation concluded by issuing arrest warrants for general secretaries Carlos Altamirano (PS), Oscar Guillermo Garretón (MAPU), and Miguel Enríquez (MIR). For more on the August arrests and the fate of constitutionalist sailors, see Magasich Airola, *Los que dijeron "No"*; Danny Monsálvez Araneda, *Agosto 1973. Proa al golpe en la Armada: El caso Asmar-Talcahuano* (Tomé, Chile: Editorial Al Aire Libro, 2010). For the memoirs of one of the detained sailors, see Ramírez R., *Memoria colectiva de los marinos anti-golpistas.*

143. Pedro Enríquez Barra, interview by author, Concepción, Chile, October 11, 2011.

144. The PS in Concepción was the first political party to denounce the mistreatment of the sailors, and more in-depth coverage in the leftist press circulated by the end of the month. Comité Regional Partido Socialista Concepción, "Declaración 10 de agosto de 1973," *Diario Color,* August 11, 1973, 6. See "Torturas en la Marina," *Chile Hoy,* August 24, 1973; "Marinero torturado: El pueblo está contigo," *Punto Final,* August 28, 1973.

145. "Libres los detenidos en allanamiento," *Diario Color,* August 15, 1973, 7.

146. "Defensa de derechos humanos," *Diario Color,* August 18, 1973, 7.

147. "Boletín Universitario: Derechos humanos," *Diario Color,* August 17, 1973, 6. The August 21 rally was planned during an open meeting held at the UdeC Institute of Art on August 17.

148. "Comité de Defensa de los Derechos humanos," *Diario Color,* August 19, 1973, 12.

149. "Rafael Merino, dirigente del PS: 'Son otros los sectores que han tratado de infiltrar las FF.AA.,'" *Diario Color,* August 13, 1973, 8.

150. Ibid.

151. "FEC Presidente: 'Nos reprimieron a golpes y palos,'" *Diario Color,* August 22, 1973, 2.

152. The southern cities of Valdivia and Punto Arenas were also controlled by the military prior to the coup. For more on preemptive military action against Mapuche peasant communities near Valdivia, see Mallon, *Courage Tastes of Blood;* Mallon, "*Barbudos*," Warriors, and *Rotos*"; Claudio Javier Barrientos, "Emblems and Narratives of the Past: The Cultural Construction of Memories and Violence in Peasant Communities in Southern Chile, 1970–2000" (PhD diss., University of Wisconsin, Madison, 2003).

153. Sanhueza interview, October 14, 2011.

154. González interview, June 16, 2011.

155. González interview, June 16, 2011.

156. "Testigos relatan acontecimientos," *Diario Color,* August 22, 1973, 2.

157. "Cris," interview by author, Concepción, Chile, May 11, 2011.

158. "El MIR probó su propia medicina," *La Crónica,* August 22, 1973, 16.

159. "Testigos relatan acontecimientos," *Diario Color,* August 22, 1973, 2.

160. They were released within 24 hours on General Carrasco's order. "En centro de Concepción: Acción militar contra provocación extremista," *El Sur,* August 22, 1973, 1.

161. "FEC Presidente: 'Nos reprimieron a golpes y palos,'" *Diario Color,* August 22, 1973, 2. For more on national press coverage of events in Concepción, see Magacisch, *Los que dijeron "No,"* 218–22.

162. Winn, "Furies of the Andes," 261.

163. General Carrasco took over Concepción and Rear Admiral Paredes, Tomé and Talcahuano. Communist governor Fernando Álvarez retained control over administrative functions and public services. "Jefes de plaza asumen mando en Concepción," *Diario Color,* August 12, 1973, 10; "Intervención militar en todo el país en huelga del transporte," *Diario Color,* August 13, 1973, 1.

164. Subsequent public demonstrations in Tomé and Concepción in protest over the August 21 incidents were similarly met with a military repression.

165. "En Concepción y Tomé: Dos allanamientos practicaron las FF.AA," *El Sur,* August 23, 1973, 1.

166. Rodríguez interview, October 31, 2011.

167. Reyes interview, October 14, 2011.

168. "En centro de Concepción: Acción militar contra provocación extremista," *El Sur,* August 22, 1973, 1.

169. "El MIR probó su propia medicina," *La Crónica,* August 22, 1973, 16; "Teatro Concepción: Show en defensa de los derechos humanos," *La Crónica,* August 22, 1973, 4.

170. "El MIR probó su propia medicina," *La Crónica,* August 22, 1973, 16.

171. "En centro de Concepción: Acción militar contra provocación extremista," *El Sur,* August 22, 1973, 1.

172. "Comerciantes de Tomé se defienden de los ataques oficialistas," *La Crónica,* August 27, 1973, 5.

173. Ibid.

174. Julio Arroyo Kuhn, "Poderoso arsenal descubrió la Armada: Numerosos violentistas detenidos en Concepción," *El Mercurio* (Santiago), August 26, 1973, 1; Julio Arroyo Kuhn, "Descubren en Concepción: Gigantesco arsenal PS," *La Segunda* (Santiago), August 25, 1973, 1.

175. "Gigantesca farsa por 'arsenal' en Talcahuano," *Diario Color,* August 26, 1973, 1. 16; "Angustia en Las Higueras por falsas informaciones," *Diario Color,* August 27, 1973, 2.

176. One of the city's dailies, the *Crónica,* first denounced a Plan Z scheme in mid-August 1973; this was subsequently followed by "breathtaking daily reports between 19 and 24 September that appeared to provide irrefutable proof of a provincial mass assassination plan." Stern, *Battling for Hearts and Minds,* 42. *El Mercurio* correspondent in Concepción, Julio Arroyo Kuhn, continued to play a prominent role in the dissemination of Plan Z stories after the coup. He received his information directly from Navy Intelligence Services. See Magasich, *Los que dijeron "No,"* 23.

EPILOGUE

1. Juan Reyes, interviews by author, Tomé, Chile, June 2 and October 14, 2011.

2. Stern, *Battling for Hearts and Minds,* 41–56.

3. Elizabeth Q. Hutchinson et al., eds., *The Chile Reader: History, Culture, Politics* (Durham, NC: Duke University Press, 2014), 435–36. Credible estimates range from 3,500 to 4,500. Stern, *Reckoning with Pinochet,* xxiii–xxiv.

4. More than 200,000 Chileans went into forced exile. Hutchinson et al., *The Chile Reader,* 436; Stern, *Reckoning with Pinochet,* 390–93.

5. Winn, "Furies of the Andes," 239–40.

6. Manuel Torres, interview by author, Concepción, Chile, September 6, 2011.

7. Jorge González, interview by author, Coronel, Chile, June 16, 2011.

8. Alondra Peirano Iglesias, *De la militancia revolucionaria a la militancia social: Los miristas en el Chile neoliberal* (Concepción: Escaparate, 2008).

9. Grecia Quiero, interview by author, Lota, Chile, May 10, 2011.

10. Reyes interviews.

11. Winn, "Furies of the Andes," 257.

12. Lautaro López, interview by author, Talcahuano, Chile, June 15, 2011.

13. Quiero interview, May 10, 2011.

14. "El Mono" Escalona, interview by author, Coronel, Chile, May 7, 2011.

BIBLIOGRAPHY

PRIMARY SOURCES
Archives

Concepción, Chile
Archivos Judiciales de Concepción
Servicios de Estudios Regionales
Universidad de Concepción
    Archivos Generales (AGUdeC)
    Biblioteca Central Luis David Cruz Ocampo, Hemeroteca and Sala Chile
    Centro de Estudios Regionales

Santiago, Chile
Archivo Oral de Villa Grimaldi
Biblioteca Nacional, Hemeroteca

Tomé, Chile
Actas del Sindicato Industrial de Bellavista Tomé

Newspapers

Chile Hoy
La Crónica
El Diario Color
El Mercurio
Noticias de la Tarde
Noticias de Última Hora

La Patria
El Rebelde
Revolución
El Siglo
El Sur
El Surazo
Tiro Fijo

Magazines

Ercilla
Mensaje
Punto Final

Oral Sources and Interviews

At the request of participants, I have included their names in the bibliography. Pseudonyms are denoted by quotation marks. I omitted those individuals I interviewed who elected to remain anonymous and were not cited in the text.

Bronx, New York
Víctor Toro, July 27, 2012

Concepción, Chile
Enzo La Mura, April 1 and 29, 2011
Alberto Vidal, April 5, 2011
Héctor Jego, April 19, 2011
Pedro Fernández, May 3, 2011
Cris V., May 6, 2011
Edith Márquez, June 14, 2011
Francisco Vergara, July 12, 2011
Nelson González, July 19 and August 28, 2011
Lily Rivas, July 26 (with Gina Inostroza), July 30, and October 11, 2011
Teresa Veloso, August 4, 2011
Arinda Ojeda, August 19, 2011
Dagoberto Reyes, August 22, 2011
Pedro Enríquez Barra, August 25 and October 11, 2011
Iván Quintana, August 26, 2011
Manuel Torres, September 6, 2011
Yerko Aravena, August 23, 2014
Makarena Paz, August 23, 2014
Gabriel Provoste, August 25, 2014
Recaredo Gálvez, August 26, 2014
Álvaro Riffo, by Eugenia Palieraki, January 10, 2005
Nelson Gutiérrez, by Eugenia Palieraki, January 13, 2005
Martín Hernández, by Sebastián Leiva, March 25, 2005
"Fernando Manque," by Gina Inostroza and Marco Contreras, July 16, 2014

Coronel, Chile
Group Interview, April 30, 2011
Juan Alarcón, May 2, 2011
"El Mono" Escalona, May 7, 2011
Grecia Quiero, May 10, 2011
Enzo La Mura, October 12 and 30, 2011
Jorge González, June 16, 2011
"Aníbal Cáceres," June 19, 2011
Hernán Reyes, by Eugenia Palieraki, March 7, 2005

Penco, Chile
Carlos Robles, August 2, 2011

Quinchamalí, Chile
Ramón Riquelme, August 28, 2011

San Pedro de la Paz, Chile
Coronel group interview, March 5, 2011
Hugo Monsalves, August 15, 2011
Manuel Rodríguez, October 7, 2011

Santiago, Chile
Patricio Bustos, January 4, 2011
Juan Carlos Feres, January 5, 2011
Marcial Muñoz, January 7, 2011
Gastón Muñoz, January 10, 2011
Antonio Mondelaers, January 18, 2011
Carlos Sandoval, January 31, 2011
"Margarita González," March 24, 2011
Alejandro Alarcón, April 13 (with Aníbal Navarrete) and April 27, 2011
Eduardo Aquevedo, October 20, 2011
Mario Garcés, December 7 and 9, 2011
Andrés Pascal Allende, December 12, 2011
Martín Hernández, by Eugenia Palieraki, October 16, 2004, and April 12, 2005
Ricardo Frödden, by Eugenia Palieraki, February 2, 2005

Talcahuano, Chile
Héctor Sandoval, March 7, April 20, and October 31, 2011
Lautaro López, June 15, 2011
Víctor Rebolledo, November 1, 2011
Ida Subiabre, November 1, 2011
Humberto Fernández, by Mariel Ruiz Muñoz, February 2012
Ana Sandoval, by Mariel Ruiz Muñoz, February 2012
Lusvenia Fernández, by Gina Inostroza Retamal, March 19, 2016
Rosa Jara, by Gina Inostroza, March 19, 2016

Tomé, Chile
Juan Reyes, June 2, 2011
Juan Reyes, Nicanor Ibáñez, and Rolando Espejo, July 10 and 20, 2011
Helmuth Goecke, July 23, 2011
"Gume Figueroa," July 23, 2011
Juan Sandoval Torres, August 16, 2011
Luisa Sandoval Torres, August 19, 2011
Eulogio Sanhueza, October 14, 2011
Darwin Rodríguez, October 31, 2011

Villa Nonguén, Chile
Gabriel S., July 30, 2011
Club de Rehabilitados, July 30, 2011
María Márquez, August 26, 2011
Nano Saez, August 31, 2011
Junta de Vecinos, November 2, 2011

Online Sources

Archivo Chile–Centro de Estudios Miguel Enríquez (CEME), www.archivo-chile.com
Memoria Viva, www.memoriaviva.com

Document Collections and Memoirs

Bastías Rebolledo, Julián. *Memorias de la lucha campesina: Cristiano, mestizo, y tomador de fundos*. Santiago: LOM, 2009.
Bitar, Sergio. *Chile: 1970–1973*. Mexico City: Siglo Veintiuno, 1979.
Bravo Aguilera, José. *De Carranco a Carrán: Las tomas que cambiaron la historia*. Santiago: LOM, 2015.
Enríquez Frödden, Edgardo. *En nombre de una vida*. 3 vols. Mexico City: UAM, 1994.
Farías, Víctor, ed. *La izquierda chilena (1969–1973): Documentos para el estudio de su línea estratégica*. Santiago: Centro de Estudios Públicos, 2000.
Frenz, Helmut. *Mi vida chilena: Solidaridad con los oprimidos*. Trans. Sonia Plaut. Santiago: LOM, 2006.
Informe de la Comisión Nacional de Verdad y Reconciliación sobre la violación a los derechos humanos en Chile, 1973–1990. Santiago: Ministerio Secretaría General de Gobierno, 1991.
Informe de la Comisión Nacional sobre Prisión Política y Tortura. Santiago: Gobierno de Chile, Ministerio del Interior, 2005.
Marambio, Max. *Las armas de ayer*. Madrid: Debate, 2008.
Ramírez R., Mariano. *Memoria colectiva de los marinos anti-golpistas: Escuela de Ingeniería de la Armada de Chile, 1973*. Tomé: Editorial Al Aire Libre, 2011.
Saavedra Gorriateguy, Juan. *Te cuento otra vez esa historia tan bonita*. Santiago: Forja, 2010.

SELECTED SECONDARY SOURCES

Aguayo Mardones, Gloria, and Margarita Mora Rodriguez. "Cambios estructurales en la Universidad de Concepción: Su relación a lo que fue el accionar de la ultraizquierda, 1964–1968." Undergraduate thesis, Universidad de Concepción, 1994.

Albornoz, César, and Claudio Rolle. *1973: La vida cotidiana de un año crucial.* Santiago: Planeta Historia y Sociedad, 2003.

Álvarez Vergara, Marco. *La constituyente revolucionaria: Historia de la fundación del MIR chileno.* Santiago: LOM, 2015.

Angell, Alan. *Politics and the Labour Movement in Chile.* London: Oxford University Press for the Royal Institute of International Affairs, 1972.

Arrate, Jorge, and Eduardo Rojas. *Memoria de la izquierda chilena.* 2 vols. Santiago: Ediciones B, 2004.

Avendaño, Daniel, and Mauricio Palma. *El rebelde de la burguesía: La historia de Miguel Enríquez.* Santiago: CESOC, 2001.

Barrientos, Claudio Javier. "Emblems and Narratives of the Past: The Cultural Construction of Memories and Violence in Peasant Communities in Southern Chile,1970–2000." PhD diss., University of Wisconsin, Madison, 2003.

Barr-Melej, Patrick. *Psychedelic Chile: Youth, Counterculture, and Politics on the Road to Socialism and Dictatorship.* Chapel Hill: University of North Carolina Press, 2017.

———. "Siloísmo and the Self in Allende's Chile: Youth 'Total Revolution,' and the Roots of the Humanist Movement." *Hispanic American Historical Review* 86.4 (November 2006): 747–84.

Beverley, John. *Latin Americanism after 9/11.* Durham, NC: Duke University Press, 2011.

———. "Rethinking the Armed Struggle in Latin America." *Boundary 2* 36.1 (2009): 47–59.

Bruey, Alison J. *Bread, Justice, and Liberty: Grassroots Activism and Human Rights in Pinochet's Chile.* Madison: University of Wisconsin Press, 2018.

Cabrera, César A., Sandra Luengo A., and José Rebolledo M. "Una aproximación histórica al estudio de los pobladores en Concepción, 1968–1973." Undergraduate thesis, Universidad de Concepción, 1995.

Calderón López, José Leonel. "La política del Movimiento de Izquierda Revolucionaria (MIR) durante los dos primeros años de la dictadura militar (1973–1975): Entre la lucha por convertirse en actor político y la lucha por sobrevivir." Undergraduate thesis, Universidad de Santiago de Chile, 2009.

Calveiro, Pilar. *Política y/o violencia: Una aproximación a la guerrilla de los años 70.* Buenos Aires: Siglo Veintiuno, 2013.

Cancino Troncoso, Hugo. *Chile: La problemática del poder popular en el proceso de la vía chilena al socialismo, 1970–1973.* Aarhus, Denmark: Aarhus University Press, 1988.

Casals Araya, Marcelo. *El alba de una revolución: La izquierda y el proceso de construcción estratégica de la "vía chilena al socialismo," 1956–1970.* Santiago: LOM, 2010.

———. *La creación de la amenaza roja: Del surgimiento del anticomunismo en Chile a la "campaña del terror" de 1964.* Santiago: LOM, 2016.

Castañeda, Jorge G. *Utopia Unarmed: The Latin American Left after the Cold War.* New York: Vintage Books, 1993.

Castells, Manuel. "La lucha política de clases y la democracia burguesa en Chile." *Documento del Trabajo No. 60.* Santiago: Universidad Católica de Chile, Centro Interdisciplinario de Desarrollo Urbano, 1972.

———. "Movimiento de pobladores y lucha de clases en Chile." *EURE: Revista de Estudios Urbano Regionales* 3:7 (1973): 9–35.

Centro para el Desarrollo Económico y Social de América Latina (DESAL). *América Latina y desarrollo social.* 2 vols. Santiago: DESAL, 1965.

Churchill, Lindsey. *Becoming the Tupamaros: Solidarity and Transnational Revolutionaries in Uruguay and the United States.* Nashville, TN: Vanderbilt University Press, 2014.

Cifuentes, Luis, and Raúl Allard. *La reforma universitaria en Chile (1967–1973).* Santiago: Editorial Universidad de Santiago, 1997.

Cofré, Boris. *Campamento Nueva La Havana: El MIR y el movimiento de pobladores, 1970–1973.* Concepción: Ediciones Escaparate, 2007.

Cosse, Isabella, Karina Felitti, and Valeria Manzano, eds. *Los '60 de otra manera: Vida cotidiana, género y sexualidades en la Argentina.* Buenos Aires: Prometeo, 2010.

Díaz Cabrera, Esperanza. "La participación de las mujeres en las Juntas de Abastecimiento y Precio (JAP) en el Gran Concepción entre 1971–1973." Undergraduate thesis, Universidad de Concepción, 2011.

Elsey, Brenda. *Citizens and Sportsmen: Fútbol and Politics in Twentieth-Century Chile.* Austin: University of Texas Press, 2011.

Espinosa, Juan G., and Andrew S. Zimbalist. *Economic Democracy: Workers Participation, 1970–1973.* New York: Academic Press, 1981.

Fabricant, Nicole, and Nancy Postero. "Contested Bodies, Contested States: Performance, Emotions, and New Forms of Regional Governance in Santa Cruz, Bolivia." *JLACA* 18.2 (2013): 187–211.

Figueroa, Francisco. *Llegamos para quedarnos: Crónicas de la revuelta estudiantil.* Santiago: LOM, 2013.

Frazier, Lessie Jo. *Salt in the Sand: Memory, Violence, and the Nation-State in Chile, 1890 to the Present.* Durham, NC: Duke University Press, 2007.

Garcés Durán, Mario. *El despertar de la sociedad: Los movimientos sociales en América Latina y Chile.* Santiago: LOM, 2012.

———. "El movimiento de pobladores durante la Unidad Popular, 1970–73." *Atenea* 215 (July–December 2015): 33–47.

———. "Prólogo." In *Miguel Enríquez y el proyecto revolucionario en Chile: Discursos y documentos del Movimiento de Izquierda Revolucionaria,* ed. Pedro Naranjo et al. Santiago: LOM and Centro de Estudios Miguel Enríquez, 2004.

———. "Recreando el pasado: Guía metodológica para la memoria y la historia local." Santiago: Educación y Comunicaciones (ECO), March 2002.

———. *Tomando su sitio: El movimiento de pobladores de Santiago, 1957–1970.* Santiago: LOM, 2002.

Garcés Durán, Mario, and Sebastián Leiva. *Golpe en La Legua: Los caminos de la historia y la memoria.* Santiago: LOM, 2005.

Garcés Durán, Mario, P. Milos, M. Olguín, J. Pinto, M. T. Rojas, and M. Urrutia, eds. *Memoria para un nuevo siglo: Chile, miradas a la segunda mitad del siglo XX.* Santiago: LOM, 2000.

Garcés Fuentes, Magdalena. "Terrorismo de Estado en Chile: La campaña de exterminio de la DINA en contra del MIR." PhD diss., Universidad de Salamanca, 2016.

García Molina, Jaime. *El campus de la Universidad de Concepción: Su desarrollo urbanístico y arquitectónico.* Concepción: Universidad de Concepción, 1994.

Garretón, Manuel Antonio. *The Chilean Political Process*. Trans. Sharon Kellum. Boston: Unwin Hyman, 1989.

———. *Las ciencias sociales en la trama de Chile y América Latina: Estudios sobre transformaciones sociopolíticas y movimiento social*. Santiago: LOM, 2014.

Gaudichaud, Frank. *Poder popular y cordones industriales: Testimonios sobre el movimiento popular urbano, 1970–73*. Santiago: LOM, 2004.

Goecke Saavedra, Ximena. "'Nuestra Sierra es la elección . . .': Juventudes revolucionarios en Chile, 1964–1973." Undergraduate thesis, Pontificia Universidad Católica de Chile, 1997.

Goicovic, Igor. *Movimiento de Izquierda Revolucionaria*. Concepción: Ediciones Escaparate, 2012.

———. "Violencia y poder en la estrategia política del Movimiento de Izquierda Revolucionaria, 1967–1986." *Cuadernos Sociológicos. Tres décadas después: Lecturas sobre el derrocamiento de la unidad popular* 3 (Universidad ARCIS, Santiago de Chile, 2004): 157–70.

Goodwin, Jeff, James M. Jasper, and Francesca Poletta, eds. *Passionate Politics: Emotions and Social Movements*. Chicago: University of Chicago Press, 2001.

Gould, Jeffrey. "Solidarity under Siege: The Latin American Left, 1968." *American Historical Review* 114.2 (April 2009): 348–75.

Gould, Jeffrey, and Aldo A. Lauria-Santiago. *To Rise in Darkness: Revolution, Repression, and Memory in El Salvador, 1920–1932*. Durham, NC: Duke University Press, 2008.

Grandin, Greg. *The Last Colonial Massacre: Latin America in the Cold War*. Chicago: University of Chicago Press, 2004.

———. "Living in Revolutionary Time: Coming to Terms with the Violence of Latin America's Long Cold War." In *A Century of Revolution: Insurgent and Counterinsurgent Violence during Latin America's Long Cold War*, ed. Greg Grandin and Gilbert M. Joseph, 1–42. Durham, NC: Duke University Press, 2010.

Grandin, Greg, and Gilbert Joseph, eds. *A Century of Revolution: Insurgent and Counterinsurgent Violence during Latin America's Long Cold War*. Durham, NC: Duke University Press, 2010.

Guerra, Lillian. *Visions of Power in Cuba: Revolution, Redemption, and Resistance, 1959–1971*. Chapel Hill: University of North Carolina Press, 2012.

Guevara, Ernesto. *Guerrilla Warfare*. New York: Monthly Review Press, 1961.

Han, Clara. *Life in Debt: Times of Care and Violence in Neoliberal Chile*. Berkeley: University of California Press, 2012.

Harmer, Tanya. *Allende's Chile and the Inter-American Cold War*. Chapel Hill: University of North Carolina Press, 2011.

Henfrey, Colin, and Bernardo Sorj. *Chilean Voices: Activists Describe Their Experiences of the Popular Unity Period*. Atlantic Highlands, NJ: Humanities Press, 1977.

Hernández Vásquez, Martín. *El pensamiento revolucionario de Bautista Van Schouwen, 1943–1973*. Santiago: Ediciones Escaparate, 2004.

Hite, Katherine. *When the Romance Ended: Leaders of the Chilean Left, 1968–1998*. New York: Columbia University Press, 2000.

Huneeus M., Carlos. *Movimientos universitarios y generación de elites dirigentes: Estudio de casos*. Santiago: Corporación de Promoción Universitaria, August 1973.

————. *La reforma en la Universidad de Chile*. Santiago: Corporación de Promoción Universitaria, 1973.

————. *La reforma universitaria: Veinte años después*. Santiago de Chile: Corporación de Promoción Universitaria, 1988.

Hutchinson, Elizabeth Quay, et al., eds. *The Chile Reader: History, Culture, Politics*. Durham, NC: Duke University Press, 2014.

Illanes Oliva, María Angélica. *La batalla de la memoria: Ensayos históricos de nuestro siglo, Chile 1900–2000*. Santiago: Planeta, 2002.

James, Daniel. *Doña María's Story: Life, History, Memory, and Political Identity*. Durham, NC: Duke University Press, 2000.

Jeffries, Hasan Kwame. *Bloody Lowndes: Civil Rights and Black Power in Alabama's Black Belt*. New York: New York University Press, 2009.

Jocelyn-Holt Letelier, Alfredo. *El Chile perplejo: Del avanzar sin transar al transar sin parar*. Santiago: Planeta, 1998.

————. *El peso de la noche: Nuestra frágil fortaleza histórica*. Santiago: Planeta, 1998.

Joseph, Gilbert M., and Daniela Spenser, eds. *In from the Cold: Latin America's New Encounter with the Cold War*. Durham, NC: Duke University Press, 2008.

Klubock, Thomas Miller. "Ránquil: Violence and Peasant Politics on Chile's Southern Frontier." In *A Century of Revolution: Insurgent and Counterinsurgent Violence during Latin America's Long Cold War*, ed. Greg Grandin and Gilbert Joseph, 121–59. Durham, NC: Duke University Press, 2010.

Kornbluh, Pete. *The Pinochet File: A Declassified Dossier on Atrocity and Accountability*. New York: New Press, 2004.

Labarca, José Tomás. "'Por los que quieren un gobierno de avanzada popular': Nuevas prácticas políticas en la campaña presidencial de la Democracia Cristiana, Chile, 1962–1964." *Latin American Research Review* 52.1 (2017): 50–63.

Landsberger, Henry A., and Tim McDaniel. "Hypermobilization in Chile, 1970–1973." *World Politics* 28.4 (July 1976): 502–41.

Langland, Victoria. *Speaking of Flowers: Student Movements and the Making and Remembering of 1968 in Military Brazil*. Durham, NC: Duke University Press, 2013.

Lawson, Steven F., and Charles Payne. "'This Transformation of the People': An Interview with Bob Moses." In *Debating the Civil Rights Movement, 1945–1968*, 170–88. 2nd ed. Lanham, MD: Rowman and Littlefield, 2006.

Leiva, Sebastián. *Revolución socialista y poder popular: Los casos del MIR y el PRT-ERP 1970–1976*. Concepción: Ediciones Escaparate, 2010.

Magasich Airola, Jorge. *Los que dijeron "No": Historia del movimiento de los marinos antigolpistas de 1973*. 2 vols. Santiago: LOM, 2008.

Mallon, Florencia. "*Barbudos*, Warriors, and *Rotos*: The MIR, Masculinity, and Power in the Chilean Agrarian Reform, 1965–1974." In *Changing Men and Masculinities in Latin America*, ed. Matthew C. Gutmann, 179–215. Durham, NC: Duke University Press, 2003.

————. *Courage Tastes of Blood: The Mapuche Community of Nicolás Ailío and the Chilean State, 1906–2001*. Durham, NC: Duke University Press, 2005.

————. "Descolonizando la historia Mapuche de la Unidad Popular." *De/rotar* 1.2 (2009): 3–13.

Manzano, Valeria. *The Age of Youth in Argentina: Culture, Politics, and Sexuality from Perón to Videla*. Chapel Hill: University of North Carolina Press, 2014.

Marchesi, Alberto Aldo. "Geographies of Armed Protest: Transnational Cold War, Latin Americanism, and the New Left in the Southern Cone (1964–1976)." PhD diss., New York University, 2013.

———. *Latin America's Radical Left: Rebellion and Cold War in the Global 1960s*. Cambridge: Cambridge University Press, 2017.

Markarian, Vania. *El 68 uruguayo: El movimiento estudiantil entre molotovs y música beat*. Buenos Aires: Universidad Nacional de Quilmes, 2012.

Martín-Cabrera, Luis. *Radical Justice: Spain and the Southern Cone beyond Market and State*. Lewisburg, PA: Bucknell University Press, 2011.

Milos, Pedro. *Historia y memoria: 2 de abril de 1957*. Santiago: LOM, 2007.

Monsálvez Araneda, Danny. *Agosto 1973. Proa al golpe en la Armada: El caso Asmar-Talcahuano*. Tomé: Editorial Al Aire Libro, 2010.

———. "La asamblea del Pueblo en Concepción: La expresión del poder popular." *Revista de Historia* 16 (2006): 37–58.

Moulian, Tomás. *Chile actual: Anatomía de un mito*. Santiago: LOM, 2002.

Muñoz Cordero, Mauricio, and Gabriel Moreno Gonzalez. "Poder popular en Chile, 1968–1973: Concepción y desarrollo de una estrategia revolucionaria." Undergraduate thesis, Universidad de Concepción, 1992.

Murphy, Edward. *For a Proper Home: Housing Rights in the Margins of Urban Chile, 1960–2010*. Pittsburgh: University of Pittsburgh Press, 2015.

Naranjo, Pedro. "La vida de Miguel Enríquez el MIR." In *Miguel Enríquez y el proyecto revolucionario en Chile: Discursos y documentos del Movimiento de Izquierda Revolucionaria*, ed. Pedro Naranjo et al., 29–88. Santiago: LOM and Centro de Estudios Miguel Enríquez, 2004.

Naranjo, Pedro, et al., eds. *Miguel Enríquez y el proyecto revolucionario en Chile: Discursos y documentos del Movimiento de Izquierda Revolucionaria*. Santiago: LOM and Centro de Estudios Miguel Enríquez, 2004.

Objectives of the Academic Reorganization and Integrated Urbanization Plan of the University of Concepción. Santiago: Editorial Universitaria, 1958.

Ogalde, Rosa, Marta García, and Mario Gutiérrez. *Coronel y ayer y hoy: Cómo vivirá el tercer milenio*. Coronel, Chile: Marta García, 2003.

Olmsted, Kathryn. *Right out of California: The 1930s and the Big Business Roots of Modern Conservatism*. New York: New Press, 2015.

Ortega, Miriam, and Cecilia Radrigan. *Con vista a la esperanza*. Santiago: Ediciones Escaparate, 1998.

Ortiz Figueroa, Matías. "Retomando las fuerzas de la historia: Lecturas del mirismo chileno en la juventud actual." Undergraduate thesis, Universidad de Santiago, 2014.

Palieraki, Eugenia. "La opción por las armas: Nueva izquierda revolucionaria y violencia política en Chile (1965–1970)." *POLIS: Revista Latinoamericana* 19 (March 2008): 1–17.

———. *¡La revolución ya viene! El MIR chileno en los años sesenta*. Santiago: LOM, 2014.

Pastrana, Ernesto, and Monica Threlfall. *Pan, techo y poder: el movimiento de pobladores en Chile, 1970–1973*. Buenos Aires: Ediciones Siap-Planteos, 1974.

Pavilack, Jody. *Mining for the Nation: The Politics of Chile's Coal Communities from the Popular Front to the Cold War*. University Park: Pennsylvania State University Press, 2011.

Peirano Iglesias, Alondra. *De la militancia revolucionaria a la militancia social: Los miristas en el Chile neoliberal*. Concepción: Escaparate, 2008.

Pensado, Jaime M. *Rebel Mexico: Student Unrest and Authoritarian Political Culture during the Long Sixties*. Stanford: Stanford University Press, 2013.

Pérez, Cristián. "Historia del MIR: Si quieren guerra, guerra tendrán . . . " *Estudios Públicos* 91 (2003): 5–44.

Pérotin-Dumon, Anne. "El pasado vivo de Chile en el año del 'Informe sobre la Tortura.'" *Nuevo Mundo Mundos Nuevos*, Debates, 2005. http://nuevomundo.revues.org//index954 .html.

Pinto Vallejos, Julio, ed. *Cuando hicimos historia: La experiencia de la Unidad Popular*. Santiago: LOM, 2005.

———. *Fiesta y drama: Nuevas historias de la Unidad Popular*. Santiago: LOM, 2014.

Power, Margaret, *Right-Wing Women in Chile: Feminine Power and the Struggle against Allende, 1964–1973*. University Park: Pennsylvania State University Press, 2002.

Pozo, José del, *Rebeldes, reformistas y revolucionarios: Una historia oral de la izquierda chilena en la época de la Unidad Popular*. Santiago: Ediciones Documentas, 1992.

Reyes Cabello, Franco. "El Movimiento de Izquierda Revolucionaria (MIR) y el Movimiento Universitario de Izquierda (MUI) en la Universidad de Concepción (UdeC): Revolucionarios y estudiantes, 1965–1974." Undergraduate thesis, Universidad de Concepción, 2010.

Ross, Kristin. *May '68 and Its Afterlives*. Chicago: University of Chicago Press, 2002.

Ruiz, María Olga. "Disciplina y desacato: Mandatos militantes y traición en el Movimiento de Izquierda Revolucionaria (MIR) en Chile." *Nuevo Mundo Mundos Nuevos* (February 2013). DOI:10.4000/nuevomundo.64899.

Salazar Vergara, Gabriel. *Movimientos sociales en Chile: Trayectoria histórica y proyección política*. Santiago: Ediciones Uqbar, 2012.

———. *Violencia política popular en las "grandes alamedas": Santiago de Chile 1947–1987. Una perspectiva histórico-popular*. Santiago: Ediciones SUR, 1990.

Salazar Vergara, Gabriel, and Julio Pinto Vallejos. *Historia contemporánea de Chile*. 5 vols. Santiago: LOM, 1999–2002.

Salcedo, Javier. *Los Montoneros del barrio*. Buenos Aires: EDUTREF, 2013.

Saldivia Manríquez, Enrique A., and Marianela B. Zapata Rodríguez. "Dirigentes políticos de Concepción, 1964–1973." Undergraduate thesis, Universidad de Concepción, 1989.

Salinas Valdés, Juan José. "Campamento Lenin: Expresión de poder popular en Talcahuano/ Concepción, 1970–1973." MA thesis, Universidad de Concepción, 2012.

———. "Poder popular provincial: Los casos de Concepción-Talcahuano y Constitución, 1970–1973." Undergraduate thesis, Universidad de Concepción, 2008.

Sandoval Ambiado, Carlos. *MIR (una historia)*. Santiago: Sociedad Editorial Trabajadores, 1990.

———. *Movimiento de Izquierda Revolucionaria 1970–1973: Coyunturas, documentos y vivencias*. Chile: Ediciones Escaparate, 2004.

———. *Movimiento de Izquierda Revolucionaria 1973–1980*. Vol. 3: *Coyunturas y vivencias*. Concepción: Ediciones Escaparate, 2011.

Schlotterbeck, Marian. "Chile: Reflecting on the Revolutionary Left." *Berkeley Review of Latin American Studies* (Fall 2015): 28–31.

Sierra, Daniel. "En la voz de sus actores: Triunfos, obstáculos y tensiones del movimiento estudiantil chileno." Working Paper, Educacion y Comunicaciones (ECO), Santiago, December 2014.

Silber, Irina Carlota. *Everyday Revoluionaries: Gender, Violence, and Disillusionment in Postwar El Salvador.* New Brunswick, NJ: Rutgers University Press, 2011.

Silva, Miguel. *Los cordones industriales y el socialismo desde abajo.* Santiago: Imprenta Lizor, n.d.

Sitrin, Marina. *Everyday Revolutions: Horizontalism and Autonomy in Argentina.* London: Zed, 2012.

Stallings, Barbara. *Class Conflict and Economic Development in Chile, 1958–1973.* Stanford: Stanford University Press, 1978.

Stern, Steve J. *Battling for Hearts and Minds: Memory Struggles in Pinochet's Chile, 1973–1988.* Durham, NC: Duke University Press, 2006.

———. "A New Century of Solitude? The Late 20th Century as a Cultural Battleground." *Latin American Perspectives* 25.6 (November 1998): 92–94.

———. *Reckoning with Pinochet: The Memory Question in Democratic Chile, 1989–2006.* Durham, NC: Duke University Press, 2010.

———. *Remembering Pinochet's Chile: On the Eve of London 1998.* Durham, NC: Duke University Press, 2004.

Sweig, Julia E. *Inside the Cuban Revolution: Fidel Castro and the Urban Underground.* Cambridge, MA: Harvard University Press, 2002.

Thomas, Gwynn. *Contesting Legitimacy in Chile: Familial Ideals, Citizenship, and Political Struggle, 1970–1990.* University Park: Pennsylvania State University Press, 2012.

———. "The Legacies of Patrimonial Patriarchalism." *Annals of the American Academy of Political and Social Science* 636.1 (July 2011): 69–87.

Tinsman, Heidi. *Partners in Conflict: The Politics of Gender, Sexuality, and Labor in the Chilean Agrarian Reform, 1950–1973.* Durham, NC: Duke University Press, 2002.

Trumper, Camilo. *Ephemeral Histories: Public Art, Politics, and the Struggle for the Streets in Chile.* Oakland: University of California Press, 2016.

Urrutia Fernández, Miguel, and Alma Barra Cáceres. "Lo social y lo político en el movimiento estudiantil de la Universidad de Concepción, 1973–1983." Undergraduate thesis, Universidad de Concepción, 1992.

Valdivia Ortiz de Zárate, Verónica. *Nacionales y gremialistas: El parto de la nueva derecha política chilena, 1964–1973.* Santiago: LOM, 2008.

Valdivia Ortiz de Zárate, Verónica, Rolando Álvarez Vallejos, and Julio Pinto Vallejos. *Su revolución contra nuestra revolución: Izquierdas y derechas en el Chile de Pinochet (1973–1981).* Santiago: LOM, 2006.

Valenzuela, Arturo. *The Breakdown of Democratic Regimes: Chile.* Baltimore, MD: Johns Hopkins University Press, 1978.

———. *Political Brokers in Chile: Local Government in a Centralized Polity.* Durham, NC: Duke University Press, 1977.

Valenzuela, Arturo, and J. Samuel Valenzuela. *Chile: Politics and Society.* New Brunswick, NJ: Transaction Books, 1976.

Vergara, Angela. "Revisiting Pampa Irigoin: Social Movements, Repression, and Political Culture in 1960s Chile." *Radical History Review* 124 (January 2016): 43–54.

Vidal, Hernán. *Presencia del MIR: 14 claves existenciales.* Santiago: Mosquito Editores, 1999.

Vidaurrázaga Aránguiz, Tamara. "Mujeres en rojo y negro: Reconstrucción de la memoria de tres mujeres miristas (1971–1990)." MA thesis, Universidad de Chile. 2005

Vitale, Luis. *Contribución a la historia del MIR (1965–1970).* Santiago: Instituto de Investigación de Movimientos Sociales "Pedro Vuskovic," 1999.

Volk, Steven S. "Salvador Allende." *Oxford Research Encyclopedia of Latin American History* (November 2015). 10.1093/acrefore/9780199366439.013.106

Wilde, Alexander. "Irruptions of Memory: Expressive Politics in Chile's Transition to Democracy," *Journal of Latin American Studies* 31.2 (May 1999): 473–500.

Winn, Peter. "The Furies of the Andes: Violence and Terror in the Chilean Revolution and Counterrevolution." In *A Century of Revolution: Insurgent and Counterinsurgent Violence during Latin America's Long Cold War,* ed. Greg Grandin and Gilbert M. Joseph, 239–75. Durham, NC: Duke University Press, 2010.

———. *La revolución chilena.* Santiago: LOM, 2013.

———. "Salvador Allende: His Political Life . . . and Afterlife." *Socialism and Democracy* 19.3 (2005): 129–59.

———, ed. *Victims of the Chilean Miracle: Workers and Neoliberalism in the Pinochet Era, 1972–2002.* Durham, NC: Duke University Press, 2004.

———. *Weavers of Revolution: The Yarur Workers and Chile's Road to Socialism.* New York: Oxford University Press, 1986.

———. "Workers into Managers: Worker Participation in the Chilean Textile Industry." In *Popular Participation in Social Change: Cooperatives, Collectives, and Nationalized Industry,* ed. June Nash et al., 577–601. The Hague: Mouton, 1976.

Winter, Jay. *Dreams of Peace and Freedom: Utopian Moments in the 20th Century.* New Haven, CT: Yale University Press, 2006.

Wood, Elisabeth Jean. *Insurgent Collective Action and Civil War in El Salvador.* Cambridge: Cambridge University Press, 2003.

Wright, Thomas C. *Latin America in the Era of the Cuban Revolution.* Westport, CT: Praeger, 2001.

Zolov, Eric. "Introduction: Latin America in the Global Sixties." *Americas* (Special Issue: *Latin America in the Global Sixties*) 70.3 (January 2014): 349–62.

INDEX